THE FLIGHT

ALSO BY DAN HAMPTON

NONFICTION
The Hunter Killers
Lords of the Sky
Viper Pilot

FICTION
The Mercenary

THE FLIGHT

CHARLES LINDBERGH'S DARING AND IMMORTAL 1927 TRANSATLANTIC CROSSING

DAN HAMPTON

WILLIAM MORROW
An Imprint of HarperCollinsPublishers

HarperCollins books may be purchased for educational, business, or sales promotional use. For information, please email the Special Markets Department at SPsales@harpercollins.com.

A hardcover edition of this book was published in 2017 by William Morrow, an imprint of HarperCollins Publishers.

FIRST WILLIAM MORROW PAPERBACK EDITION PUBLISHED 2018.

Designed by Joy O'Meara

Library of Congress Cataloging-in-Publication Data has been applied for.

ISBN 978-0-06-246440-8

18 19 20 21 22   DIX/LSC   10 9 8 7 6 5 4 3 2 1

For those with the spirit to dream, to face the unknown, and the courage to conquer fear

CONTENTS

AUTHOR'S NOTE

CHARLES AUGUSTUS LINDBERGH was a complicated man and, in later years, certainly a controversial one. *The Flight* is a detailed account of his extraordinary 1927 flight from Long Island to Paris—an achievement that captured the world's attention like few other events in history and made Lindbergh perhaps the most celebrated man of his time. Pertinent aspects of Lindbergh's childhood, character, and later years are touched upon when they serve to explain the man as we see him in 1927, but this work is not a judgment of the balance of his life. My purpose in these pages is to put the reader into the cockpit of the *Spirit of St. Louis* during those thirty-three and a half hours on May 20 and 21, 1927, and to fly along with him. No other book about this man and this flight has been written from the cockpit point of view by a fellow aviator with the desire to have us all share his triumph, to be there as the frontier of aviation is changed forever.

After coming to know Charles Lindbergh through his family recollections, personal artifacts, and most of all through his own writings, I learned that much of what I'd been taught was incorrect, or at best, incomplete. He was neither naïve nor simplistic, although in some ways he was an innocent. Lindbergh made mistakes, both personal and professional, yet who among us has not? Who among us, being thrust into instant wealth and global celebrity, would react better? Fame overwhelmed him and, though he learned to eventually take credit for his remarkable accomplishment, publicity was a curse he never quite overcame. His loss of privacy, as well as to some degree the loss of himself, is something that should have been expected from such a feat, but Lindbergh never considered how success would change his life—or what it would cost.

His name became immortal, and his fortune immense, yet was it worth the price? This is a question with no answer, at least not one we can give. The tragedy of losing a child is something no parent should have to bear, and surely this would not have occurred had he not been Charles Lindbergh. He would also not have incurred the wrath of a president, and all the ramifications that came back to him. If he had not been an eminent public figure would his politics, comments, and opinions have been amplified and distorted as they were? Very likely not. I mention these events so the intelligent reader is aware that they exist, and is aware that this book is not blind adulation, but an account of one very human man and his extraordinary flight across the Atlantic Ocean.

Regardless of what judgments are passed on Lindbergh, no one can dispute the raw courage and skill he showed the world in May 1927. Others had attempted this most dangerous of exploits, and failed, and many passed into relative oblivion. Lindbergh's epic flight brought him fame, fortune, love, and tragedy. Someone else, a Richard Byrd or Clarence Chamberlin perhaps, could have accomplished the flight first, but Charles Lindbergh was the one who did it. In the end, *he* took the chance, risked everything, and prevailed.

In writing this book I was incalculably aided by the man

himself, for having Lindbergh's own thoughts and observations with me was irreplaceable. All first-person quotes, including internal dialog, are drawn from Lindbergh's own recollections. He was a meticulous note taker, and his papers are wonderfully preserved in the Yale University Library, in New Haven, Connecticut, and the Missouri Historical Society, in St. Louis. The thoughts and expressions in the text are credited in the Notes and Sources section of this book. Most will be found in Lindbergh's 1953 *Spirit of St. Louis*, but his *Wartime Journals* was also exceptionally detailed. Perhaps the best place to start with Lindbergh himself is with the posthumously published *Autobiography of Values*; his writing had fully matured, and even accounting for the benefit of hindsight, his prose is clear, personal, and illuminating. There are other fine books on the subject, notably A. Scott Berg's *Lindbergh*, though Berg devotes just a few pages to the flight itself.

As for descriptions of the vistas and terrain he overflew, particularly Nova Scotia, Newfoundland, and the European landfalls, not to mention the vast, empty stretches of the northern Atlantic Ocean, I was fortunate to have seen them myself, having made solo transatlantic flights many times while piloting single-seat F-16s during my twenty years with the United States Air Force. Often a word from "Slim," to use one of Lindbergh's nicknames, would trigger a memory, and I felt less like an author and more like I was back in the air over the Atlantic—just another pilot along for the ride.

So in reading this book, admire the bravery necessary to survive those lonely, dangerous, and uncertain hours. Put yourself in a small, fabric-covered cockpit in a thousand-mile storm over the Atlantic at night and learn what you didn't know about the man and his dream.

Above all else, Charles Lindbergh believed in the power of aviation: its untapped potential and inherent capacity to join peoples, advance technology, and bring the world closer together. That passion and courage define a spirit that all Americans can claim through Charles Lindbergh and that we, as humans, can collectively share.

Dan Hampton
New Hampshire, 2016

THE FLIGHT

PROLOGUE

Le Bourget Field, Paris
May 8, 1927, 5:18 A.M.

THOUSANDS OF CHINS tilted back as the large, pale biplane lumbered heavily into the damp morning air above the French capital. Clearing the airfield, it began a smooth, climbing left turn away from the clouds darkening the eastern horizon. Called *L'Oiseau Blanc,* or the "White Bird," the Levasseur PL-8 had been built for a single purpose—to be the first powered aircraft to fly more than 3,600 miles nonstop across the Atlantic Ocean.

Thunder rumbled in the distance, and the plane continued turning northwest, its chalk-colored wings very plain against the gray clouds. Brighter was a brief splash of yellow from the cockpit as *L'Oiseau Blanc* rolled up steeply over the little village of Gonesse. Even though they were expecting it, the crowd gasped when the undercarriage suddenly detached, tumbling through the air into the wet fields below. Jettisoning the 270-pound landing gear was a well-publicized part of the plan as this reduced weight and drag and saved precious fuel. Besides, wheels weren't necessary to land on water and that was precisely what the two Frenchmen intended to do: set the White Bird down in New York Harbor beneath the Statue of Liberty and claim the $25,000 Orteig Prize for the first nonstop flight between Paris and New York.

It was audacious, yet in 1927 no less was expected from Charles Eugène Jules Marie Nungesser and François Coli, France's leading aviators. Both men had been French Air Service fighter pilots, with Nungesser finishing the Great War as France's third-highest-scoring ace. When asked about the dangers of the transatlantic flight, Nungesser calmly replied, "A cœur vaillant rien d'impossible." *To the valiant heart nothing is impossible.*

Handsome and scarred, Nungesser had a panache and contemptuous disregard for danger that personified the image of French military manhood. He inspired adoring coverage by the French press, who seemed to love everything about the former race car driver, stunt pilot, and military hero. After the war he had married Consuelo "Connie" Hatmaker, a glamorous American heiress, and starred in *The Sky Raider,* a Hollywood motion picture. The world, particularly France, adored him and never more than that May morning as he set out to conquer the unconquerable Atlantic Ocean.

When the biplane rolled out to level flight, the proud red, white, and blue tricolor could be easily seen on the tail. Less visible was the "Black Heart" painted on the fuselage just aft of the open cockpit. Though the crowd couldn't see the details they knew Nungesser's "Coeur Noir" well: a white skull and crossbones surmounted by a coffin and flanked by a pair of lighted candles. It was a personal crest, emblazoned on his silver Nieuport 17 fighter during the war, showing Nungesser's blatant challenge toward mankind's greatest mortal fear: death.

Heading northwest, the plane disappeared into the chilly

dawn, the roar of its Lorraine-Dietrich engine fading as it flew on toward Normandy. Without an enclosed cockpit, both men were hunched down out of the cold air behind a large, four-and-a-half-foot windscreen. Their bright yellow, heavy-weather flying suits were fur lined and electrically heated to stave off freezing winds aloft. Nungesser's navigator, François Coli, was on the right side, seated a bit behind and slightly lower than the pilot. During the war Coli had lost an eye, thus acquiring the nickname the "One-Eyed Devil," but he had also once been a sea captain and was intimately familiar with maritime navigation, particularly in the North Atlantic. An accomplished pilot himself, Coli was a superb navigator, and it was he who had worked out the route's details.

Coli's tools included the very latest technical instruments: a ground speed indicator that corrected the airspeed indicator for wind; a Le Prieur navigraph to give surface alerts over water; and a Coutinho sextant for astral navigation. Gago Coutinho, the Portuguese aviator who'd first flown across the South Atlantic in 1922, had modified a maritime sextant with an artificial horizon so it could be used effectively in flight. But the navigator's main instrument was a large Krauss-Morel compass. In *L'Oiseau Blanc* it was horizontally mounted, similar to a binnacle that Coli would've used aboard ship. Placed in front of the stick, both men could see it plainly and follow the plotted course. Day or night, with clear skies, Coli could also check their position trigonometrically using his sextant. With a precise heading, two chronometers for measuring elapsed time, and a ground speed indicator the White Bird's position would always be known.

Charles Nungesser sat in the left seat with the throttle lever and mixture control beside him on the bulkhead. The control stick was long, slim, and topped with a pommel for easy gripping. Facing him was a panel dotted with gauges for monitoring oil temperature, and fuel, and a tachometer showing the engine's revolutions per minute. Among his flight instruments were a Chauvin & Arnoux bank indicator, a vertical velocity indicator, and a Badin-Aéra flight controller.

The White Bird had been completed in early April, and both men had then spent the next twenty-two days accomplishing a series of flight tests in preparation for the crossing. Operating primarily from Villacoublay, southwest of Paris, Nungesser had reached a top speed of 124 miles per hour with a practical ceiling of 19,800 feet. During testing he hadn't attempted a fully loaded, maximum-weight takeoff, preferring to risk this only once on the actual flight. Supremely confident in his own abilities and Coli's skills as a navigator, he was certain it could be done with no issues. The French ace felt they were ready but would state to the press on May 4, 1927, "The least negligence, the least mistake, the least impatience could make everything fail."

CROSSING THE COASTLINE near Étretat, Nungesser and Coli continued over the English Channel, where they were observed and reported by a British submarine.* For the next several hours scores of keen observers spotted the paunchy aircraft as Weymouth, Exeter, and dozens of other southern English towns passed under its wings. When they reached the island's west coast, the squat white tower of Hartland Point lighthouse would have been clearly visible as the two Frenchmen flew out over the Bristol Channel. With its immense 48-foot wingspan, the 11,102-pound *L'Oiseau Blanc* was roughly the same width

---

* *H-50,* of the Royal Navy.

as current-day airliners. It was easy to see. Growling power-fully, the 450-horsepower Lorraine-Dietrich motor could be plainly heard above the crash of waves and the screaming gulls.

Without landing gear, the plane could comfortably main-tain a 110 mph cruise speed, which Nungesser intended to hold. But there were always winds, and this was one reason the pilots had chosen an east-west Atlantic crossing, rather than the con-verse. Coli had purposely waited for a low-pressure weather system when the usual westerly winds would be reversed, and today, May 8, there was just such an area over their proposed route. This would produce an easterly, quartering tailwind that would push the White Bird across the Atlantic rather than slow it down. Flying east to west also meant two-thirds of their fuel load would be consumed by the time they reached Newfound-land, so the plane would be much lighter and better able to cope with severe weather in the area.

When asked why he'd planned such a route, Coli simply shrugged and said, "Because we are French! If we go there to come here it would appear that we were coming to visit our-selves."

Most critical for his navigation, especially after flying sev-eral thousand miles at night, was the challenge of "finding the earth," as Coli called it: determining their exact position. This problem would be simplified by a landfall near Belle Isle, New-foundland, which was more than 1,000 miles from New York. If any course corrections were necessary, there would be suf-ficient time to do so, while in contrast, anyone flying to Paris from New York would only have 500 miles after Ireland to make course corrections. A landing in Paris would also be at night, a considerable challenge on a strange field after flying for forty-odd hours.

The reciprocal argument was also very true. The Frenchmen

only had a 500-mile outbound leg to ensure an exact course before departing the Irish coast. But Coli had picked prominent landmarks across the British Isles to guarantee a solid north-westerly heading. Twelve miles off the Devon coast in the Bristol Channel, Lundy Island was just such an ideal navigation point. Having long been a pirate haven, the reputation of the rugged little speck may have appealed to the pair of renegade Frenchmen.

Shortly after 10 A.M. the White Bird crossed St. George's Channel and struck the Irish coast at Dungarvan. Taking his bearings from the Cunnigar, a long finger of land sticking into the bay, Coli corrected their course, and they passed just south of the town. Sunday mass was under way so many people caught sight of the white aircraft, including J. Dunphy, a retired Royal Navy officer, who clearly saw French markings through his field glasses.

For the aviators all was well; deep vales trapped the low mist, but the sky was perfectly blue a few hundred feet up. Waterford, Tipperary, and Limerick counties rolled by, their lyrical Irish names strange to French ears. Countless gray rocks speckled the emerald meadows as Ireland, soft and green in the morning light, concealed the threat that lay ahead. *L'Oiseau Blanc* was positively spotted over Sugar Loaf mountain, Cappoquin, and Glin as it flew steadily on, always northwest.

Just before 11 A.M. it was sighted a bare fifteen miles from the Atlantic coast over Kilrush, near the Shannon River. As the plane passed over Scattery Island both pilots could see the vast blue shimmer of the open ocean. Off Nungesser's left wing the stark, hard cliffs of Loop Head peninsula jutted forward into the cold Atlantic; enormous waves slammed against the granite rocks, throwing spray hundreds of feet into the air. A white lighthouse perched near land's end, like the nail on a green finger pointing the way west.

At 11 A.M. an eight-year-old boy named H. G. Glynn was climbing Knocknagaroon Hill, near Carrigaholt on the west Irish coast. Hearing a strange sound he looked up, shading his eyes against the glare. The boy watched, transfixed, as a large white biplane serenely crossed the shoreline, chasing the sun to the west out over the Atlantic.

It was never seen again.

PART ONE

Now, I'm giving up both land and day. Now, I'm heading eastward across two oceans, one of night and one of water.

—CHARLES LINDBERGH

ONE

THE FIRST HOURS

Roosevelt Field, Long Island
May 20, 1927, 7:50 A.M.

GLUE AND GASOLINE.

The snug cockpit reeked, but the pilot ignored both smells. Slowly pushing the throttle forward he brought the roaring engine to its takeoff revolutions. The frame shook as the aircraft strained against the wheel chocks, desperate to pull man and machine through the wet, clutching clay. Leaning far left against the fabric-covered fuselage, Charles Lindbergh peered through the open window and down Roosevelt Field's narrow runway. Not that there was much he could see on this drizzly Long Island morning. Shredded curtains of rain hung from low, heavy clouds and he could barely see the tree line at the field's eastern edge.

Despite being packed with cinders, the runway was soggy

and the damp, sea-level air wasn't giving as much power to the Wright Whirlwind J-5C motor as it should. The tachometer, which measures engine revolutions per minute, showed thirty revolutions low. That worried him, as did the slight tailwind. Lindbergh had planned a sunrise takeoff facing into the easterly nighttime wind, but he was late. Now the breeze was from the west, and he either had to have the aircraft moved to the other end of the runway or live with the problem.

He could die from it, too.

3610 miles to Paris. Following twelve days after the Frenchmen Nungesser and Coli's doomed attempt at the Orteig Prize in *L'Oiseau Blanc*, Lindbergh's flight was to be the first to try it nonstop and alone, and the first and only American attempt. Crowds had begun gathering at Roosevelt Field at midnight. Now a reported five hundred stood expectantly in the rain, "in the hope that they might see one of the great dramas of the air," wrote the *New York Times*'s correspondent Russell Owen, who had made his name covering polar exploration. Like the conquest of the poles that a generation earlier had consumed the attention of the masses and made global celebrities of explorers like Peary, Shackleton, Mawson, Scott, and Amundsen, flying nonstop across the Atlantic had emerged as the signal quest of the time, emblematic of civilization's expanding limits.

Lindbergh had served in the Army Air Service and was an experienced contract airmail pilot. In fact, it had been while flying the mail eleven months earlier that aviation's vast commercial potential became clear to the young pilot. In 1919, a kindred spirit, French-born American hotelier Raymond Orteig, proposed his eponymous prize for the first non-stop Paris-to-New York flight, hoped that in spurring pilots to win the prize money, aviation would be taken seriously and its technology advanced. Eight years later Charles Lindbergh had drawn the attention of the world to this latest attempt to prove the world-shrinking possibilities of aviation.

His maps were the best available, and he had planned the flight for a year, reviewing the route until he felt every detail was familiar. But he also understood the flight required an accep-tance of the unknown. Something would happen. While others had crossed the Atlantic piecemeal or in airships, the pilot was aware that very few believed he, so young and unproven, pos-sessed much of a chance. His backers in St. Louis had confi-dence, of course, as did his mother Evangeline in Detroit. Most importantly he, Charles Augustus Lindbergh, believed it. Not that anyone outside of his rather insular world had ever heard of him before he'd shown up here on Long Island.

It didn't matter.

Inevitably known as "Slim," the tall, lanky former mail pilot was committed now. To reduce stress on the under-carriage, his five fuel tanks had only been partially filled at neighboring Curtiss Field, and then the aircraft had been towed nearly a mile across open country to Roosevelt Field.* Fueling was finished at Roosevelt with bright red, five-gallon cans passed up to Ken Lane, Wright Aircraft's chief engineer. With one foot on the nose and another on the wing, Lane had carefully filtered the gas through a 200-mesh wire screen. Losing the engine somewhere over the North Atlantic due to a clogged fuel line was a nasty thought. Almost as bad as having it quit during a heavyweight takeoff with an audience,

---

* Named for President Theodore Roosevelt's youngest son, twenty-year-old Lieutenant Quentin Roosevelt. A fighter pilot with the 95th Aero Squadron, Quentin was killed in a dogfight over Chamery, France, on July 14, 1918. Sagamore Hill, the Roosevelt estate in Oyster Bay, lies about ten miles north of Lindbergh's take-off point.

in the rain. But that was the nature of flying: dangerous and unforgiving.

Lindbergh's boots slipped a bit on the plain, metal rudder pedals, as he hadn't thought to wipe them before squeezing into the narrow cockpit. With smooth foot movements he "walked the rudder," keeping the plane aligned along the runway's northern edge, but without a view forward it wasn't easy. Slim had had the main fuselage tanks moved forward of the cockpit, which was safer in the event of an accident—Lindbergh had seen too many pilots crushed or burned in crashes because they'd been sandwiched between fuel tanks and an engine. But this meant he had to use a three-by-five-inch periscope to see straight ahead. There was no front window.

His eyes darted inside again to the tachometer. If anything was subtly wrong with the engine it would show here first, but the needle was steady at 1,825 revolutions. The plane skidded a bit, and as his heart skipped a beat Slim's blue eyes flashed back to the runway's edge . . . *I must hold the plane straight . . . and not take my eyes from its edge for an instant!*

He wasn't moving fast enough to fly yet. Men were still running alongside the plane, their hands on the struts, pushing it through the muddy mess. His mechanic had actually greased the tires so they wouldn't stick as much, but he couldn't tell if it helped. The engine sounded muted, almost weak, compared to previous test flights and his trip here from the West Coast. Slim could feel the stick wobble in his hands, which wouldn't happen if enough air was passing over the control surfaces. Faster . . . he had to get the plane moving quicker. It felt more like an overloaded truck than an airplane.

Built by Ryan Airlines in San Diego and named *The Spirit of St. Louis,* the plane was heavier than ever before; 450 gallons of California gasoline—compliments of Standard

Oil—produced a gross weight of 5,250 pounds. This was an astounding number, more than two and a half tons, and though Lindbergh knew the J-5 Wright Whirlwind was theoretically capable of overcoming it, he'd never done it before. Lieutenant Commander Noel Davis and Lieutenant Stanton Wooster had tried a heavyweight takeoff three weeks earlier in Virginia. On April 26 their Keystone Pathfinder *American Legion,* a full ton overweight, stalled on takeoff and both died after smashing into a mud bank.

"TRANSOCEAN FLIERS DOGGED BY BAD LUCK; All Serious Contenders Here in Dash to Paris Have Met With Reverses, Some Fatal," the *New York Times* had reported. "MANY TRAGEDIES RECENTLY . . . 13 Deaths Reported in This Month Alone."

His face pale, Lindbergh stared from the little window searching for a tiny white handkerchief he'd tied on a stick set in the ground. It was there as a warning; half the runway was gone and only 3,000 feet remained. He'd extrapolated a 2,250-foot takeoff distance from his test data, but that had been on a dry runway with a seven-knot headwind. What had he been thinking? Did he, Charles Lindbergh, possess some magical quality that the others before him lacked? They were certainly older than his twenty-five years, and much more experienced. Why did he think he could succeed where they failed?

Nearly a mile long, Roosevelt Field was the only choice for such an attempt, but was it even long enough? Yards from where he'd started, just off the runway's western edge was an ugly, black scorched area at the bottom of a ravine. A bent propeller blade was stuck upright in the middle of the burn, poignantly marking the crash of the last pilot who tried to reach Paris from New York. René Fonck, the great French flying ace, had rumbled down this very runway eight months ago in September, crashing an expensive aircraft and causing the horrible deaths of two crewmen.*

Lurching forward, the *Spirit* feels heavy and ungainly to the pilot. Lindbergh bounces in the wicker seat, like riding in a buckboard wagon, and details jump out: mist hovering off the ground, mud slapping against the aircraft, blue violets clustered in the grass. But he felt a difference. At 300 feet down the runway the plane is faster and the last men have let go of the struts. Should he have waited? A takeoff seemed hopeless, Lindbergh would later write, and the wrong decision would mean a crash. Should he have waited another day or swallowed his pride and had the heavy aircraft towed around to the other end of Roosevelt Field?

A thousand feet down the runway now and the stick is tighter. Slim feels air pressure pushing on the rudder through his boots. Spinning hard into the thick air, the propeller is trying to bite, to hold, and pull the *Spirit* into the sky. Is it enough? Will the wings take the heavy load before the thirty-four-inch, wire-spoked wheels snap?†

The handkerchief!

A brief white speck flutters in the gray air, then vanishes into the mist. Halfway now . . . 3,000 feet down and still not fast enough. He should've been airborne more than 500 feet back. Too much fuel? The extra twenty-five gallons added 153 pounds. Or is it the tailwind? Or the mushy runway? Too many variables . . . he knows that. He knows better. Lindbergh pulls the stick back an inch and the wheels rise off the ground.

But the *Spirit* immediately sinks back to the mud, hitting a

---

* Charles Clavier, a radio operator, and Jacob Islamoff, a Sikorsky mechanic, were killed. Fonck and U.S. Navy lieutenant Lawrence W. Curtin escaped. The $80,000 craft ($267,259.88 in 2016 dollars) was not insured.
† B. F. Goodrich Silvertown tires.

puddle and splashing cold, dirty water along the cotton fabric fuselage. The wings wobble; his right hand and both feet play the stick and rudder to keep the plane straight. Lindbergh can feel the *Spirit* tremble, an animal crouched to spring, and then the right wing suddenly dips.

Pull up!

The wings level . . . now, ease back to the runway . . . softly . . . a little rudder and the plane settles . . . more splashes and he feels the wheels slip in the mud. The roar fills the cockpit now as the engine churns out power, and his gloved fingers hold the throttle forward. It's like being inside a drum. The wheels lift off again and he senses the ground falling away a few feet. *I could probably stay in the air. . . .*

But he doesn't.

Letting the *Spirit* sink, Lindbergh feels the wheels mush again, but this time it's different and the earth can't hold him down. The plane wants to fly. Sliding over the ground, controls taut, Slim feels all 223 horses throbbing through the stick. Staring through the silver spinning blades, Slim knows he's much too close to cut the power and far too fast now to stop. Does he have the speed to clear the wall of trees and telephone wires a thousand feet ahead?

Up . . . *up!*

The propeller bites, wings lift, and the *Spirit* claws itself off the ground at 7:52 on that Friday morning. As the plane staggers slowly into the air, twenty feet high now, the trees are rushing up. So are the wires, shining in the rain like a spiderweb. Forty feet. The Whirlwind's powerful growling thickens his hearing, and water droplets splatter across Lindbergh's goggles—no choice now but to fly or die. From the corner of his eye, the pilot glimpses a small knot of men at the end of the runway. The president of Ryan Airlines, B. F. Mahoney, and

others are gathered around a big Lancia sedan, waiting with
fire extinguishers, just in case.*

Suddenly trees flash beneath the gleaming wet wheels.
Manicured grass . . . pale faces looking up . . . the golf course!
He's over the links past the east end of the airfield. But through
the spinning eight-foot, nine-inch propeller he sees another hill
ahead. The stick trembles and he knows the plane is telling him
not to turn. There's not enough altitude to trade for airspeed,
and not enough airspeed to maneuver. They're on the ragged
edge of a stall and his breathing quickens again. If he tries to
avoid the hill the *Spirit* will likely stall and they'll spin in, just
like Wooster and Davis. Tapping the rudder Slim gently nudges
the stick to the right. The aircraft answers ever so slightly,
almost reluctantly, and they barely clear the hill.

I'm above the trees. . . .

"LINDBERGH LEAVES NEW YORK AT 7:52 A.M. With
Cool Determination He Braves Death to Get Off in the Misty
Dawn," Russell Owen breathlessly reported to the *Times*'s
readers. "Hundreds gasp as unconquorable youth [Lindbergh]
by sheer wizardry lifts machine carrying 5,200 pound load,
with failure a few yards off."

Cautiously he climbs, watching the rolling hills of Long
Island flatten out to the south and east. Then, realizing that
he's at least a hundred feet in the air now, Lindbergh begins to
breathe normally. If the engine quits now there's enough altitude and speed to make a controlled landing somewhere. His
eyes flicker toward the tachometer on the black-painted wooden
instrument panel and is relieved to see it still steady at 1,825
revolutions. Below it is the Boyce Motometer, which displays

---

* Tony Fokker, aircraft designer and part of Commander Byrd's *America*
team at Roosevelt Field, loaned Mahoney the vehicle.

engine oil temperature, and it's fine, too. On the lower edge of the panel, directly in the center, is a large, T-shaped inclinometer. Filled with liquid like a builder's level, the gauge contains a horizontal crossbar that shows left and right turns while the vertical arm displays altitude changes. On either side of the T are the tachometer and airspeed indicator, respectively.

Lindbergh eases the oak throttle knob back slowly and the revolutions fall to 1,800. Airspeed still indicates over 100 miles per hour, so he inches the throttle back a bit more to hold 1,750, and it stabilizes. Finally, able to look left and right from the small windows, Slim is startled to see another airplane in loose formation with him: a Curtiss Oriole. He knows it's full of reporters, and his eyes harden at the cameras sticking out of every window.

Even now they pester him. Charles Lindbergh isn't prone to anger, but it surges through him now. Newspapers printed lies about him in California; reporters made up conversations with his mother; they even broke into his room and tried to photograph him in his pajamas. "Lucky Lindy," they called him, as if luck had anything to do with it. Or the "Flying Fool." He liked that even less. French newspapers like *La Presse* and *Le Journal* had run detailed stories describing Nungesser and Coli's arrival in New York; utterly fraudulent, including the French ace's fabricated first words to the American press. Why smother the flavor of life in a spice of fiction?

Nudging the stick left, he booted the rudder and the *Spirit of St. Louis* came smoothly around to the northeast, leaving the newshounds briefly behind. The newly installed Pioneer earth inductor compass seemed to be working perfectly, and he rolled out heading 065 degrees. Peering outside to compare landmarks against his fifty-cent Rand McNally railroad map, Lindbergh swept his eyes over Long Island, or what he could see

of it.* At 150 feet altitude he faced a three-mile visibility and
patches of low fog. He couldn't make out Manhattan fifteen
miles off his tail, or Oyster Bay, where he'd lunched with Theodore Roosevelt Jr. just days earlier.† Nor could he see Great
Neck, or much of Long Island's North Shore. It was the fabled
Gold Coast, captured by the decade's most celebrated writer,
F. Scott Fitzgerald, in his masterpiece, *The Great Gatsby*. Slim
knew it firsthand, having visited Falaise, a vast Sands Point
estate owned by his new acquaintance Harry Guggenheim. An
accomplished naval aviator himself, Guggenheim was director
of the Daniel Guggenheim Fund for the Promotion of Aeronautics and had met Lindbergh at Curtiss Field the previous week.

At 8:07 A.M., fifteen minutes after the takeoff, Smithtown
Bay appeared off his left wing. Craning his neck the other way,
Slim could see Setauket under the right wing and a harbor
full of boats. Port Jefferson. Beyond the shore lay Long Island
Sound and then thirty-five miles farther the Connecticut coast.
I've never flown across that much water before. I'm also a mile
or two southeast off course, he thought, but decided not to cor-
rect the heading until reaching the New England shoreline.

Scanning the gauges he saw the oil pressure was good at 56
pounds, and the engine temperature was cool. Fuel pressure was
steady, and with 1,750 revolutions set, the *Spirit* comfortably
held 105 mph just a few hundred feet above Long Island. Below
the instrument panel was the Lukenheimer distributor, a network of exposed vertical and horizontal fuel lines that allowed
him to feed his 450 gallons of gas from any of five tanks. There
was a 200-gallon main tank on the other side of the panel and
a nose tank beyond that containing another 80 gallons. Farthest

---

* Lindbergh bought four of these maps from a San Diego drugstore.
† The oldest son of President Theodore Roosevelt, he was Quentin Roosevelt's
brother and had served with distinction during World War I.

forward was a 25-gallon oil reservoir doubling as a firewall, a barrier between the engine and himself. Finally, three wing tanks held the last 145 official gallons, though his mechanics had somehow managed to stuff an extra 25 into the *Spirit*.

Using adjustable valves called petcocks, he could open or close any fuel line to trim, or balance, the aircraft throughout the flight. He planned on feeding from each tank for fifteen minutes to ensure they were all functioning, and then to alternate the feed every hour until he reached Paris. Twisting the petcock for the nose tank until it paralleled the fuel line, he waited a few moments then shut off the center wing tank by turning its petcock perpendicular to the pipe. Altogether, Lindbergh had taken off with 2,745 pounds of gas, enough for more than 4,000 miles of flight if the winds in his face weren't too stiff. And if he didn't get lost.

No use thinking about that now.

Suddenly the *Spirit* was tossed upward and Lindbergh's stomach dropped. Then the plane plummeted back down. Wide-eyed, he peered outside and saw *Spirit*'s wingtips bending from the invisible turbulence. Gripping the stick, he fought with the rudder to keep the aircraft generally level, and then they were through the patch of turbulence. Air was usually unsettled where land and water met, but he hadn't been thinking of it, and didn't have much experience flying near water. As heavy as the *Spirit* was, such turbulence could easily rip the wings off. But it didn't happen.

Flying out over the sound's glassy waters, Slim relaxed a bit, and settled back in the wicker seat. The pesky plane full of reporters had turned back at the shore. He knew the type of pictures they'd wanted, death and disaster, a burning wreck in the trees at Roosevelt Field, or Lindbergh dead on the grass of some great estate. But he had left all that behind, and now the air, the clouds, the sky—these elements were his alone.

"One boy's a boy," his father used to say, promoting the

virtues of individualism. "Two boys are half a boy. Three boys are no boy at all." And he was correct.

When a pilot flies alone he can't be undone by another's errors—there is only himself to depend upon. One extra man in his flying clothes with all his equipment might weigh 170 pounds. Gasoline weighs 6.1 pounds per gallon, so he'd sacrifice nearly thirty gallons, more than 200 miles of flight, for an unnecessary body. Lindbergh also rejected a second or even third engine. In his mind that was twice the components that could malfunction, and if one engine failed could the other support all that deadweight anyway? He didn't think so.

He had confidence in Ryan Airlines and B. F. Mahoney. With his backers in St. Louis, Lindbergh had officially ordered the plane on February 25, 1927, and first took it into the air sixty-three days later over Dutch Flats, on the outskirts of San Diego. Thirty-two flights and nearly twenty-eight flying hours later, here he was over the East Coast attempting to cross an ocean and claim the Orteig Prize. They had commemorated the event by painting RYAN NYP, for "New York–Paris," on the tail. Under the right wing was another new marking: N-X-211.*

In 1926, Congress had passed the Air Commerce Act, mandating that U.S. aircraft be registered with the Department of Commerce's Aeronautics Branch. Due to the federal push for compliance with safety regulations, pilots also now needed a license to fly. Luckily for Slim, his friend and reserve commander, Major Clarence Young, had been appointed as chief of the Air Regulations Division of the Aeronautics Branch and had expedited the procedure. According to License No. 69, Charles A. Lindbergh was rated as a "Transport Pilot" on April 21, 1927, and the *Spirit of St. Louis* was granted a special

---

* N for North America, X for Experimental, and 211 is the hull number. "Gus the Sign Painter" of San Diego did the work on April 26, 1927.

license six days later. He also made a personal request to Bill McCracken, the Assistant Secretary of Commerce for Aeronautics, to fly without the required aircraft lighting. "Well, you probably won't encounter much night traffic up where you're going," McCracken had smiled. "I think we can give you a special dispensation, just this once."

By the new rules he was legal to fly now and the plane was ready. Time, as he well knew, was short. Nungesser and Coli could depart from Paris at any time, and here in America Chamberlin and Byrd were poised to make the crossing. But Lindbergh's bold—many would say reckless—act wasn't really about winning the Orteig Prize. True, the winnings would pay off his investors with a bit left over for himself, but this wasn't really about the money.

Raymond Orteig had become fascinated with aviation during the Great War when many pilots frequented his Lafayette Hotel in New York. He heard a 1919 speech by Eddie Rickenbacker at the Aero Club of America, where the U.S. flying ace spoke of a day when France and America would be connected by air. Inspired, Orteig initiated the prize that would bear his name, writing in a letter to Alan Ramsay Hawley, president of the Aero Club,

> *Gentlemen: As a stimulus to the courageous aviators, I desire to offer, through the auspices and regulations of the Aero Club of America, a prize of $25,000 to the first aviator of any Allied Country crossing the Atlantic in one flight, from Paris to New York or New York to Paris, all other details in your care.*
>
> *Yours very sincerely,*
> *Raymond Orteig*
> *May 22, 1919*

The challenge was initially intended to run for five years but when 1924 arrived with the money still unclaimed, it was renewed for another five-year period. By now the contest was open to aviators from all nations, and the rules had been carefully codified. The aircraft could be either a seaplane or land plane, but it had to take off and land within fifty miles of either city. The gasoline tanks had to be sealed and the Fédération Aéronautique Internationale required that a barograph record the flight.* Carl Schory of the National Aeronautic Association personally installed the 1924 PN-7 barograph into the *Spirit of St. Louis* while it was hangared at Curtiss Field.

Orteig was inspired to promote aviation, and that was the real reason Lindbergh was risking his life on this flight to prove aviation's worth. Despite the technological advances there were still many who regarded manned flight as a fad. The transatlantic air crossing was the most dramatic possible display of aviation's promise to connect the world as no technology had before, to prove that planes could be for the twentieth century what railroads had been for the nineteenth. Lindbergh's backers in St. Louis were caught up in the spirit of the event, and when Slim pointed out that the requisite sixty days hadn't elapsed between filing and the actual flight, his foremost investor, banker Harry Knight, had replied, "To hell with the money. When you're ready to take off, go ahead."

And here he was.

FORTY MINUTES AFTER takeoff Long Island Sound was glassy and smooth: gray water under gray skies. Forcing his shoul-

---

* A barograph measures atmospheric pressure, and its altitude readings would prove that the flight was uninterrupted.

ders back to relax, Lindbergh knew fatigue would be one of his worst enemies, and he'd have to do what he could to alleviate it. Checking the heading again, he squinted at the earth inductor compass and wondered, not for the first time, just how accurate the new instrument was. Brice Goldsborough of the Pioneer Instrument Company had installed it himself shortly after the *Spirit* arrived at Curtiss Field. There was obviously a magnetic compass for backup but it was mounted over his head and he could only read it backward from a mirror on top of the instrument panel. Magnetic compasses were notoriously fickle, difficult to use, and often unreliable.

Holding his northeast heading of 065 degrees, Lindbergh glanced at the New York State railroad map spread across his knee. It seemed he left Long Island a bit southeast of the planned route, but he'd be better able to check the course on the other side of the sound. He ought to cross the Connecticut shoreline over Clinton Bay; with Cedar Island running through the middle, it should be an unmistakable landmark. He'd then continue northeast to hit the 100-mile mark on the Thames River north of New London, Connecticut.

A pilot could only plan so far in a theoretical, flat-world sense, so fixing this first 100-mile position was a critical assessment of his navigation. Headings, courses, times—these were all necessary, and they had to be accurately plotted, but he'd been flying for five years now, long enough to know they rarely matched reality. Nevertheless, Lindbergh was certain that if he was to survive the night, if he was to have the slightest chance of eventually making landfall in Ireland, then he must stay as close as possible to the black line calculated in California weeks ago. This was easier said than done, since the route on the map was a "course," a planned direction of travel. A course was always expressed in degrees, with three digits, beginning at north and working clockwise around the compass. Plotted on the map his course was 066 degrees but his "heading"—where the aircraft physically pointed—was 065 degrees. Usually the difference was due to winds, though at this stage he simply elected to use Dead Reckoning: to fly from landmark to landmark while he could.

While flying along the eastern states he would use his four railroad maps, and these were indispensable as long as the ground was visible. Even when it wasn't, a pilot could get fairly close by maintaining his course and keeping track of the time: so many minutes along a plotted line that could then be compared to the map. Geographical features, and very often water towers or city signs, were also used whenever in doubt. Headings and courses rarely coincided due to instrument or pilot errors, which was why cross-checking with landmarks was so vital.

Still, dead reckoning was really the only practical way to fly over land in 1927. Very shortly, however, the *Spirit* would leave the American coast for Nova Scotia and Newfoundland, where maps were not to be trusted. Beyond that, east of the Avalon Peninsula, lay the open ocean and no references at all. In his case, he'd have to be absolutely certain of his last position on the Newfoundland coast as there would be no updates over the Atlantic. The only way to cross an ocean with any accuracy was as ships did it with a course corrected against the earth's magnetic field, and timing. He'd have to account for winds, and keep the *Spirit* on a compass heading that would get them to Ireland.

The difficulty with any type of map is that it's a flat representation of a sphere, and one cannot travel in a truly straight line over something rounded, such as the earth. There will always be some distortion, like peeling an orange and trying to flatten the pieces. Thus a course plotted between New York and Paris would appear as a straight line, but in reality it was not.

It was a slice through the globe, called a great circle, which cut through all lines of longitude, or meridians, at the same angle. To hold that same angle over a curve, periodic course changes had to be made and Lindbergh decided to do so at hundred-mile increments. As he planned to maintain a 100-mph air speed, this made the calculations relatively simple. The two biggest challenges would be staying awake and accurately correcting for the effects of weather and wind. Why, the *Spirit* was already several miles south of the planned route and he wasn't even thirty miles from Roosevelt Field.

Slim leaned back, gazed around the cockpit, and again tried to relax. It's a compact place to live, he thought of *Spirit*'s interior. I can press both sides of the fuselage with partly outstretched elbows. The wicker seat was curved along the back so hunching forward a bit was natural. That also helped with his headroom and, in fact, a rib in the fuselage had been modified so he could sit upright, more or less. As it was, his head brushed against the celluloid skylight installed above him, but when he looked up Lindbergh could see the stars and add another verification for his nighttime navigation.

The control stick was little more than a bare rod. Beyond a slight bulge at the top there was nothing else on the plain wooden cap to keep his fingers from slipping. A grip . . . why not a knurled grip of some sort with a small ledge on which to rest his right hand during the long hours ahead? Most everything else that needed manipulation was on his left: throttle and mixture controls, each with simple wood knobs, and a sliding lever that extended or retracted the periscope. Albert Clyde Randolph, a Ryan employee, came up with the idea and made it work. The forward visibility through the simple mirrors wasn't much, but he could see hills or telephone wires ahead. It was enough.

The inside of the cockpit was completely exposed, with no weight wasted for paneling or unnecessary finishes. Each ounce saved was an extra ounce of fuel carried, a few more precious moments in the air that could mean the difference between success and failure. Lindbergh knew Commander Dick Byrd's huge *America* had three 220-horsepower Wright engines and could lift a four-man crew with nearly the same poundage in fuel as the *Spirit* weighed altogether. Though Nungesser's *L'Oiseau Blanc* was a single-engine aircraft, its motor was an immense, twelve-cylinder Lorraine-Dietrich that could generate 450 horsepower. René Fonck's enormous, three-engined Sikorsky S-35 boasted red leather seats, extra clothes, a bed, and duck à l'orange to celebrate their arrival in Paris.*

Lindbergh couldn't afford the weight.

He had a few sandwiches in a brown paper bag that Dick Blythe, a Wright Corporation public relations man, bought for him on the way back to Roosevelt Field the night before.† Frank Tichenor, who edited the *Aero Digest,* had asked, "Are you only taking five sandwiches?"

"Yes," Slim had replied. "That's enough. If I get to Paris I won't need any more, and if I don't get to Paris I won't need any more, either."

Flying the mail, he'd remained awake longer than the thirty-odd hours this flight would require. He didn't eat much anyway, as his slight frame evidenced. Fuel and navigation mattered more.

Switching hands on the stick, he folds up the Rand McNally map of New York and shoves it into the chart bag by his left leg. It also contains a pair of dark green sunglasses, a first-

---

* Fonck's plane was also overweight by two tons: a staggering 24,400 pounds gross weight.
† Two ham sandwiches, two beef, and one of hardboiled egg, according to Kenneth Davis in *The Hero* (Garden City, NY: Doubleday, 1959), p. 181.

aid kit, and smelling salts, but he just extracts the next map: Connecticut.

Shifting left again, he squints ahead into the haze. As shore approaches, the gray is darkening to blue, then to green as the misty haze becomes the New England coastline. One of the pitfalls with dead reckoning is the tendency of a pilot to make what he observes outside match what he hopes to see on paper. By holding the 065-degree heading, and leaving Long Island somewhat south of his route, Slim figures he's closer to the Connecticut River than to the planned point at Cedar Island. If that's true, then he should see a nearly perfect corner of land off the nose: the right angle of Old Saybrook sticking into the water. Follow it north to the yawning mouth of the river, maybe a mile wide, emptying into the sound.

The *Spirit* pitches a bit again as the air changes, but Lindbergh is less bothered than before. Passing along Harvey Beach he notes the time, 8:42, and decides to hold this heading. As long as he can see the ground he can get a good fix on *Spirit*'s position. But the engine could be "leaned" out a bit, he thinks, running an eye over the gauges. By manually adjusting how much fuel and air is mixed together he can directly control the motor's performance. A richer mix of fuel to air is necessary for higher throttle settings, such as on takeoff or climbing to higher altitudes. A leaner mix contains less fuel so the engine operates more efficiently in cruise flight. Under stable conditions with the throttle set, less gas is burned, so there is less waste, and the motor is cleaner. This is important with a combustion engine that depends on spark plugs and valves for smooth, consistent operation. Less fuel also means higher engine temperatures that must be monitored closely, and of course if the mixture is too lean the motor will quit.

Slim wants to lean the mixture until the tachometer needle fluctuates, or the motor begins to lose power. More art than science, this operation is affected by many variables: the type of motor, its maintenance, and the aircraft's parameters. There is less pressure at higher altitudes so the air molecules spread out, making the air less dense. Leaning out air that is already thin quickly becomes problematic so the mixture is kept richer. At 150 feet, where he is now, air pressure is greater so the molecules are more closely packed. Temperature makes a difference as hotter air will also force the molecules apart somewhat. Holding the engine at 1,750 revolutions per minute, he eases the mixture knob down another inch until he can hear the difference. The motor is less throaty, and the roaring decreases. When the tachometer fluctuates, he nudges the mixture lever back up a hair until it is steady again.

Ten minutes later, approaching the Thames River valley and rising hills, he climbs gradually to 600 feet. Leveling off, throttling back, and leaning out, Lindbergh holds the airspeed as New London, Connecticut, passes under the right wingtip. Norwich is somewhere upriver to his left, but he can't see it and it doesn't matter anyway. Noting the instrument readings in the log he then switches to the fifth fuel tank and is pleased. A successful takeoff, the first one hundred miles behind him, and everything is working as planned. Nudging the stick left, he angles north five degrees knowing that now is the time to correct toward his great-circle course. If he can get on course the *Spirit* will cross the Blackstone River just north of Providence, Rhode Island.

Pulling out his third railroad map, Slim stares from the window at New England, struck again by the closeness of these eastern states. Morrison County, Minnesota, where he grew up, was bigger than the entire state of Rhode Island.* The land here is so green, the rolling hills heavy with trees, and what

---

* Morrison County is 1,153 square miles while little Rhode Island covers a mere 1,214 square miles. Lindbergh's childhood home of Little Falls was the county seat.

fields he can see are small, irregularly shaped, and filled with cattle or crops. Towns, railroads, and roads clutter the map, and he gives up trying to sort them out. The big landmarks are unmistakable and they're enough. So at five past nine, with Narragansett Bay spreading out off the nose, he finds his exact position. Providence is to the left, and as several bay islands pass to his right Slim figures he's about six miles from Massachusetts. Less than a half hour to the ocean.

Lindbergh is also ten miles off course to the south, but that's not a worry right now as there are ample opportunities ahead for corrections. The sky is clearing just as James "Doc" Kimball from the U.S. Weather Bureau had said it would, and Slim was confident he'd get a good position fix prior to departing the Massachusetts coast. Tilting his head back, he looks up through the skylight and feels a surge of optimism. The lead-colored overcast is thinning in places so the sun's dazzling light begins burning through. Fall River, Taunton, Middleborough, and scores of other towns all slide south beneath the *Spirit*'s wings. Ahead the pilot sees the sky split: lighter gray above with the darker Kingston Bay shoreline below. North and south of the town, about a half mile offshore, a pair of beaches reach inward to form a natural breakwater. A narrow gap allows ship traffic, and through his right window he can see a squat, rust-colored lighthouse. Shaped like a spark plug, it's perched near shoals at the center of the channel.*

Looking back as the coastline disappears under the tail, Lindbergh folds up his last Rand McNally map and stows it. With the immense, curving fishhook of Cape Cod Bay off his right wing, he tugs out the chart he'll use for the rest of the flight. Called a Mercator projection, it essentially unrolls, or

---

* Duxbury Pier Light, built in 1871. Also called the Bug, it is, in fact, the first spark plug lighthouse in the United States.

projects, the three-dimensional earth onto a two-dimensional surface. The orange peel again, but this time stitched together. Because of this, the longitude and latitude lines appear straight, at right angles to each other, and though unrealistic it allows huge distances to be plotted on a single chart. If periodic corrections are made that account for the earth's shape then the Mercator gives accurate compass bearings between two points. For this reason it's the best tool available for the *Spirit*'s journey.

His second 100-mile point was just ahead, between the dark smudge of Boston to his left, and Race Point on the right. The great Cape Cod fishhook ends here, at Provincetown, curling around 270 degrees to point back east. Lindbergh couldn't see it, but he knew there was a stone tower in the harbor commemorating the *Mayflower*'s first anchorage.* The thought of those Pilgrims spending two months at sea in a hundred-foot ship had once seemed outrageous, yet now he was going to cross that same daunting ocean in a 27-foot, eight-inch-long aircraft.

With the cape off his right wing, Slim nudges the stick and gently kicks the rudder, watching the compass wobble around until 071 degrees appears under the line. He'll hold this heading for the next hundred miles, then check to the right again, adjusting for the earth's curve. Still at 150 feet over the waves, Slim absorbs the sense of sheer space that would likely overwhelm a pilot unused to it. Years of flying over the vast American Midwest proved to be good practice for open-water flying. The Wright Whirlwind is steady at 1,760 revolutions and the other gauges read normal as he carefully switches to the nose

---

* The 252-foot Pilgrim Monument. On November 11, 1620, Captain Christopher Jones anchored the *Mayflower* here after failing to find Virginia. Another sixteen days passed before the Pilgrims took a small boat across the bay to land on the site of present-day Plymouth, Massachusetts.

fuel tank. His course is set, his chart is open and ready, and the *Spirit* is performing perfectly.

As America fades away behind him, he stares down at the Mercator projection; so many points on a map, so carefully calculated and plotted. They must have seemed almost arrogant now. Paris, still just a distant, impersonal black dot, is over 3,000 miles away. Thirty-five more heading changes over unknown spots. Well, unknown to him, but the marks between Long Island and Cape Cod had been strange a few hours ago, too. Now they're real memories of actual places, just as those points ahead will be. As the world rotates beneath him the pilot takes comfort in knowing that each degree of turn, each foot and mile traveled, brings Paris closer. Slim is struck, not for the first time, by the power and magnificent potential of flight. What better way to demonstrate that the world can truly be opened to man than by safely flying between continents? Staring ahead toward the shimmering horizon Charles Lindbergh knows this is the real reason for accepting this challenge, and the terrible risk to his own life.

TWO

HOPE

FEAR DIDN'T PLAY much into Lindbergh's thinking, and independence, toughness, intelligence, and stubbornness were inherited traits. His paternal great-grandfather, Ola Mansson, personified these attributes that would surface throughout Charles's life. Born in the village of Gardlosa, Sweden, on the southern tip of the Scandinavian peninsula, in 1808, Mansson grew up just miles inland from the Baltic coast. It was a region rich in Norse mythology, home to the legend of Beowulf and Viking excursions, and bred a particularly hardy, resilient population.

Elected to the Riksdag, the Swedish parliament, in 1847, Mansson served on the Appropriations Committee and was appointed to the State Bank of Sweden. Outspoken and a bit self-righteous, he acquired enemies in proportion to his rising power; his ardent support for social reform didn't help. He backed rights for Jews, the infirm, and for women, whose company Mansson enjoyed while in Stockholm away from his wife and growing family.

Despite some success, by 1858 Mansson's life began to un-ravel and in January a dalliance with a teenager named Lovisa Carlen produced a son. A maid in Ola's Stockholm residence discovered a letter from Lovisa disclosing the birth and implor-ing him to meet his boy; the maid promptly forwarded this to Mansson's wife, Ingar, who was obviously displeased. Later that year, Ola's political enemies arranged for a government prosecutor to charge him with embezzlement. It was subse-quently revealed that he had violated banking regulations by acting as a loan agent, and pocketing a 1 percent commission, while serving on the board for the Bank of Sweden.

Just before Christmas 1858, the courts ruled against him, and Ola learned he was to be dismissed from government ser-vice. Mansson appealed to the Supreme Court to gain a bit of time, but he also began learning English and planning his exit to North America. Securing a passport in the spring of 1859, Mansson and Lovisa were gone by the time he lost his appeal in June.* With eighteen-month-old Karl August, the couple left for England, then sailed from Liverpool to Quebec. As with many beginning a fresh life in the New World, Mansson de-cided to change names upon arriving in Canada. In *Lindbergh*, A. Scott Berg states that "he adopted the surname his older two sons had acquired at the University in Lund."

This is certainly possible. In *One Summer: America, 1927,* Bill Bryson writes that "Lindbergh" means "linden tree moun-tain," which it more or less does in several languages, but not in Swedish. If this is what occurred, the name would have likely been "Lindenbergh," though it could have been shortened with mistranslations. In fact, there are no linden trees in Sweden,

---

* Mansson did ask his wife, Ingar, to leave with him, but understandably she refused. Before departing, Ola deeded his property to his legal Swedish family so they would be with means of support.

though they do grow in parts of Canada. Reeve Lindbergh, Ola's great-granddaughter, admits she was told the latter version, and it was family lore. But she concedes that the Anglicized etymology was probably granted after the fact and adds, "I doubt that this meaning, lovely as it is, has anything to do with the name change itself, though it certainly is in the family tradition. I understood and repeated this from my childhood onward, wherever it came from."

Another explanation for the name that became a household word is a combination of both theories. Adopting "Lund" seems reasonable as it was one of the oldest, most prominent cities in Sweden. Barely fifty miles from Gardlosa where Ola was born, its university is the largest in the country. *Borgh* is defined as "fortress" or "city" in Old Swedish, and Ola may have been paying homage to his ancestry with the name Lundborgh. Or maybe he simply liked the way it sounded. Given Mansson's accent, the name could be easily heard as Lindbergh and subsequently written this way on the new Canadian or American documents.

However they were named, the newly christened Lindberghs traveled west and in July 1859 they crossed by train from Windsor, Ontario, into the United States. Continuing deeper into the frontier, the Manssons, now August and Louisa Lindbergh, passed Chicago headed for Dubuque, Iowa, on the Mississippi River. A steamboat, considerably more comfortable than the trains, brought them three hundred miles north to St. Anthony Falls in the infant state of Minnesota.* Pushing deeper to the very edge of civilization by wagon and cart, August finally stopped some ninety miles northwest of the falls and built a sod home for the winter near Melrose.

---

* Present-day Minneapolis.

Working hard and expanding his home, August lost his left arm to a saw blade in 1861, yet he survived to sire six more children in addition to Karl August, the boy he'd brought from Sweden. Now known as Charles August, or "C.A.," the eldest Lindbergh son grew up tall, and was independent, if a bit narrow in his thinking, much like his father. Hunting and roaming the land from a young age, he had no real schooling until early adolescence, when, for six dollars a week, he attended Grove Lake Academy. Two years of studies enabled C.A. to gain entrance to the University of Michigan at Ann Arbor, where he matriculated with a law degree in 1883. Extremely handsome, the twenty-four-year-old C.A. had high cheekbones, a dimpled chin, and clear, hard eyes that left little doubt of his determination. For several years he moved around, exploring possibilities and gaining experience, but in 1885, at the age of twenty-seven, he returned home to Minnesota. The young attorney hung up a shingle in a town called Little Falls, about thirty miles northwest of his parents, and went to work.

While living at the local boardinghouse he met a girl, Mary LaFond, and they were married two years later. Two children soon followed and by 1890, Charles August Lindbergh was the picture of success and the embodiment of the American dream. A son of immigrants, he'd survived life on the frontier, earned a university degree, and was now Morrison County's attorney. C.A. also began to acquire real estate: substantial holdings throughout the county, including the first creamery and a large brick home for his family.

Eight years later Mary succumbed to a cancerous abdominal tumor, leaving C.A. with two young daughters: ten-year-old Lillian and six-year-old Eva. In the fall of 1900, after eighteen months of quiet grief for his wife, he sent the girls to Stanley Hall, a Minneapolis boarding school, rented out his house, and moved into Little Falls' Antlers Hotel. He threw himself into the real estate business and his law practice, and with characteristic toughness C. A. Lindbergh persevered with his lonely life. Yet a poet once said "solitude is fine but you need someone to tell you solitude is fine," and certainly this was about to happen for the forty-one-year-old widower.

C.A. had a younger brother, Frank, and two sisters, Juno and Linda, all living in the area. Little Falls was now a county seat with a growing school system to meet the needs of its five thousand strong population, and the school superintendent was his brother-in-law, Joseph Seal, Linda's husband. One afternoon in September 1900, Superintendent Seal was in the Antlers Hotel to meet a teacher newly arrived from Detroit, and he introduced the young lady to C. A. Lindbergh.

A blue-eyed, twenty-four-year-old graduate of the University of Michigan, Evangeline Lodge Land had come to Minnesota looking for adventure. Accepting a position to teach chemistry, she found herself instructing a total of five courses, including botany and physics. Feisty and confrontational, Evangeline was soon at odds with the school officials and she was not particularly enamored with Minnesota. She had been born and raised in Detroit, a positive metropolis compared to Little Falls, and certainly a great deal more cosmopolitan.

Dr. Edwin Albert Lodge, Evangeline's maternal grandfather, was the nation's foremost proponent of homeopathic medicine. Undoubtedly quite intelligent, he was also opinionated, stubborn, and a minor religious fanatic. After joining the Church of the Disciples of Christ, a fundamentalist movement dedicated to restoring Christian unity, Lodge prohibited dancing within his family, hot meals on Sunday, and generally fun of any sort. Hardly a loving man at any time, Dr. Lodge was also quarrelsome and frequently verbally abusive. The only one of his eleven children with whom he had a workable relationship was his daughter Evangeline, who married Dr. Charles Henry Land in 1875.

Regarded as one of the most progressive dentists of his time, Charles Land, though eccentric, had several dozen patents granted in his name and pioneered the use of porcelain in dentistry.* Outspoken, he encouraged diversity in thought, independence in attitude and, above all, education. It was no surprise then that his daughter, also named Evangeline, would earn a degree in a time when many women were barely literate and expected to devote themselves to bearing children. Nor was it surprising that she inherited his self-confidence, disdain for authority, and considerable fearlessness. It *was* surprising that such a girl would become smitten with a widowed lawyer seventeen years her senior in a place like Little Falls, Minnesota. Yet she did just that.

When C. A. Lindbergh, rising attorney, wealthy landowner, and Morrison County's most eligible bachelor, proposed in December 1900, Evangeline Lodge Land did not refuse him outright. However, she did resign from her fifty-five-dollars-per-month teaching job and return to her parents in Detroit to consider his offer, which she accepted.

At the time of his second marriage on March 27, 1901, C.A. was doing quite well. He practiced a bit of criminal law, but made most of his money by managing business affairs for large corporations with local interests. These included the Singer Manufacturing Company, the McCormick Harvesting Machine Company, and the Weyerhaeuser Syndicate's vast timber holdings. Though most of his wealth was in land, C. A.

---

* Dr. Charles Henry Land is credited with inventing the all-ceramic, porcelain jacket crown.

Lindbergh was worth approximately $200,000, a considerable fortune in 1901.* On 110 acres south of town he built one of the finest homes in Morrison County for his bride, which featured five bedrooms, a billiard room, indoor plumbing, and hot water radiators against the brutal Minnesota winters. After returning from their ten-week honeymoon through Colorado, Oregon, and California, the couple camped out on the bluffs overlooking the Mississippi while their home was finished. That summer Evangeline announced she was pregnant, and at 1:30 a.m. on February 2, 1902, at her parents' Detroit home, she gave birth to a nine-pound, eight-ounce infant named Charles Augustus Lindbergh.†

THE WORLD CHARLES A. Lindbergh entered on that cold midwestern morning was changing rapidly. During the month of Charles's birth, Robert Falcon Scott, together with Ernest Shackleton and the rest of the Discovery Expedition, arrived in the Antarctic and would reach a record 82 degrees latitude south by the end of the year. The Nile, then considered the world's longest river, was dammed at Aswan. King Edward VII was crowned in August, following the reign of England's longest-serving monarch, Queen Victoria. In Nice, France, an automobile driven by Léon Serpollet would reach 74 miles per hour, a new land speed record, and the world's first movie theater opened in Los Angeles. In Vietnam the Paul Doumer Bridge was completed, connecting Hanoi on both sides of the Red River, and Denmark was negotiating the sale of the Virgin

---

* About $5.5 million in 2016 dollars.
† He is often listed as a "junior" but this is erroneous as his middle name was Augustus, not August like his father's.

Islands to the United States. Teddy Roosevelt was in the White House following the assassination of William McKinley the previous September, and the Philippine-American War would end.* A pair of South Carolina congressmen had a fistfight in the Senate, and Charles Lewis Tiffany, founder of Tiffany & Company in New York, died.

New technologies were beginning to capture the American imagination and transform daily life. Just twenty-five years earlier a scant 7,500 telegraph offices existed in the entire country, but now there were more than 23,000. American Telephone & Telegraph routed nearly 2.5 billion calls per year for the 2,525,606 telephones in the United States. And in a satisfying twist of fate, just months after Charles Lindbergh was born, Wilbur Wright made the final flights in his 1902 glider over Kill Devil Hills, North Carolina. With the addition of a steerable rudder, the aircraft could now truly maneuver and would be ready for the first historic, powered flight the following year.

Young Charles, of course, was blissfully unconcerned with all this, recalling later in life only the carriages, dinner parties, and his mother playing the piano. C.A. was briefly happy, caught up with his pretty wife, his young children, and apparently successful career. He seemed to truly love Evangeline, yet historians agree the elder Lindbergh had a profoundly difficult time demonstrating his feelings, not just for his wife, but also for the girls—and Charles. However, given his own father's temperament, his upbringing in rural Minnesota, and a natural stoicism, this was understandable. However, for a young, passionate woman like Evangeline it was difficult, especially when

---

* Roosevelt would also be the first U.S. president to ride in an automobile; a Columbia Electric Victoria.

the honeymoon glitz had worn away and life in Little Falls with a man old enough to be her father loomed ahead.

Life for the Lindberghs began to unravel in 1905. Scrupulously honest, C.A. lacked a businessman's killer instinct and often held promissory notes in lieu of cash for property transactions. Habitually buying too high and selling too low tends to make one popular with those on the other end of the deals, but it was a sure way to bleed assets dry. Nor did C.A.'s idealism mix well with financial realities. He launched a quarterly magazine of sorts, *The Law of Rights, Realized and Unrealized, Individual and Public,* and as the title would suggest, the publication was not successful.

Like his father before him, C. A. Lindbergh was a genuine supporter of the working class. Somewhat ironically, given his own business dealings with large corporations, he was rabidly opposed to big business. Why, he asked, should a handful of corporate entities be permitted to dominate entire markets like railroads, oil, and telephones, and through them manipulate the economy? Banks especially earned C.A.'s enmity and he created the Industrial Adjustment Company in 1905, basically a rural cooperative, to fight them. The company would buy local animals, butcher them in Little Falls, and ship directly to merchants, thereby eliminating the middleman.

Businesses in the area were encouraged to join together and this would, it was hoped, eliminate unnecessary competition while presenting a unified front against big corporate encroachment. This essentially socialist approach was not well received among the fiercely independent local merchants, nor were they willing to go bankrupt in the name of Lindbergh's "masses against the classes" philosophy. The company predictably went bust by early 1907, costing C.A. $20,000, which represented most of his liquid assets. Dr. Charles Land, Evangeline's father,

and Frank Lindbergh, C.A.'s younger brother, lost their investments as well.

Adding to the year's misery, the Lindbergh home burned
to the ground. An exact cause was never determined, but the
maid's oil lamp was suspected as the house burned from the
top down. Neighbors managed to save the piano and quite a
few downstairs furnishings, including Evangeline's prized blue
willowware, but the structure would have to be entirely rebuilt.
Bundling his family—six Lindberghs, two dogs, and a nurse-
maid for little Charles—around to several locations, they eventually settled into a suite at the Buckman Hotel in Little Falls.
Pressing her husband to immediately rebuild the home, Evangeline soon realized the extent of C.A.'s financial troubles. By the
end of the year, he himself admitted, "We are exceedingly poor
in cash, and will be for some time to come."

Whether money was the culprit or not, the original grand
home on the banks of the Mississippi was never truly resurrected. A one-and-a-half-story house did eventually go up,
but there was neither central heat or indoor plumbing. Then
in June a bit of hope appeared. Local Progressives were not
happy with Clarence Bennett Buckman, the incumbent Republican congressman from Minnesota's Sixth District.* Among
other things, he was apparently using his congressional position
to secure timber contracts on land he happened to own. Such
perfidy infuriated the Progressives who soon enlisted C. A.
Lindbergh, champion of the common man, to fight corruption.
Whether motivated by idealism, ambition, or a desire to distance himself from rural Minnesota, C.A. announced his intention to run for Congress and won the September Republican

---

* Buckman also owned the hotel that housed the Lindberghs, and his daughter was married to C. A. Lindbergh's younger brother Frank.

primary by seven percentage points. He was then victorious in November's general election by a narrow margin.*

Eager to escape Little Falls, C.A. moved his family to Washington, D.C., well in advance of the Sixtieth Congress's December 2, 1907, opening. Located at 1831 Vernon Street, between Kalorama and Lanier Heights, the newly built Romaine Hotel seemed an ideal location. Close to parks, shopping, and Dupont Circle, perhaps C.A. hoped his family would enjoy the impressive surroundings and their new situation would dispel past unhappiness.

It did not.

The elder Lindbergh immersed himself in the job, as he had always done, eating breakfast in his office and sometimes working from dawn till midnight. Had Evangeline been able to join the D.C. cocktail circuit and partake in the glittering public life open to congressmen, perhaps their relationship would have improved. But C.A.'s terse, stoic façade was hardly conducive to friendships, nor did he drink, gamble, or otherwise socialize. Even if he had, nothing would have likely improved between his daughters and their stepmother. Willful and independent teenagers, Lillian and Eva had borne the brunt of C.A.'s tumultuous life and apparently resented their step-mother Evangeline, who was closer to their ages than to her husband. Both returned west and Lillian met Dr. Loren Roberts while attending the University of Michigan, eventually marrying him. Eva attended Carleton College in Northfield, Minnesota, then rejoined C.A. as an intern in Washington before her own marriage to George W. Christie, a journalist.

At five years old Charles was oblivious to most of this and

---

* The Sixth Congressional district tallied 16,762 for C. A. Lindbergh against Buckman's 13,115.

what he did recall, he usually suppressed. This denial, this mental shutdown of painful emotional situations, would develop into a lifelong habit that sometimes worked to his advantage, but often did not. Berg agrees, writing in *Lindbergh* that Charles "simply learned at a young age to see and hear only that which he wanted to." Yet the boy hunted Easter eggs on the White House lawn and was appointed as a special Senate page so he could have a front-row seat for Woodrow Wilson's inauguration. There were trips to Philadelphia, New York, and even the Panama Canal. Summers were spent with his grandparents in Detroit or back in Little Falls, where Charles relished his outdoor life of camping, skinny-dipping, fishing, and hunting. He was growing up physically tough, mentally introspective, and emotionally reclusive. Charles also developed the habit of internalizing his conversations, quite possibly since there was no one but himself and his dog Wahgoosh in whom to confide. The fox terrier slept with the boy and often shared his breakfast.

Proud of his father, Lindbergh wrote that C.A. always called him "Boss." Despite the public persona, there was quiet humor in the man and whenever possible C.A. would take his son on "expeditions to rivers, creeks and lakes." A solitary man, separated from his wife and increasingly isolated by his politics, C.A. reached out to his son in the only way he knew. Charles recognized this and recalled that "I became his partner."

The situation between his parents remained publicly polite. They attended White House receptions and occasionally dined in the congressional dining room, yet privately the marriage was finished. Evangeline had asked C.A. for a divorce in 1909 but agreed to keep up pretenses for the sake of "the boy" and her husband's flourishing political career. A man of complexities and contradictions, C.A. refused to be buttonholed as a Republican, even though that party elected him. He would not attend caucuses, nor subject himself to party discipline. Congressman Lindbergh voted his conscience; he opposed the establishment of the Federal Reserve and supported women's suffrage. Though he unequivocally favored an individual's right to consume alcohol, C.A. fervently believed in Prohibition, stating that the sale of liquor was "attended with practices that are extremely detrimental to good government."

Blossoming intellectually, though regrettably not emotionally, C.A. found his niche in Washington within the movements for American social and economic change. Outspoken and uncompromising, he was either respected or reviled, depending on one's point of view. Rivals back in Minnesota dug up his numerous land transactions and insinuated that the champion of the common man, the antitrust warrior and bank hater, had profited from farm foreclosures. Lindbergh responded by selling off his property, and within a few years his net worth was half of what it had been when he left Little Falls. Fearing perceptions of hypocrisy, C.A. dissociated himself from lucrative corporate clients, neglecting his law practice and generating a cash flow crisis that would last the rest of his life.

Like his father in the Swedish Riksdag, Congressman Lindbergh seemed to cast himself as a contemporary Don Quixote, charging against the windmills of the powerful and wealthy. He may have gloried in the fight, but Evangeline certainly did not. She was not willing to sacrifice herself, or her son, on the altar of politics and this irreparably widened the schism between them. By now C.A. and his wife were maintaining separate residences in Washington, which meant a string of boardinghouses for Charles and Evangeline. When they were together, civility eroded quickly. Enraged during one violent confrontation, Evangeline held a gun to C.A.'s head. He merely shrugged and said, "If you must do it, do it."

She'd also discovered that her husband was having a long-term affair with his stenographer, who'd joined his D.C. staff from Little Falls. Isolated and lonely, Evangeline transferred her energies and affections to Charles. Lindbergh's reserve, loathing of politics, and overdeveloped introspection all had their roots in the decade he spent as a congressman's son. Nonetheless, Evangeline and Charles immersed themselves in the capital's culture: the memorials, art galleries, and, of course, the Smithsonian Institution.* At age eleven, he was enrolled in the Friends School, an exclusive Washington, D.C., Quaker academy, his first encounter with rigorous academics.†

Then, in June 1912, C.A. arranged for Charles (with Evangeline) to attend the yearly Army Aeronautical Trials to evaluate new aircraft. This one, like the first such event in 1908, was being held just across the Potomac River at Fort Myer, Virginia. Lindbergh would recount, "One of the planes took off and raced a motor car around the oval track in front of us. You could see its pilot clearly, out in front—pant's legs flapping, and cap visor pointed backward to streamline in the wind." ‡ Electrified, the boy later admitted it was there he realized that he wanted to be a pilot himself. "I used to imagine myself with wings," he wrote more than forty years later, "on which I could swoop down off our roof into the valley, soaring through the air from one river bank to the other."

TWO SUMMERS FOLLOWING Lindbergh's epiphany, a motorcade carrying a beribboned, middle-aged man and his portly

---

* Lindbergh would later lend the *Spirit of St. Louis* to the Smithsonian, where it was put on public display on May 13, 1928, and still resides today.
† Later known as Sidwell Friends School. Among his classmates were President Teddy Roosevelt's sons, Kermit and Quentin, the latter of whom would posthumously give his name to Roosevelt Field on Long Island.
‡ Likely a Curtiss Model D biplane.

wife threaded its way through the warm streets of Sarajevo. Archduke Franz Ferdinand, heir apparent to the Austro-Hungarian Empire, was smiling and waving when a young Bosnian Serb stepped from the crowd and drew a pistol. Gavrilo Princip calmly fired several shots, mortally wounding both the archduke and his consort, Princess Sophie.

Dominoes began falling around the world a month later.

Austria-Hungary, a member of the Triple Alliance with Italy and Germany, declared war on Serbia. Russia, seeking to bolster a battered national image and distract its people from internal misery, mobilized to protect her Slavic "brethren." Germany immediately responded by gearing up for war, all the while demanding that France remain passively neutral. Allied with Britain under the Entente Cordiale, Paris rejected the ultimatum, and the Kaiser now had a pretext for picking a fight with everyone. Russia was first, followed by Luxembourg, and on August 3, 1914, Germany declared war on France then promptly invaded Belgium. What was to be called the "Great War" began in earnest when British troops landed on French soil in fulfillment of the Entente Cordiale. Four bloody years later, with some thirty million dead, wounded, or missing from the industrialized slaughter of the western front, an armistice was signed in Compiègne, France. Hostilities were over, at least temporarily, but there would be no lasting peace.

Back on the farm and too young to fight, Charles Lindbergh had listened to the distant war with rapt attention. His interests in aviation had been growing steadily and, like many young men, he was enamored with tales of the Red Baron or Eddie Rickenbacker and could see himself in a fighter cockpit over a far-off battlefield. By necessity, the war had taken flying to new levels through astounding advances in technology, training, and tactics. The first Royal Flying Corps aircraft to arrive in France were a mismatched collection of mechanized canvas kites held together by varnish and wire. Used for scouting and artillery spotting, they had temperamental, underpowered engines barely capable of 75 miles per hour under ideal conditions.

Four years later everything had changed. In 1914 it was not uncommon for pilots to enter combat with five hours of flight time and no tactical training at all. The resulting casualty rate—sometimes 100 percent—resulted in drastic changes to pilot selection, academic instruction, and flight training. Optical, hermetically sealed gunsights employed with metallic belt-link ammunition transformed aerial gunnery into a deadly reality.

Through the practical and unforgiving laboratory of war, the science of aerodynamics leapt forward. Aircraft became more maneuverable as ailerons were added and designs streamlined. Structural and material innovations led to lighter, more efficient wings, which, when combined with better engines, exponentially improved aircraft range, flight endurance, and possibilities.

Engine technology radically advanced. The 80-horsepower rotary motors of 1914 were outclassed by stationary radial engines with bigger pistons and higher compression ratios. Mercedes, Hispano-Suiza, and Bentley were among those capable of 200 horsepower or better, and airspeeds greater than 135 miles per hour. Through its use in war, aviation could no longer be dismissed as a fad, so it rapidly entered mainstream life and fired the imaginations of young Americans.

While attending a farm auction on November 11, 1918, young Charles Lindbergh heard the news that a treaty had been signed, and discovered he now lacked a direction in life. Excused from his final two periods of high school to raise food for the war effort, Charles was ambivalent about life as a farmer. It was back-breaking and monotonous, risky work that could be wiped out by the vagaries of weather or disease. He could be injured, even killed, by a sudden storm, an animal, or a piece of equipment.

"As I grew older," Lindbergh later recalled, "I learned that danger was a part of life not always to be shunned. It often surrounded the things you liked most to do." Charles wasn't afraid of risks, but there was no excitement, no adventure, in a farmer's life. His high school grades seemed to indicate a path, or at least a general direction, that would capitalize on his abilities. At six feet three inches, Charles was strong and slender, with a natural aptitude for mechanics and science. He earned high marks in physics and chemistry, in particular.

Nineteen eighteen was a traumatic and unsettling time for Americans in general and the sixteen-year-old specifically. Bombs and bullets aside, the war continued killing for another two years through the spread of a deadly new virus that the medical community identified as H1N1: known today as influenza. Inaccurately termed "Spanish flu," the pandemic most likely began through infected pigs kept in the squalor of the western front trenches.* Troops transiting through a huge British Expeditionary Force depot at Étaples-sur-Mer spread the virus within the enormous hospitals, the railheads of northern France, and then across the English Channel. Ships returning to the United States from Europe brought the virus with them, and through the nation's expanding rail network soldiers heading home quickly spread the disease.

"It was explained at the Department of Health," the *New York Times* reported, "that New York City could not be charged with these cases, as there were men in the army and navy service who contracted the disease at camp, cantonment or on board ship."

Cheap entertainment was now plentiful—some eight hundred movies were opened in 1918 alone—and crowded

---

* Wartime censors exaggerated the flu virus's impact in neutral Spain to keep up morale in Britain, France, and the United States.

theaters helped spread the disease. Dockworkers also retransmitted the flu to vessels from every nation and it rapidly traversed the globe. In the end, more than 500 million people were infected and at least 50 million died.* Life expectancy for an American adult dropped by twelve years in a single twelve-month period.†

Inevitably, social upheaval accompanied the health disaster. To begin with, Congress poorly handled the deflation of a wartime economy so production fell and America plunged into a pronounced recession, inflamed by hyperinflation in Europe. Jobs disappeared and those that remained were now at a premium. This was exacerbated by millions of young men who had enlisted to fight and whose jobs were taken by women and 500,000 black males. Tensions were further inflamed by D. W. Griffith's popular film *The Clansman* (later renamed *The Birth of a Nation*), which resurrected a nearly defunct Ku Klux Klan.‡ When soldiers returned home they wanted their jobs back and, unprotected by unions who didn't accept them, mobs of young black men were now unemployed or in direct competition with white males for scarce jobs. Race riots broke out in thirty-eight cities during 1918.

Drastically empowered during the war, the government seemed analogous to a teenager who, discovering his muscles for the first time, runs amok. Five years earlier a Democrat-controlled Congress and White House permitted the passage of the Sixteenth Amendment, which in turn led to the Revenue Act of 1913 and a reinstatement of federal income tax.§

---

* Commonwealth Pier in Boston was likely the main North American hub for the virus's dispersion.
† Before the epidemic this was about fifty-three years of age for an adult male.
‡ Griffith's *The Clansman* was based on a 1905 book and play of the same name by Thomas Dixon Jr., a Southern Baptist minister.
§ The first amendment in forty-three years. The Fifteenth Amendment, passed in 1870, granted suffrage to black males.

The same administration enacted the Espionage Act, granting itself broad powers to contain any sort of domestic support for Germany or Italy. A 1918 amendment often erroneously termed the Sedition Act expanded this to also prohibit "disloyal, profane, scurrilous, or abusive language" concerning the flag, the military and, of course, the U.S. government itself. Thousands were jailed and held indefinitely. On December 21, 1919, the U.S. Army transport ship *Buford* steamed out of New York Harbor with 249 "undesirables" aboard. Nearly a month later the ship anchored in Hanko, Finland, and the deportees were escorted onto Russian Bolshevik soil. The news media heralded the government's action, with the Cleveland *Plain Dealer* writing, "It is hoped and expected that other vessels, larger, more commodious, carrying similar cargoes, will follow in her wake."

Closer to home Congressman Lindbergh's life gradually disintegrated. Deciding to run for the Senate after a decade in the House, he placed fourth out of four candidates. C.A.'s vitriolic diatribes left him increasingly isolated and he made powerful enemies among the members of the Federal Reserve Board who were resolved to end his career. He had vehemently opposed America's entry into the war, a stance that was perceived as unpatriotic and his oldest daughter, Lillian, died of tuberculosis in California. After recovering from a hernia operation, C.A. then chose to run in the 1918 Minnesota Republican gubernatorial primary. Supported by the Nonpartisan League, founded by A. C. Townley, organizer of the American Socialist Party, Lindbergh lost the election by a humiliating margin.

Because of his opposition to America's entry into World War I and his attacks on the Federal Reserve Board, C.A. was hanged in effigy in Red Wing, Minnesota, with talk of tarring and feathering. Printing plates for his two books were destroyed at Washington's National Capital Press and his next attempt at publishing, *Lindbergh's National Farmer,* was a failure. Uncompromising, controversial, and evidently unlikable, C. A. Lindbergh was sliding into the twilight of his life.

YET AMID GLOBAL and national turmoil, aviation had the power to give hope and inspire, particularly to a youthful Charles Lindbergh.

On May 8, 1919, three U.S. Navy Curtiss Flying Boats, *NC-1, NC-3,* and *NC-4,* lifted off from Naval Air Station Rockaway in Queens, New York, bound for Newfoundland, to attempt the first powered aircraft flight across the Atlantic. Leaving very little to chance, the Navy arranged for warships to be spread out between the American East Coast and Plymouth, England, the ultimate destination.

The planes departed from Trepassey, on the southern edge of Newfoundland's Avalon Peninsula, on May 16, 1919, bound for the Azores. American warships were positioned at fifty-mile intervals, spotlights illuminated and star shells blazing, to guide the aviators through the night. *NC-1,* flown by Lieutenant Commander Marc Mitscher, went down but the five-man crew was rescued.* *NC-3* managed a water landing and Commander John Henry "Jack" Towers taxied across the waves for two hundred miles toward the Azores before being towed into harbor. Lieutenant Commander Albert Cushing Read, flying *NC-4,* made it safely to Horta, in the Azores, on May 17, and

---

* Marc Mitscher would later command the aircraft carrier USS *Hornet* during the battle of Midway, and retired as an admiral. Jack Towers, piloting *NC-3,* would command the very first American aircraft carrier, the USS *Langley,* and would also rise to the rank of admiral.

within days departed for Lisbon, Portugal; then Ferrol, Spain; finally landing in Plymouth on May 31, 1919.

LONDON GIVES READ AND CREW OF NC-4 A GREAT RE-CEPTION, ran the *New York Times* headline on June 2. The *London Chronicle* added, "The congratulations of all Britain will go out to these plucky representatives of the United States."

After returning to the States, Commander Read stated, "It soon will be possible to drive an airplane around the world at a height of 60,000 feet and 1,000 miles per hour." Truly prophetic, this extraordinary vision was ridiculed by an editorial in the *Times,* which stated, "It is one thing to be a qualified aviator, and quite another to be a qualified prophet."

Yet Read's feat fired the imaginations of others, including a seventeen-year-old Charles Lindbergh. He had never forgotten the experience at the 1908 Army Aeronautical Trials and was seriously considering an engineering career. In any event, the Navy wasn't interested in publicity or fame; the flight was a challenge to be met. Though a spectacular achievement for the time, using fifty-three warships and multiple aircraft certainly wasn't feasible for anyone other than the U.S. government.

The Navy event was quickly eclipsed, for two weeks later, during the week of June 14, two Englishmen lifted off from Lester's Field near St. John's, Newfoundland, and headed east toward Great Britain. Former Royal Flying Corps pilots Captain John "Jack" Alcock and Lieutenant Arthur Whitten-Brown set out across the Atlantic in a modified Vickers Vimy long-range bomber.

The June 15 *Times* headline read: GIANT BIPLANE IN AT-TEMPTING TO RISE FOR THE START BARELY CLEARS TREES AND FENCES IN FIGHTING THE WIND. NO MESSAGE FROM VIMY AFTER ELEVEN HOURS.

Flying through the night in fog so heavy they couldn't see their propellers, the men lost all heating and hit turbulence so severe they dropped from 4,000 feet to the wavetops in seconds. A snowstorm caused such severe icing that "Teddy" Brown had to crawl out on the wings to chip away at the stuff before it brought the plane down.

Fifteen hours after leaving Newfoundland the pair found themselves over Ireland's Galway coast near Clifden and decided to land. Alcock chose a fertile green pasture south of town that unfortunately happened to be the soft ground of Derrygimla Moor. The Vimy ended up on its nose in the bog, but both men were uninjured and the first nonstop, non-airship crossing of the Atlantic had just been successfully accomplished.* Their landing hardly mattered, though, as both men became instant international celebrities, claimed the *Daily Mail* prize of £10,000, and were knighted by King George V.

THE DAWN OF the 1920s offered some hope to a weary world. There was a sense that the millions who had died in the carnage of the Great War had proven the "old" world order was wrong, and that everything it stood for could be discarded. All over the world people were shaking off the figurative dust of irrelevant beliefs, discarded morality, and, perhaps most of all, past limitations. As Ronald W. Hull would later write:

> The war to end all wars was over,
>   and so was the deadly flu.
> It was time to think of life and living,
>   a time for me and you.

---

* Three weeks later, on July 2, 1919, the British airship *R34* would make the first nonstop east-west crossing from East Fortune, Scotland, to Long Island, New York. It landed on Roosevelt Field after a 108-hour, 12-minute flight. Zachary Lansdowne, future commander of the USS *Shenandoah*, was aboard.

Anything seemed possible.

This was especially true in the United States, which prized independence, change, and innovation. Throughout the next few years more than 40 percent of global manufactured goods would be made in the United States. Half of the planet's recovered gold reserves were in American banks, and 85 percent of the world's automobiles were made in U.S. factories. Technological advances of all types were invented, designed, and manufactured into reality in America: iceboxes, the washing machine, electric fans, the vacuum cleaner, and that marvel of modern communications, the radio. As Charles Lindbergh headed off to college, one in five hundred families owned a radio set. Just a few years later it would be one in twenty.

In this spirit, eighteen-year-old Charles Lindbergh rode his Excelsior motorcycle 365 miles southeast to the University of Wisconsin in Madison to study mechanical engineering. He would later write, "I don't want to go to college very much. Both Father and Mother went to the University of Michigan, and they think I ought to be a college graduate too. Everyone says it's important to have a diploma. It helps you get along in later life."

Arriving late, he failed to impress his instructors and seemed to find the classroom atmosphere stifling. Like his parents, Charles was a rebel in a quiet, stubborn sort of way. He chafed against the constraints placed on fledgling university students, such as nonsensical traditions like wearing a green freshman beanie and the arcane, at least to him, rules of formal education. In a satirical English essay penned by Lindbergh, St. Peter refuses admission to a man due to a missing comma in his passport: "[a] pity, to permit so many mechanical errors to bar good material from eternal commendation."

Failing English, Lindbergh also ended the first semester on probation in mathematics and chemistry, yet he performed well enough in his other subjects. Surprisingly, given his social aloofness, he excelled in the Reserve Officer Training Corps as a field artillery cadet. Charles also ended the academic year as the top marksman on the nation's university rifle team. He was known for consistently perfect scores and for shooting silver Liberty quarters out of a teammate's fingers. Though he returned to school in the fall of 1921, Lindbergh was again considering life as a farmer if his scholastic situation didn't improve. It did not.

Recalling those times, he later stated, "Why should I continue studying to pass examinations to get into a life I didn't want to lead—a life of factories, and drawing boards, and desks. . . . I know that civilized progress depends on education. Without it, I'd have had no motorcycle to ride, no tractor to run on our farm . . . why learn mathematics of the planets if we lose appreciation of the earth?"

Already planning his escape from the drudgery of school, he'd been learning all he could about flying and flight schools. With his aptitude for drawing, Charles might have tried to formally study aeronautics, but he was realistic enough to dismiss the thought. Instead, throughout the fall of 1921 he applied to various flying programs hoping for a break and an optimistic end to a generally unhappy year. Academic woes aside, Charles's family issues had not improved; C.A. and Evangeline were still estranged and his father was nearly broke.

SINCE HIS SON entered college, the elder Lindbergh had lost thousands of dollars through bad decisions, poor investments, and unsecured loans. He'd lost his final bid for Congress in April 1920. The following year, as Charles was failing a second semester, C.A.'s redoubtable mother, by then called Louisa, who had survived immigration, the Sioux uprising of 1862, and more than thirty years of August Lindbergh, passed away.

Combating deepening depression and trying desperately to recoup his financial losses, C.A. departed for Florida.

Nearly a decade earlier, foreseeing the radical changes the automobile would have on America, an entrepreneur named Carl Graham Fisher had developed the Lincoln Highway, a 3,389-mile permanent, paved road connecting San Francisco to New York City. Based on that success he proposed building a "Dixie" Highway from Chicago to Miami, though it eventually extended as far north as Sault Saint Marie, on Michigan's Canadian border. After it opened, Fisher decided to create a sun-drenched paradise at its southern terminus, which he named Miami Beach.*

Thanks to the automobile and the Dixie Highway, Florida was no longer just an escape for the wealthy. Land prices shot up and there were rumors the state's income and inheritance taxes would soon be repealed. An opportunistic C. A. Lindbergh sought to capitalize on Florida's impending boom. Having little success he deeded land in Little Falls over to his wife and managed a fifty-dollars-a-month sustainment for his son. With no income and no credit from the banks, sixty-two-year-old C.A. had little else to offer to his family.

In the wake of all this, Charles realized that his own future, for better or worse, would not be won at a university. After he failed three of five courses in the fall 1921 semester, his academic career officially ended. He'd been corresponding with several aviation schools during the fall semester and decided on the Lincoln Flying School, part of the Lincoln Standard Aircraft Company in Nebraska.† For five hundred dollars, Charles could spend a month in their factory learning aircraft design, maintenance,

---

* Fisher Island, about three miles offshore from Miami, was named for him. In 1925 he traded the island to William K. Vanderbilt II for a yacht.

† Formerly the Nebraska Aircraft Corporation, the name was changed when the company was acquired by aviation legend Ray H. Page on August 6, 1920.

and the basics of flight. Arriving by motorcycle on April 1, 1922, he moved into the Hotel Savoy and spent the first week tearing down engines, modifying cockpits, and "doping" fuselages.*

Eight days later, on April 9, the young man stood on the airfield, excited and focused. Fresh from the factory, a plane was being carefully assembled; wings were attached and riggers connected the rudder and ailerons. Mechanics tuned the 150-horsepower Hispano-Suiza engine, straining the fuel, then adding oil. It was a Lincoln Standard Tourabout, a 2,900-pound aircraft with wings a bit over 44 feet long. Left over from the war, the plane was ungainly and slow, but to Charles it looked beautiful.

And why not? On that day, the company's chief pilot, Otto Timm, was taking him up for his first flight, an adventure that would change his life forever. But that was all still far ahead and this fine Nebraska spring day was simply about a young man discovering his love of flying. Like almost all pilots he would never forget that thrilling first experience, and decades later it was still sharp in his memory.

"Behind every movement, word, and detail," he recalled fondly, "one felt the strength of life, the presence of death. There was pride in man's conquest of the air. There was the realization that he took life in hand to fly."

---

* Before metallic skins were widely used, fabric-covered metal or wood framing had to be strengthened and tightened using brushed-on lacquer, or "dope."

THREE

HOUR FIVE

THE SUN BATHED the cockpit in bright white light, washing out the black instrument panel to gray and making the gauges difficult to see. It was also very warm. Slim unzipped his flying suit and pulled the halves apart, letting cooler air flow onto his chest. Made by A. G. Spalding, the heavy brown flight suit had faded to a khaki color but was still sturdy and intact. Built for warmth and utility, it was insulated with wool, and had a fur-lined collar and two big pockets handy for maps and food. Underneath he wore a light jacket over a white shirt and Army officer's riding breeches. Teitzel-Jones & Dehner boots completed his ensemble and the only bit of color was Slim's red-and-blue-striped regimental tie, purchased at the Scruggs-Vandervoort-Barney department store in St. Louis.

Straightening his legs against the rudder pedals, Lindbergh yawned and tried to stretch out the cramps. *I'm a little tired,* he admitted. It *would* be pleasant to doze off for a few seconds. This was always the worst part, around the four- or five-hour point, before his muscles became accustomed to their unnatural, enforced positions. In a few more hours they'd conform to the seat and the aches would fade. Of course, he'd never flown a forty-hour flight before—so would he reach a point where his body began protesting again? Were there worse hours ahead?

Too far off to worry about.

Nearly two hundred miles past Cape Cod into the Gulf of Maine, Slim was truly out to sea for the first time in his life. He marveled at that since his previous over-water record flight had been thirty miles between Long Island and the Connecticut coast. That was an amusing thought, and no doubt after he reached Ireland the distance he was now flying would seem trivial. That was how to look at it, though; each piece of land was just another stepping-stone across the Atlantic. Despite the noise and blowing air the warm cockpit was making him drowsy. The constant humming vibration didn't help and as his mind wandered Slim peered outside, hoping to see land.

No land.

He noticed mud splattered under the right wing. Hunching a bit to see from the other window he spotted another clump beneath the other wing. How much did the mud weigh? A few ounces, no more than that, yet those ounces would cost how much in fuel? It was more than 3,600 miles to Paris, so if the extra weight was, say, half a pound, then how much more gasoline would it cost to land New York mud in France? When he extended the periscope, how much drag did that generate and how much extra fuel to overcome it? The airspeed indicator showed no difference yet he knew there was. Even slight resistance was still resistance; everything cost *something* in fuel and distance. Why should he tear leaves from a notebook to save weight and then be weighed down by mud? Higher power settings to overcome these things meant more fuel burned. Was there enough?

I'm half-asleep!

Stop it.

Slim stuck his hand out the left window, cupping the fingers and letting fresh air hit him in the face. Blinking hard and shaking his head Lindbergh knew he couldn't afford this now, only a few hours into the flight. He should have slept during the past thirty-six hours but hadn't been able to do it. Too many details, too many interruptions, and, to be honest, too much apprehension. *I've let myself be caught off guard at a critical moment* . . . a pilot must be fresh for the start of a record-breaking transoceanic flight.

Well, this is one of the emergencies that fill a flying life. Wriggling in the seat, Lindbergh forces himself to look from the instruments, to the gauges, and then the horizon. Then back again. He retracts the periscope by sliding the lever sideways and then concentrates on the black panel. The throttle is set at 1,725 revolutions per minute which holds 104 miles per hour. Fuel is feeding from the right wing tank and Slim figures he's burned about sixteen gallons after four hours of flying. So at 6.1 pounds per gallon the sixty-four consumed from the 450 at takeoff leaves *Spirit* . . . 391 pounds lighter.

Reaching Nova Scotia on course is his first true test of navigation, so he focuses on the Mercator chart across his knees. The true course was 058 degrees, but that had been plotted on paper over a nice, flat desk back in San Diego, not on an aircraft compass. The problem was the earth itself; a solid iron core surrounded by molten metal, it acts as a giant magnet. A free-floating magnetized needle like the one in Lindbergh's conventional compass theoretically points toward the magnetic concentration near the earth's poles. Unfortunately, the metallic surfaces in and around the aircraft, like the steel tubing and engine block, interfere with the magnetic field. This "needle error," or deviation, might be a degree or two, negligible for a quick jaunt, but potentially disastrous in the cumulative effects over the distance from New York to Paris.

And since the *Spirit* had no line of sight to the pole, every piece of interference between the aircraft's compass and magnetic north added error. The needle's horizontal mounting also reacted inaccurately to the planet's spherical shape and the lines of magnetism curving around it. This induced more error since the earth's magnetic field isn't horizontal except near the equator. Last, and most significant, the magnetic pole itself isn't stationary. Like water in a bucket, the molten area around earth's core "sloshes" as we spin, so the magnetic pole is usually at least 200 miles from the planet's geographic pole.*

The geographic pole, physically the "top of the world" on maps, is true north. At this point all geographical meridians, or lines of longitude, converge. This "true north" is used for cartography and charting, but magnetic north was essential for real-time navigation in 1927. Both must be understood for the plotting of accurate courses. Meridians, the vertical lines of longitude read on charts, are drawn between both poles. The angular difference between both parallel sets of lines is declination, and is expressed in degrees east or west on maps. This value is then added or subtracted to a magnetic course, and the result is a "true" heading corrected for magnetic errors.

As Lindbergh approached Nova Scotia in May 1927, the declination was 20 degrees west, which he added to his plotted map course of 058 for a compass course of 078 degrees. This had to be corrected for the wind, which was blowing steadily from the northwest at 15 miles per hour and pushing the *Spirit*

---

* It has actually been measured as far as 1,200 miles from the geographic pole.

right, or southeast. Countering by crabbing left 10 degrees into the wind, Slim was able to hold the true compass heading of 068 degrees that would put him on course. More or less. At best, magnetic navigation could get a pilot, explorer, or ship captain fairly close, and then the destination could be pinpointed by landmarks—hopefully. A better method was needed and with this in mind the earth inductor compass was developed.

Switching hands on the stick, Slim reaches down to the earth inductor compass dial mounted horizontally near his right thigh. The very latest in navigation technology, it had been installed personally by Pioneer Instrument's Brice Goldsborough, and this 236-mile leg between Provincetown and Nova Scotia would reveal whether it truly worked. It looked like a conventional compass face: a controller dial marked at 10-degree increments with a large white numeral at each 30-degree point. A permanent line was etched from the middle of the dial to the top, where it met a small white triangle. Twiddling a little burled knob, Slim rotates the controller dial until his map course of 058 degrees is set beneath the triangle.

Of course, this is uncorrected for deviation, inclination, or declination, but that is precisely the point. The earth inductor compass is independent of anything magnetic and derives its directional information by electricity. As the earth is a giant magnet, its lines of force run from pole to pole; that is, north to south. Whenever those lines are intersected an electric voltage is produced, and this can be indicated on a display. For the *Spirit,* a small generator mounted in the fuselage behind the pilot's seat contains a coil and a pair of armature brushes. When the dial next to his thigh is rotated the brushes contact the coil at the desired angle, in this case 058 degrees, and voltage is produced.

Now, when the coil is at a right angle to the pole it is not cutting magnetic lines of force at a measurable rate so no voltage is produced. The angle off the pole is displayed by an inner ring painted with gold numbers, zero through ninety, which indicate the aircraft's offset from magnetic north. So if 90 degrees is directly off the pilot's shoulder then the angle will decrease as the plane angles inward, and this is what Slim does. After dialing in 058, he continues banking slightly left until the zero on the inner yellow ring is firmly at the top of the dial. This tells him that he is holding the correct heading to remain perpendicular to the earth's magnetic pole. With this and the magnetic compass he should be very close to his plotted course.

And at 11:52 A.M., New York time, there it was–land!

How accurately have I held my course? When flying low one sees only individual landmarks, gaining intimacy but losing perspective. Altitude will help locate his exact position, Slim knows, so he nudges the throttle forward and climbs to 1,000 feet. Walking the rudder pedals he yaws the *Spirit* from side to side to see from both windows. The charcoal-colored coastline up ahead is low and just flattens out gradually into the Gulf of Maine's waters. Inland the land slopes upward, rising up into pine- and spruce-covered hills. He's over the mouth of a medium-sized, north–south oriented bay. To his right is a small cape, with little gray houses dotting a curving, scalloped shoreline.* Under the left wing is a long, narrow spit of land forming the western edge of the bay. Peering through the open window, Slim realizes the end of the peninsula is actually an island, like the tip of a finger.†

Squinting at the map, he matches printed lines against

---

* Cape St. Mary's.
† Brier Island. Home to renowned sailor Joshua Slocum, who completed the first solo circumnavigation of the globe in a 36-foot sloop in 1898.

the land below and knows by its shape this can only be St. Mary's Bay. His plotted course ran up the west side of the bay to the town of Digby, just six miles northwest of his land-fall. Six miles! Slim leans back and stares out the window again. Relief envelops him, warm and relaxing. The relief only pilots and mariners feel when they find themselves exactly where they'd planned to be. Well, almost exactly. But six miles . . . it was close enough.

Back in San Diego Slim had figured he could live with a 5 percent navigation error, say five miles off during each 100-mile segment. It was correctable. But six miles in the 230 or so since Massachusetts was about a 2 percent error. It was more than 2,000 miles from St. John's in Newfoundland to Ireland, and with this level of navigational accuracy he'd be no more than 50 miles off course when he reached Ireland. Was it luck, or had he learned to navigate?

Optimistic, Lindbergh wriggled down in the wicker seat and shifted his inflatable cushion a bit. This landfall had proven that penciled courses could bring him safely to land after hours over water. It proved that earth inductor and magnetic compasses could be used together with a higher degree of accuracy than previously believed. His instruments had worked; a course plot-ted in the California sun had brought him safely to Nova Scotia. Taking a swallow of water to celebrate, the pilot knew he'd also passed his second self-imposed line. The first had been actually making it off the ground alive at Roosevelt Field and the second was this, a successful landfall after two hours of open water. He had one more, the point of no return: halfway across the Atlan-tic, when Europe became closer than North America.

But this was Nova Scotia!

Below, the harsh terrain unrolled beneath the wings and he knew that the whole peninsula, plus Sable and Cape Breton islands, measured just 21,300 square miles, smaller than West Virginia. Named "New Scotland," the land had been colonized by the French in 1605 and they'd called it "Acadia." The British conquered the land a century later and it became a shipbuilding center to serve the Royal Navy's endless requirements for timber. The vast stretches of trees and lakes remind him of home. Like pieces of blue glass, thousands of ponds mirror the sky and hills rise ahead toward a mountain range. *What amazing magic is carried in an airplane's wings,* he muses, looking out over the desolate, tree-covered landscape. New York at breakfast; Nova Scotia for lunch. *There hasn't been time enough between to prepare my mind and body for the difference,* he realizes. Flying has torn apart the relationship between space and time; it uses our old clock but with new yardsticks.

Adding more power, Slim angles toward a saddle along the ridgeline and switches to the nose fuel tank. He'd flown up the middle of the peninsula with the Bay of Fundy on his left and the Atlantic on the right. After an hour, the *Spirit* is in the center of the peninsula over Mount Uniacke. Halifax lay beyond the mountains under his right wing, and another hour northeast lay the Strait of Canso, separating Nova Scotia from Cape Breton Island. Beyond that was a 200-mile leg to Newfoundland. Strange how a few hundred miles over the ocean seems normal now.

As Slim hangs up his canteen, wind suddenly catches his chart, lifting and fluttering it toward the open window. Startled, he jerks it back then tucks the chart firmly under his leg. What would he say to that? "On course, plenty of fuel, all readings normal, but the chart blew out the window." *That* would truly be an embarrassing calamity, to be forced back in failure because of a sheet of paper. It had happened before, though. He'd lost a flight data card through the very same window during one of his California test flights. If the detachable windows were in place there would be no breeze in the cockpit. *No, I'll leave the windows in their rack,* Slim decides. *They'll form a barrier between me and elements outside my plane.* They'd interfere with the crystal clarity of communion with water, land, and sky.

Easing his shoulders back against the seat Lindbergh feels the hollowness in his gut fade a bit. He has two celluloid windowpanes in a little rack behind the seat, and can slide them in place anytime, so why not right now? *Why didn't I put them in before?* Why have I wasted their streamlining value for these five hours of flight? After all, streamlining was the main reason for enclosing the fuselage and a natural evolution of the *Spirit*'s design.

Don Hall, the plane's creator, had designed "an enclosed cockpit that doesn't have any projections from the fuselage and ought to increase the cruising speed two or three miles an hour. We might pick up an extra hundred miles of range that way." To Hall the logical solution was simply enclosing the cockpit from that position, so the top of the fuselage became the top of the cockpit.

Quite a man, Don Hall. He had designed and built the *Spirit of St. Louis* in sixty days, often working more than eighty hours a week. Son of a Western Union telegraph operator, he'd grown up in working-class Brooklyn and graduated from the Pratt Institute. Hall began as a draftsman for the Curtiss Aeroplane and Motor Corporation before moving to Santa Monica, California, to work for the Douglas Company.

Quiet and unassuming, he was a long-distance swimmer and a photographer, and like Lindbergh, he loved the outdoors. Hall designed a fine aircraft. Slim had watched the entire Ryan crew, under B. F. Mahoney and Bert Tindale, painstakingly construct the *Spirit* down to 1/32 of an inch tolerance in some areas. Lindbergh had remained in San Diego the entire time, contributing his expertise throughout the design and construction process.

In his 1927 engineering report on the *Spirit of St. Louis,* Don Hall wrote, "The presence of Charles Lindbergh, with his keen knowledge of flying, his understanding of engineering problems, his implicit faith in the proposed flight, and his constant application to it, was a most important factor in welding together the entire factory organization into one smoothly running team. This group was unusually conscientious, co-operative [*sic*], and hard working."

Suddenly the plane bolted upward and Slim's hand instantly tightened around the stick. Everything loose in the cockpit bounced: the chart, canteen, and his gloves. Sinking toward the saddle in the mountains he watched the wingtips flex, and out of habit Slim wrapped his left hand around the throttle, ready to power out of the turbulence. Then the summit abruptly fell away, and as the plane lurched back to level flight, eastern Nova Scotia opened up beneath him.

The wings were never designed for such a wrenching, he thinks, staring at the ground. It's certainly bad country for a forced landing; there's not a farmer's field in sight and wicked gray boulders are everywhere, like warts across a green face. A lake would be best, but there aren't any in this rough terrain so young trees would have to do. Their supple trunks and thick, green boughs would break much of the impact shock, but with four hundred gallons of fuel remaining, Slim figured he was too heavy to crash-land anyway. *Spirit* would likely catch fire and Lindbergh, like all pilots, dreaded fire most of all.

"It was a mistake not to put dump valves in the tanks," he

said aloud, frowning and shaking his head. Solitary conversation was a habit nurtured from childhood, from long periods with no friends or parents around. "Now, if you could dump three hundred gallons of fuel, you could probably stall-in there with nothing worse than a blown tire and a bent propeller."

Dump valves were simple vents under the tanks that the pilot could manually open from the cockpit. Gravity then drained the fuel into the wind stream and, depending on the altitude, it would evaporate. But such a system added weight and cost, so Lindbergh had refused it.

"Yes," Slim continued his internal debate, "but we considered all that at the factory while the plane was being built. Dump valves might have leaked. No one was certain how to make them, not to mention the additional weight. Suppose one of the valves accidentally opened halfway across the ocean?"

Fuel was life.

Lindbergh had run out of gas eight months ago and didn't care to repeat the experience. In September 1926, while he was flying the mail from St. Louis to Chicago, the fog had rolled in, cutting visibility to nothing. He'd circled, vainly trying to see the beacons installed by the government for such an occurrence, but the weather was too thick. When his reserve tank ran dry, Slim unbuckled, dove out of the cockpit into the opaque mess, and pulled the ripcord three seconds later. He'd been parachuting since his barnstorming days so floating down through the foggy blackness didn't bother him much, but the plane he'd just deserted did. Slim hadn't cut the De Havilland's switches because the engine had quit for lack of gasoline, but without a pilot's weight the nose dropped and trapped fuel spilled forward into the carburetor. The Liberty engine continued running and the DH, as it was called, circled its floating pilot all the way to the ground.

Where fuel was concerned, having more than enough was

a tremendous advantage, so he needed that, even if this meant risking fire during a forced landing. Not installing the valves had been the correct decision since it saved weight, and if he did go down he would have other problems. Staring from the window at the thickening sky he thought about that. Did anyone even know he was here? Surely he was visually spotted all the way up the eastern seaboard and hopefully someone in Plymouth or Provincetown saw the *Spirit* head out to sea.

Surely.

But what about here? He'd really only seen small clusters of houses just off the coast near St. Mary's Bay, and the few structures between there and here very likely had no radio or telegraph. He didn't even have a radio; radios were simply too heavy.

On either side of *Spirit*'s nose the horizon had vanished. A solid wall of cloud reached from the ocean upward, the shade of gray darkening as it rose higher. The wind was rising, too, and Slim's earlier sense of well-being drained through his boots. It now took a 25-degree crab to hold course into the gathering wind so he decided to let the weather push him southeast. He could get a position fix before striking out for Newfoundland, as long as Cape Breton's eastern coastline was visible.

But that didn't look good, either, at the moment.

Shimmering curtains of rain were sweeping across the ground ahead, fragmenting the horizon while streaking the lakes with whitecaps. Wet, warm air was rising fast, cooling as it soared upward, and the saturated bits became rain while others were flung so high and fast they froze into ice. Both plummeted back down, cooling and unsettling the air as they fell. As *Spirit* bucked and yawed in the turbulence, Lindbergh throttled back a fraction to hold 1,625 revolutions, then watched the wings. Each workman at the Ryan factory had signed the front wing spar around the phrase "to ride along on the flight for good luck." He certainly hoped his luck would hold.

For the first time this flight, Slim was truly alarmed, and for good reason. Don Hall had added ten feet to the standard Ryan M-2 design so *Spirit* could lift the 2,500 pounds of extra load, mostly fuel, needed for the 3,610-mile flight. The modified 46-foot span provided a 33 percent greater wing area, but it also meant the longer wings would bend more as they protruded farther from the fuselage. The airfoil, or cross section, of Hall's wing, allowed additional room for fuel tanks and made the wing structurally much stronger. Called a "Clark Y" type after its designer, the airfoil was curved, or cambered, along the top surface, but the underside was flat.* Air racing over the top of such a surface would have to accelerate, and its pressure was less than air flowing along the flat bottom. This greater pressure pushing upwards made the wing fly. Strong, stable, capacious, and generating lift, it was the best of all worlds—unless unforeseen and immeasurable turbulence was encountered. Just like now.

Like a coyote shaking a rabbit, the storm tossed the little aircraft up, down, and sideways, all the while blowing it farther southeast off course. *If only I had a parachute!* Slim's eyes were wide now as he fought for control and struggled to buckle the safety belt. With the rudder pedals smacking his soles, he tightened the throttle lock to hold it in place and grabbed the stick with both hands. But a parachute weighed twenty pounds: three gallons of fuel, fifteen minutes of flying time. It was left behind. *I can't carry everything.*

The squalls got worse. He could see through the first one,

---

* Colonel Virginius Clark, a 1907 Naval Academy graduate who later transferred to the U.S. Army Signal Corps. His design was an adaptation of the highly successful Gottingen airfoil used by Tony Fokker for the German Air Service during the Great War.

but others swayed across the sky like dark sheets. Water beats furiously against the *Spirit* and the propeller is just a whirling silver disk with vapor spinning off the edges. Droplets splash inside the cockpit, over his flight suit and charts, and the glass-faced instruments glisten. He's again reminded of how fragile his existence is at the moment; just a few feet of steel tubing, wood, and grade A cotton fabric between him and nature. Giving up trying to hold a heading, Slim begins threading his way east through the storm, coming back on course when he can, but giving up when he must. Maybe it breaks up closer to the coast. Maybe by avoiding the worst parts, the wings won't collapse. Maybe.

Don Hall built the spars utilizing a Warren truss, like a bridge span, for strength. The Warren looked like a series of alternating triangles held between a longitudinal frame and it was designed to spread the wing loading so no single section would bear the full force. The "I" spars were made of spruce, then reinforced and braced with a double line of piano wire, all contained within a SAE 1020 carbon steel frame. Hall had also moved the spars closer for increased strength, eleven inches on center instead of the usual fourteen—but was it enough? The spars were glued, and only the area from the wing's leading edge back to the first spar was plywood. The rest of the structure was covered with Flightex grade A pima cotton, coated six times with aluminum cellulose acetate dope just like the fuselage.

Suddenly the *Spirit* shoots into clear, bright sunlight and Slim blinks. Rain gleams on farmhouse roofs and he can see dirt roads twisting through the trees beneath him. Then it's dark gray again: shredded clouds and more rain. In and out of the squalls, he spots a few lakes, their surfaces blown to foam, a condition that takes at least fifty knots of wind. Towns are down there someplace, and their names betray the peninsula's Scottish origins: New Glasgow, St. Andrews, and Sherbrooke.

Water bothered him because it was everywhere in the cockpit and Slim wondered how the engine's magnetos would hold up under the constant drenching. The moisture might interrupt or even extinguish them altogether. Magnetos were vital; they kept the engine running by supplying continuous electrical pulses to the spark plugs. Independent of the aircraft electrical system, they utilized permanent magnets to generate electricity, hence the name, but if they malfunctioned then the engine would run rough or even quit. *Spirit*'s Whirlwind engine had a pair of them, both AG-9D types made by Scintilla in Sidney, New York, and Slim had figured that if they were good enough for Wright Aeronautical they'd work for him.*

I don't dare check the magnetos now. He wiped the rain from his lips knowing full well he couldn't spare a hand from the controls. But not a single cylinder had missed, so the mags seemed fine. Of all *Spirit*'s complex components the Wright Whirlwind engine worried him least; it was so good that both Chamberlin's *Columbia* and Byrd's *America* used it.

Officially designated the Model J-5C, it was a nine-cylinder radial engine rated for 220 horsepower though this one actually put out a bit more. He'd been in San Diego when it arrived from Paterson, New Jersey, its cosmoline-coated parts carefully packed in a big wooden crate.† The radial design aligned the cylinders in a star-shaped pattern with the crankshaft and propeller in the center. Such an arrangement had been around since the turn of the century but wasn't widely used until after the Great War. Ryan's Fred Rohr hand-hammered the metal cowling, then covered the blemishes with burnished, scalloped swirls that had become a company trademark.

---

* Scintilla was originally a Swiss firm and their magnetos generated an exceptionally fat, reliable spark at high speeds, ideal for aircraft engines.
† Cosmoline is basically a brown, waxy grease used to protect or preserve.

With a better power-to-weight ratio and improved metallurgy, the radial became more practical and reliable than
its predecessor. Besides simplicity, the great advantage to
the radial was that it was air cooled and much lighter than
water-cooled engines. Liquid-cooled engines had other issues;
nearly one-fifth of their failures were attributed to coolant
plumbing, and they were heavier, so less powerful than their
air-cooled counterparts. Nungesser's giant twelve-cylinder
Lorraine-Dietrich was a prime example; true, it was capable
of 450 horsepower, but its sizable cooling system contrib-
uted to the White Bird's 11,000-pound gross weight, twice as
heavy as *Spirit*.

Heavy, rain-fresh air filled the cockpit and Slim gazed outside as the wilderness flashed beneath his wings. Along with
losing an engine or running out of gas, weather was a constant,
deep source of anxiety for a pilot. Fuel can be monitored, and
much of the uncertainty about engines can be overcome with
sound maintenance and good equipment, but weather is different. It can be forecasted, but only to a point, and was still
a black art. Nature was still nature. Its unpredictability made
it dangerous and frequently lethal. He'd gotten only a slight
taste of a small storm in the past hour, but it was eye-opening
and frightening. To think of flying through that at night, over
the water . . . Slim nudged the stick forward and *Spirit* dropped
lower. He concentrated on flying here and now, not on the
night, which was still four or five hours ahead.

At fifty feet above the hilltops he was low enough to see pine
needles on the branches and watch them sway in the breeze. The
wind had shifted around and was now blowing from the southwest, a good sign he was on the back side of the storm—at least
this one. Cumulonimbus clouds towered to the north, rolling
away from Nova Scotia, and Charles thought the storm front
must stretch all the way to the Canadian mainland. Maybe a

similar storm had gotten Nungesser and Coli. It would have to
be something like that, or a catastrophic mechanical failure,
to bring the Frenchmen down.

Maybe both.

Slim flicks his right wrist several times, peering out to the left
as the *Spirit*'s wings rock. Ailerons, the small, hinged surfaces on
the wing's trailing edge, were used for lateral control. They were
interconnected so as the stick moved left or right, one aileron
would rise while the other fell. The "up" aileron decreased lift on
its wing, so it would drop as the "down" aileron increased lift,
simultaneously raising the opposite wing. When the stick was
centered so were the ailerons, and the side-to-side roll movement
of the aircraft was neutral. If the stick was pulled back, both
elevators moved up, forcing the tail down, therefore air pressure
decreased along the top of the wing, and lift was generated so
the aircraft climbed. When the stick was pushed forward the
reverse occurred.

When he reengineered *Spirit*'s wings, Don Hall had moved
the ailerons thirty-eight inches closer to the fuselage. Worried
about the added ten-foot span, he calculated that placing the ailerons nearer to the structural center would help keep the wingtips from bending under the combined strain of turbulence and
control movements. The trade-off was a "heavier" stick; more
pilot muscle was needed to physically move the ailerons. The
aircraft was certainly less maneuverable than others Lindbergh
had flown, but the *Spirit* wasn't a fighter plane. Both Hall and
Lindbergh had correctly reasoned that agility was much less
important than safety.

Craning his neck sideways in what has become a familiar
position, Slim stares ahead through the silver propeller disk, his
fatigue and muscle aches replaced with sudden dread. A floating white band stretches across his field of vision exactly along

the Nova Scotia coastline. From the Atlantic off his right wing, north to St. George's Bay, an opaque belt hovers just off the ground, obscuring everything behind it.

Fog.

Low lying and insidious, it can form in moments when the dew point, or saturation level, and air temperature are within 4 degrees Fahrenheit of each other. It's a pilot's nightmare. With no warning, fog effectively cloaks everything beneath it, and Lindbergh knows well the lonely feeling of circling above the white blanket waiting to land, running out of hope and fuel. But *Spirit* is just passing over Nova Scotia, so landing isn't an issue unless something goes wrong.

Slim pushes the throttle up, adding another fifty revolutions, then gently pulls back on the stick and begins to climb. If the fog will hold off a few hours more, he silently pleads, if I can only check my course over Newfoundland, it won't matter what happens after that. *I'll ask for nothing more until I reach the other side of the ocean.* But Lindbergh knows he's already pushed his luck. First was the overloaded takeoff from a wet field in Long Island; then the East Coast cleared so he could set himself up across the Gulf of Maine; finally, his navigation got him to St. Mary's Bay pretty much on course.

Maybe, he hoped, the fog would be limited to the narrow straits between the peninsula and Cape Breton Island. Squinting at the Mercator chart, he sees it's called the Strait of Canso, barely sixteen miles from end to end. *Yes!* The fog is localized right there. Slim relaxes the pull, levels off at 300 feet, and can clearly see a large lake off the nose that, according to his map, must be Bras d'Or. Rising up beyond it toward the north are the bleak Cape Breton highlands. A wild and beautiful place. He'd read about it while preparing the route and now, after seeing it, isn't surprised that some fifty thousand Scots immigrated here

to this land of rainswept cliffs, rocky, bare hills, and very few
people.

Of course, if the winds are bad across the Atlantic or his
navigation is off he just might see Scotland, or the Norwegian
fjords . . . or even Spain for that matter. All the more reason
to stay alert and to stop daydreaming. For sixty minutes Slim
focuses only on his instruments and flying. The Lukenheimer
fuel manifold is feeding from the fuselage tank, and he'll keep
it there for the next two hours. Cape Breton is extraordinarily
beautiful; like the Nova Scotia peninsula it is speckled with
lakes and ponds sparkling brightly through heavy forests. The
northern part of the island is mountainous, stacked like dark
green loaves through the mist. Above the trees there is snow
along the stark ridgelines.

Flying up Bras d'Or Lake, Lindbergh crossed over a
U-shaped body of water and continued northeast for the coast.
The salty air was fresh with unlimited visibility and he marveled that a few miles could make a remarkable difference.
Somewhere off his left wing was the port of Sydney, and as he
crested a line of low hills, Cape Breton's western edge spread
out off *Spirit*'s nose. Like a big thumbprint, the green waters
of a bay pushed inland toward him and Slim could make out
an island just offshore. Scatari Island, according to the chart,
at the mouth of Mira Bay. Smoothing the Mercator with his
left hand, Lindbergh hunches over and squints at the plotted
course. If he remains south and simply parallels the planned
route he'll strike Newfoundland near Hermitage Bay. But that
isn't close enough, he decides, flexing his right hand against the
stick and glancing up at his instruments.

A mirror had been mounted at the panel's top edge, dead
center above the earth inductor dial, and fastened to the plywood with chewing gum. One of the Pioneer technicians had

installed the magnetic compass just aft of the skylight, right near Slim's head—it was the only place to put it, he had said. Any more forward and the engine's metal parts would cause interference. The problem was, there was no way to see it from the pilot's seat.

"I don't mind reading it through a mirror," Lindbergh had stated calmly. "The most important thing is to have it accurate and steady."

"Will this do?" a woman had called from the knot of spectators standing beyond the roped-off hangar entrance. She was young, like a college girl, and held out a two-inch-round mirror. The technician thanked her, pulled a piece of chewing gum from his mouth, and stuck it on the back. Pressing it onto the plywood panel, he held the mirror a moment then let go, and it remained firmly in place.

Now, more than eight hours into his flight, Slim stares at the reflection, reading the numbers in reverse. Deviation at this longitude is 27 degrees, so correcting for drift gives . . . a 086-degree compass course. Eyeing the chart, he figures that should put *Spirit* over the Miquelon Islands, near the mouth of Newfoundland's Placentia Bay. As long as the magnetic course is maintained and he remains right of the earth inductor course, then all is well. But what if there's fog again, or bad weather over Newfoundland? What if he can't fix his position before heading out over the next 1,900 miles of open ocean, at night?

No. It will be all right. Slim knows self-doubt often curses pilots who fly alone. The Mercator plot shows a landfall over White Bear Bay, on Newfoundland's south coast, then across to Cape Bonavista and the Atlantic. The weather, at least what he can see of it, seems to be moving in from the north, so it's best to stay south if possible. After reaching Placentia Bay on the island's southeast edge, he could fly up it instead and pass directly over St. John's, the capitol city. Surely someone there would see and report the *Spirit*'s passage. They would wire New York that the silver plane marked N-X-211 made it at least this far. His mother, teaching in Detroit, his partners in St. Louis, and all the men at the factory in San Diego deserved to know. That is the plan then, and Slim feels another surge of optimism.

The sea is no longer a stranger and he revels in that thought. *As I struck Nova Scotia, I will strike Newfoundland; and as I strike Newfoundland, I will strike Europe!* A pebbled beach looms ahead and Slim noses over, roaring across the dead weeds and breakers at a bare twenty feet. Flying down Mira Bay, four minutes later he passes the eastern point of Main-à-Dieu, and as Scatari Island disappears beneath the right wing *Spirit* again heads out to sea.

FOUR

DOORWAY TO THE ATLANTIC

"YOU DON'T PLAN on making that flight alone, do you? I . . . I thought you'd need somebody to navigate and be relief pilot."

Don Hall, like everyone else, had been taken aback by Lindbergh's insistence on flying solo across the Atlantic. After all, Nungesser, Byrd, and the others hadn't even considered it; they all had a crew.

"I'd rather have the extra gasoline than an extra man," Slim had replied at the time, in February 1927, at the Ryan Airlines factory on the San Diego waterfront. He had been poring over design details in Don Hall's drafting room and the subject of a navigator had inevitably arisen. But Slim was certain that flying alone was the right thing to do. With another set of eyes and hands in the cockpit there is a tendency to relax, to trust that if you miss something the other man will see it, to rely on another's skill or knowledge. Maybe that was what got the Frenchmen. A pilot alone knows that it all rests on his shoulders and if he doesn't do it, or does it wrong, he'll never survive.

Flying alone had sounded so logical in St. Louis, San Diego, and New York, but now? *I'm beyond the stage where I need a bed, or even to lie down,* Slim thinks, fighting the overwhelming urge to let his head droop. *My eyes feel dry and hard as stones.* It's miserable; the lids scrape as you squeeze your eyes shut and thousands of white pinprick flashes shoot across the pink backdrop of your lids. The burning slowly subsides, like jumping into a cool pool on a hot day, and relief relaxes you a bit. You can feel the aircraft through the stick and rudder pedals. Your inner ear tells you the plane is banking slightly, and you hear the air rush over the cotton-covered fuselage. You *must* open your eyes, but it feels so good. Just another moment. Straining, the lids fight gravity and try to rise but . . .

Open your eyes!

Slim's eyelids reluctantly lift and he shifts position, leaning forward more, then blinking rapidly he levels out and checks the instruments. His legs feel fine, as he knew they would after a few hours, but his back and shoulders ache. Not the sharp kind of pain that would help keep him awake, but the deep, clenching ache that remains no matter what position he chooses. Adding power, Slim pulls the stick back a few inches and *Spirit* climbs up several hundred feet above the cold, green ocean. He had been too close to the wavetops. A few seconds of dosing would put him into the water.

Sleep is winning.

And the sun is sinking.

How can I get through the night? Slim wonders, to say nothing of the dawn, and another day. Another entire day! *I must think about problems,* he knows. Now more than ever Slim is glad the plane isn't too easy to fly, that it constantly requires hands and feet on the controls. It's easy to become complacent gliding along on a soft cushion of air with the engine's consistent vibration, the propeller's steady thrumming, and the near-floating sensation of simply flying. These are delightful on a clear day over land, but it all changes at night and especially over water. Flying ceases to be beautiful. Any variation in sound from the engine sends your heart into your throat. A tiny lurch or bounce might be a spar cracking, and the sky instantly becomes dangerous and life threatening, just as the sea is to a sailor. Both are natural obstacles that man has tried to tame, or at least temporarily overcome, but never without risk. Death is a constant companion for the sailor.

And the pilot.

FORTUNATELY FOR LINDBERGH, the *Spirit of St. Louis* always required a hand on the stick. Most aircraft could be "trimmed" to hold level flight by using small tabs built into the ailerons, horizontal tail, and rudder. This was usually done with a wheel, about the size of a saucer, in the cockpit that the pilot rotated. It would extend or retract a rectangular piece of the control surface, called a trim tab, which would lightly alter the airflow. It was possible, with a balanced, trimmed aircraft, to fly "hands-off." A pilot could eat or drink, stretch, even change clothes. Splash some water on his face or just relax a bit. Flying alone, farther and longer than any aviator before him, Slim was rightfully concerned about becoming too comfortable, especially with no sleep in the past thirty hours or so.

When Don Hall increased the wingspan to accommodate the extra fuel load, he had to extend *Spirit*'s empennage, or tail section, by two feet, which moved the plane's center of gravity (CG) too far aft for stability. The CG, as it is known, is the theoretical point where an aircraft would balance if suspended, and is a fundamental aeronautical design consideration. Each design has longitudinal and lateral centers of gravity that indicate fore-and-aft and left-to-right stability, respectively. Stability means an aircraft can maintain a generally level flight, which is essential to controllability. Some degree of instability makes a plane more maneuverable, and this is desirable in designing a fighter, but not for ordinary aircraft.

The *Spirit of St. Louis,* never intended to haul passengers, mail, or cargo, was definitely not a normal aircraft. It had a single purpose: to cross the Atlantic Ocean. In order to compensate for the new aft CG, Don Hall had lengthened the fuselage by eighteen inches so the 500-pound Wright engine could be mounted farther forward. This put the design stability within limits for flight, and Slim could fine-tune it by burning fuel in a certain order. More or less weight in certain tanks affected the *Spirit*'s balance, which was why he was systematically using up gas from the nose tank. This made the plane a bit tail heavy, but in the event of a forced landing it might keep it from flipping over.

The main fuselage tank, directly in front of his instrument panel, had a design capacity of 200 gallons; there were 80 additional gallons in the nose, and 145 gallons split between three wing tanks. Somehow the Standard Oil folks had squeezed in an extra 25 gallons and he wasn't sure where it all went. Slim suspected the tanks had been manufactured slightly oversized, so there was probably a bit of extra fuel in each.* The main tank's interior looked like a big wine rack; its four levels joined through a series of twenty holes, or baffles, which reduced the sloshing that could alter the center of gravity.

---

* This is exactly what happened; the nose tank actually held 88 gallons, the main tank 210, and the three wing tanks together 152 gallons, for a total true capacity of 450 gallons.

All the tanks were made from terneplate, thin sheets of steel dipped in zinc chloride, then a lead-and-tin alloy, and finally palm oil. Terne metal was as strong and malleable as steel, but unlike steel it was noncorrosive and easy to solder. Fuel was gravity fed by Lindbergh's tank selection through his Lukenheimer manifold. The Wright engine utilized a Viking-type fuel pump, which had the great advantage of a bypass valve that enabled a pilot to hand-pump gasoline directly into the carburetor if needed.

This hadn't yet been necessary on this flight, but it was during the trip from San Diego to St. Louis. Slim had taken off during the afternoon of May 10 intending to fly all night to Lambert Field in St. Louis. It would be good practice, let him shake out the *Spirit* a bit, and demonstrate to his backers that Charles Lindbergh was quite capable of top-notch piloting. Five hours into his flight, in pitch blackness over northern Arizona, the engine began to splutter. From 8,000 feet in the moonlight he could just make out the earth's contours and it was not good; he was over the Mogollon Rim, with nothing but mountains below and the Grand Canyon somewhere off his left wing. He would never forget that feeling: envisioning a forced landing, over mountains, at night without a single light visible on the surface.

But as he spiraled down to several thousand feet above the jagged rocks his engine began to respond. Twenty minutes later, by skillfully working the mixture control and throttle, Lindbergh was able to maintain level flight. Climbing out slowly, he headed on to St. Louis and considered the problem. Slim concluded that the thin, cold air at high altitude had formed ice in the carburetor, and if he hadn't been able to descend to warmer air the engine could have failed.

Spirit's Wright Whirlwind used a three-barreled Stromberg

NA-T4 carburetor; each barrel feeding a correct fuel-air mix into three of the engine's nine cylinders. Air, and liquid too, moves faster through a constricted space and in this case it was a Venturi tube. Slim used the cockpit mixture control lever to adjust fuel feeding to the carburetor, where it then combined with air regulated by the throttle. This metered fuel-air mix is fed into the cylinders for combustion, and the engine responds accordingly. The engine's revolutions per minute, and the power generated from this both depend on the carburetor's fuel-air mixture.

But as fuel vaporizes it cools the surrounding air, and if that air is below freezing then whatever moisture remains can form into ice, with catastrophic effect. The cockpit throttle lever is physically linked to a plate in the carburetor that increases or reduces airflow depending on the throttle's position. If ice forms here it can restrict the plate, or even freeze it shut, thus cutting off airflow into the engine. Ice can also build up on the carburetor's inner walls and physically block fuel, or air, or both. Any of these situations will at least cause the engine to run rough and splutter, or quit altogether. After the Arizona incident, Slim decided to have a carburetor heater installed in New York and now, gazing ahead, he was glad of it.

ICE.

Slim hadn't expected to see it so soon. He was barely 100 miles past Cape Breton Island, and the ocean's surface shimmered brightly in the sun. Halfway to Newfoundland the Atlantic filled his horizon to the right; off his left wing the Cabot Strait, gateway to the Gulf of St. Lawrence, was stuffed with broken cakes of ice. This must have something to do with the Labrador Current meeting the Gulf Stream, Lindbergh realizes, wondering why he hadn't thought of it during flight planning. *I feel that I'm entering the Arctic,* he thinks, staring at the black water peeping through the cracks. Those patches of snow on the bleak hillsides of Cape Breton Island had not prepared him for this. He flies down the southern edge of the field a quarter mile past the blocks and noses over toward the ocean. Nothing moves on the ice, no waves or birds, just the wavering shadow of the *Spirit of St. Louis* jumping from cake to cake.

Nine hours.

Back in New York it was dinnertime, and here . . . well, the ice was interesting and keeping him awake. Centering the earth inductor compass needle, Lindbergh throttles back to 1,600 revolutions, leans the mixture a half point, holds 95 miles per hour, and watches the blinding white sheet. Ice floats because it's less dense than water, so how many billions of floating crystals had joined up down there to create those shifting pancakes? *More important, what would I do now if my engine failed? How could a pilot land on such a surface? Well, God and gravity would take care that.*

Hopefully the top layer is softer than it looks, and he knows there is a word for the slushy part, but can't think of it. Slim remembers that if ice has turned white then it has thickened, and might be sturdy enough to land on after all. How would that even work? Ice looks smooth, but down close the surface is a nightmare of ridges and cracks and it wouldn't take much to completely wreck the *Spirit*. Certainly the landing gear would shear off immediately, though the fuselage might survive intact. It would slide, of course, but protected by the engine he might live through the impact.

Under such conditions, could anything he carried save his life? Slim had been having that debate with himself since San Diego. Everything in his plan, in Hall's design, had been dictated by weight. Safety versus load, which translated directly into fuel capacity. It was impossible to increase safety at one point without detracting from it at another and, after all, wasn't his greatest insurance having enough fuel to turn back, divert, or alter his route?

Yes, right up until the time the engine quit, or a spar broke, or ice forced him down. In the end, he'd decided that the bare minimum of survival equipment was justified just in case everything else went wrong. That was a consequence of being a pilot; you always had to plan for things going wrong despite your best efforts and skill. He had a ten-pound black rubber raft that he'd purchased in a San Diego sporting goods store. No rubberized cover sheet, though. Slim figured he could cut away a strip of doped fabric and that would work just as well. He could wrap up in it and hopefully survive until his clothes dried out. Lindbergh had worn wool, instead of cotton or leather, since it would still keep him warm when wet.

Slim had a big, fixed-blade hunting knife, though he wasn't sure how much use it would be with cold fingers. There was also a flashlight, a ball of string with a needle, matches, a ball of tough cord, and one hacksaw blade. He had a four-quart canteen of water and five cans of dubious, chocolate-like Army rations, most likely left over from the Great War. Slim had struggled to find suitable signal devices and finally had purchased red railroad emergency flares. Worried about their exposure to the elements, he'd cut a bicycle tire into four sections and sealed a flare in each one.

Lindbergh knew that a quick rescue was very unlikely, and that highlighted the problem of drinking water. The canteen wouldn't last long, and at eight pounds per gallon water was too heavy to bring extra. Slim had read about a man named C. W. Armbrust, who had invented a device for procuring fresh water for survival. The eight-inch by four-inch pouch was designed to be hung around the neck; the individual breathed directly into a rubber mouthpiece. The idea was to "recycle" moisture from breath into fresh water that was accessed through a port on the pouch's bottom.* Slim purchased a handmade prototype for fifty dollars.

But another half hour of flying right over the ice is enough, and his right hand aches. Gently climbing to 150 feet to lessen the ice's glare, Slim adjusts the stabilizer trim a notch, and the stick lightens immediately. For a few miles now he has been aware that the seemingly endless ice field is changing, veering off past the right wing south toward the Grand Banks. The water ahead is open again, and he notices a strong west wind is flattening the waves. This is good for him, however, as it adds a tailwind of maybe fifteen knots, pushing *Spirit* along that much faster. The clouds have all been blown away by the wind, so hopefully the weather is improving. Mist and blowing spray keep visibility to about ten miles, but it's good enough to see the low, dark outline of a few islands directly ahead.

Craning forward, Lindbergh peers at his chart then leans left, squinting again at brown coastlines blurred by surf. A harsh place to live, no doubt. The longer island looks like a dog bone . . . Miquelon, it's called on his chart. Both islands belong to the French, he recalls, which seems a bit strange. Or maybe not. The Grand Banks off Newfoundland had always been prized fishing grounds for the Normans and Basques, and were still man's biggest source of fish on earth. To his east lies the small island of St. Pierre, named for the patron saint of

---

* This would never prevent dehydration and, in fact, didn't work. Lindbergh always believed it did, though, and carried an Armbrust cup on his subsequent flights.

fishermen.* Squinting past the whirling propeller Slim knows there must be more land ahead. Yes! Along the horizon he can just barely see purple, rugged mountains rising from the sea.

Newfoundland—his final, great stepping-stone before two thousand miles of dark ocean. The huge, 42,000 square mile island was once called "Vinland" by the great Viking explorer Leif Eriksson for its wild cranberry and gooseberry vines.† The inhabitants were a fiercely independent mix of Mi'kmaq natives with French, Portuguese, Spanish, and English settlers. As St. Pierre passes off his left wing, Lindbergh gazes at the windswept coastline and cold, merciless water. Men from English Harbor, Marystown, and Trepassey had put to sea for centuries to fish the Grand Banks or the Flemish Cap.

Slim was immensely relieved with his navigation, though. The adjusted course he'd calculated over Nova Scotia put him within a few miles of where he needed to be. So maybe finding Ireland wouldn't be so daunting after all. Maybe now, by paralleling the Burin peninsula, *Spirit* would pass directly over Placentia Bay, and from there he could easily find St. John's. Off his left wing a wall of reddish cliffs thrust upward from the pounding beaches. Rock, barren and hard, tapered off onto a mottled green peat plateau; from there the land sloped up to the Annieopsquatch Mountains. A fishing schooner bobbed in the swells below like a child's toy. The sun dropped nearer

---

* Portuguese explorer João Fagundo named them the Virgin Islands, after "St. Ursula and the 11,000 Virgins," just as Columbus did for those in the Caribbean. The islands were also a smuggler's haven and did quite well during the U.S. Prohibition years, often bringing in more than one million gallons of whiskey annually.

† It is also likely that Eriksson, and other Vikings, made repeated visits to North America around A.D. 1000. Ivory statuettes, runestones, and even a coin have been found, though traditional historians are reluctant to confirm their authenticity.

to the horizon and the land darkened, with black shadows filling the gaps between the cliffs. *I've never been as conscious of
the minuteness of my plane or the magnitude of the world,* he
thinks, bending forward and looking out the other window. To
his right, the seemingly limitless ocean curved over the earth,
chasing the horizon east to Europe.

Minutes later the cliffs on his left abruptly fall away. Small
islands dot the coast, with countless coves and inlets scar-
ring the shoreline like claw marks.* Fifteen or so miles off the
nose is another shoreline marking the eastern edge of Placentia
Bay, green and flat down to the granite-capped southern tip.
Cape St. Mary's, Slim determines, peering at the chart. Fishing
boats spread out beneath him, triangular white wakes moving
across the dark water as they head into port, possibly Argentia or Petit Forte. The bay's surface undulates gently compared
to the violent waves of the neighboring Atlantic and the blue-
green shades are lighter here as well, belying the shallower floor
compared to the deeper ocean. At 6 P.M. Eastern Time the setting sun is nearly directly over the tail and flickering across the
mirrorlike waves.

The coast looms ahead and Lindbergh sees tiny houses,
mostly either red or white, scattered along the shoreline. A
small, beak-shaped harbor lies about four miles off the left
wing, and an odd spit of land juts away from it like a rooster's
comb. Buildings and houses are clustered in the little port and
there are even a few lights visible, but it is not marked on his
chart.† The pilot switches from the nose to the fuselage fuel

---

* One of these, Oderin Island, was a base for Peter Easton. Very likely the
most successful privateer turned pirate of all time, he was never captured and
in fact retired to France with his loot as the Marquis of Savoy.
† The town is Placentia. Fourteen years later Winston Churchill and President
Franklin Roosevelt would meet in Little Placentia Bay to discuss fighting Nazi

tank and touches the throttle, but leaves it set at 1,600 revolutions. At this latitude the difference between true and magnetic north is significant, so he compensates accordingly and crosses the breakers heading 093 degrees. From the whitecaps near the shore he figures the wind to be at least 20 miles per hour from due west and he crabs the *Spirit* left to hold course.

If he holds this course then St. Mary's Bay should appear off the right wing in about ten minutes and he should pass the southern end of Conception Bay in another half hour. Lindbergh is confident that from that point he can align himself perfectly to hit St. John's, twenty miles northeast past the bay. That would be nearly 7 P.M., forty-five minutes from now, with just enough time before sunset to get an accurate fix before heading out into the Atlantic. Slim's heart quickens a bit at that: this time the crossing is for real. Not that the shorter trips today weren't real, and he learned a great deal from each segment, but in the back of his mind he knew there was always more land ahead. Chances to salvage bad navigation, or save himself if things went wrong—but not this time. There was nothing past St. John's but open ocean and, very soon, darkness. Then, hopefully, Ireland.

Gazing from the windows there's nothing to see now but rolling moors speckled with thousands of dark ponds to the right and rising hills, almost mountains, to the left. Near the southern tip of the peninsula is Trepassey, the launch point for the U.S. Navy flying boats eight years ago. Nungesser may also have crashed somewhere down there, too, he thinks. If so, it would explain why they hadn't been found—and might

---

Germany and to sign the Atlantic Charter. The northern spit of land is Argentia, which briefly became the largest American naval base outside the United States before closing in 1994.

never be recovered. A plane is hard enough to locate in the wilderness even when you have some idea of where it crashed. Still, a search had to be attempted—a gesture, the payment of a debt felt by living men to their lost brothers who, by some miracle, might not be dead. Slim had seen the famous ace once in St. Louis. Compact and quietly intense, the Frenchman was quick, polite, and clear-eyed. How unsettling to think that somewhere ahead he would cross over Nungesser's remains— or join them beneath the waves.

But what a sight below!

Adding power, Lindbergh nudges the *Spirit* higher over the Avalon Peninsula's steeply rising terrain—Nova Scotia and Newfoundland form the northernmost part of the Appalachian mountain range. Sunset is spectacular, a deep golden band along the horizon that melts into bronze before washing upwards into a thin, bright layer of red. High cirrus clouds reflect the light, and for a few minutes they glow like white claws, tearing at the darkening sky. The mountains north of him are stark, a hard silhouette against this magnificent backdrop. It's breathtaking to be caught between heaven and earth, night and day. Sometimes flying feels like man is intruding upon the divine, Lindbergh muses, staring at the panorama below. Up here the world can seem too beautiful and too vast for human eyes.

Spirit rocks a bit from the normal turbulence over high terrain while the warm daytime air cools. Earlier today that made him nervous, but with experience the mind has a remarkable ability to adapt. He can hear the wind along the fabric, fingers of air scratching down the fuselage as the stabilizer lifts—just like a powerful current pushing a boat. With the wind just angled off the tail he doesn't have to hold a crab so much, and Slim relaxes his left leg a bit.

He can imagine Nungesser and Coli circling over this same

area looking for a place to land, feeling hopeless and lost. The ground below is rough, alternately heavy forests and rocky moors. Still, they wouldn't have tried to come down on land, would they? After all, Nungesser had jettisoned their landing gear, so why not come down on the water if they had an emergency? There were lots of lakes around and big bays, yet the weather had been bad a few weeks ago so Newfoundland could have been covered with fog or low clouds. What a lonely, bad time that would be, circling endlessly, praying for a break in the weather while you inexorably run out of fuel. Then that sick, hollow feeling when the engine quits and you inevitably glide closer to the thick, gray quilt below. Then the fog covers your aircraft, robbing you of the one essential sense a pilot must have—sight. Do you break out in time to see the ground, or plow into a hillside, leaving a tangled wreck and smashed bodies?

Fifteen minutes later Slim passes a crest, the terrain ahead falls steeply away, and to his left a big body of gray water shines in the weak sun. Conception Bay. There are several dark smudges close to the shoreline that must be small islands, though he doesn't know their names. A much larger island lies farther out, and even from here he can see its high, steep cliffs. Another twenty more miles northeast, about twelve minutes, and he should find St. John's by 7 P.M.

Then what?

Spirit has covered 1,100 miles in eleven hours. Slim is well aware that he's indulged himself by voluntarily deviating from the planned Great Circle route, and now he must deal with it. He had planned on obtaining his last navigational fix from Cape Bonavista, some 90 miles to the north, and would now have to correct back to course from St. John's instead. Slim calculates that if he angles slightly left, say to hold 083 degrees, *Spirit* will intersect the planned course a thousand miles from the Newfoundland coast: ten hours into the night. Nearly a third of the 3,610 total miles is behind him so he'd be well over halfway to Paris by then, but there will be no way to identify that point, except by timing.

It will have to do.

Skimming over the hills, Lindbergh suddenly crosses a pocked ridge and there it is—St. John's. The harbor looks like a deep stab wound, a narrow cut through the coast that widens and turns inland. Sheltered by hills on three sides, the harbor is shielded from the ocean on its eastern edge by a huge breakwater. The town is built right up to the water and boats line the docks. It's colorful, he's surprised to see, with scores of wooden buildings painted in yellows, reds, and all shades of blue. The place looks like pictures of harbors in the West Indies, and is unexpected here over the last North American city he'll see today.

Slim had thought of this moment hours before and doesn't hesitate. Pushing the stick forward, he tugs the throttle back with his left hand and dives toward the flat, mansard rooftops. There are a lot of churches for a town of thirty thousand or so. Two big ones are directly ahead and their burgundy-colored gables make them easy to see. One is red, probably brick, and the other one is stone, with startling green high, narrow windows.* Alcock and Brown took off from somewhere nearby, Lindbergh knows, but he hasn't time to dwell on this.

As the ground rushes up, Slim levels off just above the chimneys, shoves the throttle forward and the Wright's throaty roar fills the cockpit. Hopefully someone down there will hear it, too; someone will *surely* see him and send a wire out. New York will know where he was, and St. Louis, too.

---

* St. Andrew's Presbyterian, and the Anglican Cathedral of St. John the Baptist, respectively. Both were damaged by the Great Fire of 1892 and had been rebuilt by 1927.

• • •

IN FACT, LINDBERGH and the *Spirit* had been seen many times over the past eleven hours. Chester Rice, a clerk at the Middleboro, Massachusetts, police station, saw "a monoplane, believed to be that of Captain Lindbergh . . . over West Middleboro at about 9:15 this morning flying northeasterly."

From Yarmouth, Nova Scotia, a cable confirmed, "Captain Lindbergh passed over New Tusket, about forty miles from here, at 12:45 o'clock this afternoon [11:45 Eastern Daylight Saving Time]. He was flying low, but traveling very fast." A banner from Halifax, Nova Scotia, ran proclaiming, "Captain Lindbergh passed over Mulgrave on the Strait of Canso, which separates the mainland of Nova Scotia from Cape Breton Island, at 4:05 Atlantic Day Time [3:05 Eastern Daylight Saving Time]. He was flying high and the markings on his gray monoplane could not be seen."

From Sydney, Nova Scotia, it was reported in the May 20 *New York Times* that "Captain Lindbergh got his last sight of the American continent at 5 o'clock [4 P.M. Eastern Daylight Saving Time] this afternoon when he passed out into the Atlantic over Main-a-dieu, Cape Breton. The plane was flying low and at great speed, and her number, 211, was plainly visible to watchers with powerful glasses."

Finally, as the evening editions went to press in the United States, President Coolidge said that in common with the rest of the American people he had the greatest interest in Charles Lindbergh's flight across the Atlantic. "He has my best wishes for his success."

That night 40,000 people gathered at Yankee Stadium in New York City to watch a boxing match boasting a $250,000 purse. "The remarkable thing about last night's fight crowd was that they were all wondering how the transatlantic flight would come and not who would be knocked out," the *New York Times* reported the following day. "On the subways, on the sidewalks, in the stadium, the conversation was all about Lindbergh . . . wondering whether a motor high over the Atlantic would keep going until Europe was reached."

Between fights it was announced that Lindbergh was safely on course, 300 miles at sea.

"He is the greatest fighter of them all," yelled a single voice from the crowd, followed by a deafening chorus of affirmation.

The ring announcer pleaded for silence. "When he got it he requested all to rise in a moment of prayer that Lindbergh might land safely in France." At that, "40,000 persons rose as one and stood with heads bared. Looking back from the ringside on the upturned faces at this moment, there was none who did not show anxiety in his or her face."

WITH HIS FACE in the window, Slim sees scores of white dots below, faces turned upward at the noise and the sight of the shiny airplane. Snapshots fill his eye: colored awnings along the busy waterfront streets, telephone poles with sagging wires crisscrossing the town, and ships in the harbor. Wharves pass below, a rowboat loses its rhythm, and the *Spirit* is suddenly over the harbor's dark water.

Up ahead the hills come right down to the sea, then reluctantly spread out a bit to allow ships in and out. The northern side is steeper and a boxy, stone tower is just visible on top. A watchtower? Castle?* He banks slightly toward the middle of the harbor's mouth and stares through the gap. A doorway out

---

* Cabot Tower atop Signal Hill. On December 12, 1901, Marconi flew a kite some five hundred feet from this tower and received a wireless transmission that had originated in Poldhu, Cornwall, more than 2,200 miles away.

into the Atlantic. There are no more reassuring islands ahead, Slim realizes with cold finality, and the moment he's dreaded is here. The engine's snarl is lost in the crash of great waves breaking against the rocks that hurl white sheets of spray high onto the hillsides. The dying light catches the little silver plane, and for a long moment the *Spirit of St. Louis* is perfectly framed by the rocky pillars, feathery salt spray, and angry gray water.

Then suddenly it's gone. One machine, one man—swallowed up by the darkness filling the eastern sky.

PART TWO

A minute ago, I was a creature of the land, thinking of the ocean ahead . . . now, I'm a creature of the ocean. . . . I've given up a continent and taken on an ocean in its place—irrevocably.

—CHARLES LINDBERGH, MAY 20, 1927

FIVE

INNOCENCE LOST: SNAPSHOTS OF A DECADE

IT HAS BEEN said that the times make the man, but for a young Charles Lindbergh this wasn't strictly accurate. Lindbergh made Lindbergh; his upbringing, temperament, and complex family characteristics all formed the outline of the man who took off from Roosevelt Field on May 20, 1927. However, his decade, the 1920s, provided the stage upon which he found himself, and the events from this time molded him into the man the public viewed. Variously known as the Jazz Age or the Roaring Twenties, the ten years following the Great War were seminal in American history. As a nation, the United States turned a corner and much of the world followed. Technology changed people's lives; incredible fortunes were made and spent; old morals faced modern challenges; and new heroes, like Charles Lindbergh, came of age.

F. Scott Fitzgerald, prophet of the decade, wrote that his generation of Americans was "dedicated more than the last to the fear of poverty and the worship of success; grown up to find all Gods dead, all wars fought, all faiths in man shaken." The catalyst for much of this, though certainly not the sole cause, was the Great War and its immediate aftermath. From 1914 to 1918 the conflict cost 30 million dead, wounded, and missing; 14 million from Germany and Austria Hungary alone. Among the Western Allies, France and England lost 9 million between them and were in no mood for moderation or reconciliation.

Much of the fighting in the west had been on French soil, and after four years of bombs, gas, artillery, and mines, millions of acres were obliterated. Destruction of land and farms, combined with the loss of so many able-bodied men, put Europe's economy into a tailspin. All told, the war cost the Allies some $125 billion directly, and at least as much again indirectly.

Entering the war in April 1917, the United States nevertheless spent in excess of $22 billion, half of which was owed by fifteen European allies. Because the United States Congress never ratified the Treaty of Versailles, Washington had no claim to reparations from the defeated Central Powers, and of the Allies, only Finland repaid its $8 million debt. This left many Americans unenthused about Europe and bred an isolationist attitude that would largely endure until the 1941 attack on Pearl Harbor.*

With the industrial expansion to manufacture war material spiking prosperity, and a comparatively light loss of 53,402 combat deaths, the United States ended the war in a relatively strong position. On November 11, 1918, the State Department announced to newspapers on the American East Coast that the war had officially ended. Bells began to toll, and as the coun-

---

* Great Britain ceased making payments on her $4.4 billion Great War debt in 1934, though she paid off her loans from World War II in 2006.

try awakened people in every city began celebrating. Businesses closed "For the Kaiser's Funeral." The Kaiser was burned in effigy and his dummy was washed down Wall Street with fire hoses. Sirens wailed and horns blared while people cried and laughed. Eight hundred female students from Barnard College snake-danced in Morningside Heights and a young girl sang the Doxology in Times Square.

The first 3,500 American soldiers arrived home at New York's West Fourteenth Street pier aboard the Cunard liner *Mauretania* on December 1, 1918. Other ships followed in quick succession to bring back the two million troops deployed to Europe. Amid flags and colored bunting the soldiers marched down Fifth Avenue, swinging in step with fixed bayonets under an immense plaster arch at Madison Square.

Lights blazed again and Broadway was once more the "Great White Way." Wartime censorship ended, sugar was no longer scarce, and real bread reappeared. Women were still wearing their hair long with high patent leather shoes over black or tan stockings, and skirts still stopped a modest six inches up from the ground, but all of this was changing. The 1920s were alive with change of every sort and, as is usually the case, it was unsettling to those living through it. To begin with, the normal intergenerational rebellion was exacerbated by a wartime mentality that wasn't particularly interested in looking far into the future. What was the point, young men who became soldiers asked, if they had an excellent chance of dying on a battlefield? And why, young women then wondered, should we wait for men who might never come home? Why not, both sexes asked in increasing numbers, live for today and enjoy life while we have it?

Automobiles were becoming more common and were a way to escape supervision of parents, neighbors and, of course, spouses. Only 10 percent of cars were enclosed in 1919, but by the time Lindbergh flew the Atlantic this had jumped to nearly 83 percent. "Sex and confession" magazines were popular; Bernarr Macfadden's racy magazine *True-Story* sold two million copies annually by 1926 and was wildly successful. Yet the decade was hardly as gloomy and crass as it is often viewed. Walt Disney incorporated his first film company, Laugh-O-Gram, and Olympian Johnny Weissmuller swam the 100-meter freestyle in under a minute. The Lincoln Memorial was dedicated, carvings on Mount Rushmore began, and an eighteen-year-old named Ralph Samuelson became the first water-skier.

Illiteracy would decrease from 6 percent overall in 1920 to 4.3 percent by decade's end. Capitalizing on the trend, *Time* magazine would begin publishing in 1923 and create its "Man of the Year" in 1927.* The *New Yorker* hit the street in 1925, and by the summer of Lindbergh's flight more than 36 million newspapers were read each day. This newfound voracious appetite for the written word made it possible for the nation to closely follow Lindbergh's flight, though, as he himself would ruefully discover, journalists sometimes placed sensationalism above accuracy.

Automobiles sat outside 10 million homes, and there were more cars in New York City alone than in Germany, and France had fewer automobiles than Kansas. Home to the largest publishers and banks, New York's Woolworth Building at 792 feet was the world's tallest structure, and the 8,558-foot Hudson River Vehicular Tunnel was the longest underwater tunnel on earth.† New York had also surpassed London in terms of

---

* Charles Lindbergh was *Time*'s first "Man of the Year."
† Renamed the Holland Tunnel, it opened on November 13, 1927.

population, and 40 percent of U.S. international trade passed through its port.

It would be simplistic and incorrect to believe the nation suddenly rejected its values and, as is popularly portrayed, abandoned its past and future for the present. Many certainly did not go on benders, cut their hair, wear short skirts, or ditch prewar notions of morality. But many did. A tremendous labor shortage had occurred when the men joined up to fight, and the vacuum was largely filled with women and black men, who had become temporarily accustomed to the relative independence provided by a steady income.

When the soldiers came home and were demobilized, they wanted their jobs back and a return to the old social order. But many women resisted falling back into domestic servitude, and black men had shown they could perform as equals in every facet of American life—if they were permitted to do so.

Labor unions, highly influential at the time, found themselves at a crossroads. Should they protect only white workers, which would reduce their collective bargaining power with big business—or should they represent all workers regardless of color? By generally choosing the latter, they fed racial resentment among whites, bringing organizations like the Ku Klux Klan back to life. By 1920 the Reverend William J. Simmons, a former Methodist minister from Alabama, had increased the Klan's membership to more than four million. As their influence grew, so did their sense of self-importance; like the Taliban of a later era, they saw themselves as the sole guardians of "pure" American life. "Native, White, Protestant supremacy" became a motto, with dancing, drinking, religion, and any moral issues falling within their self-appointed purview.

They were not alone in this myopic, intolerant Puritanism. Some of the fanatics, like Wilbur Glenn Voliva, were silly. Head of the Christian Apostolic Church, Voliva stated in 1922 that "the sky is a vast dome of solid material, from which the sun, moon and stars are hung like chandeliers from a ceiling." Others were not so easy to dismiss. During the war's closing years, and those immediately following the armistice, enthusiasm for various forms of extremism was viewed by many as a counterweight to social change. Speaking German was made illegal in several states, books were burned, and in Boston, of all places, Beethoven was banned. In Collinsville, Illinois, a young man named Robert Prager, who happened to be born in Germany, was stripped, wrapped in an American flag, and lynched. His murderers were acquitted of this "patriotic crime" in only twenty-five minutes.

The Anti-Saloon League and the Woman's Christian Temperance Union (WCTU) were both given a new lease on life through the politics of the Wartime Prohibition Act. Ostensibly created to control critical resources like mines, factories, railroad rolling stock, and all manner of raw materials for the war effort, the act was meant to last only "for the duration" of the war. Taxes gained from the manufacture, import, and sale of liquor were to be a major source of revenue and, since Washington had imposed similar acts to pay for the Civil War and Spanish-American War, there was little concern. After all, Americans were fighting in the Great War.

The main problem was that it went into effect *after* the armistice was signed on November 11, 1918. But the "drys," as they were called, saw the act for what it was: a slightly open door through which a full-scale assault on "wet" America could be launched. In this they had a willing, powerful, and energetic partner in the United States government. Since the creation of a permanent federal income tax by the 1913 ratification of the

Sixteenth Amendment, Washington had shown an enthusiasm to intrude in public life as never before and a perfect opportunity, under the cover of war, now existed to expand its control. Four separate revenue acts had been passed since 1913, raising the tax rates to an astonishing 77 percent on those in the highest bracket, and four more would be passed between 1921 and 1928.

Cracked open by the Wartime Prohibition Act, the doorway to civil liberty and freedom of choice was kicked off its hinges a minute past midnight on January 17, 1920. The Eighteenth Amendment, stating in part that "the manufacture, sale, or transportation of intoxicating liquors within . . . the United States and all territory subject to the jurisdiction thereof for beverage purposes is hereby prohibited," was now in effect. The National Prohibition Act, also known as the Volstead Act, was also passed that year in an attempt to enforce the Eighteenth Amendment.

On its surface this was called a "noble experiment," but in truth it was a graphic illustration of the power of the political lobby. Where there is government there is always some degree of influence peddling and corruption, yet for the most part the United States had avoided these perils, at least on a large scale. Not so after 1920. Interest groups learned that if they were well organized, well financed, and extremely vocal about their desires they could influence, and actually create, legislation to their liking. It is a trend that has continued to this day, and was born during the Prohibition years.

The postwar loosening of morals, the influx of immigrants, and the faltering economy all fostered a rise in evangelical Protestantism that was determined to save America from itself, even against its will. Billy Sunday, a former professional baseball player turned itinerant preacher, declared that alcohol was

"God's worst enemy and hell's best friend." Unable to explain biblical contradictions on that subject, he and others like him hired scholars to actually rewrite the Bible and remove such passages.

A number of like-minded groups sprang up to purge America of its booze: the Anti-Saloon League, the WCTU, and the Orwellian-named Methodist Board of Temperance, Prohibition, and Public Morals. Spreading the evangelical word included a proposition to hang up alcohol offenders by their tongues, and sterilization. Other punishments were advocated that ranged from exile to execution. In a country desperately trying to rest a bit after the war, weary of spreading democracy and saving the world, there was initially little resistance to this sort of fanaticism. Most Americans then, as they do now, had a laissez-faire attitude toward the cranks as long as they left other people alone.

But they didn't.

The dry movement quickly capitalized on its success with Prohibition and began trying to remove other types of public evils: Catholics, Jews, immigrants, city dwellers, businessmen . . . basically anyone who wasn't a white, rural Protestant. By turning the Prohibition cause into a crusade against anyone beyond their narrow worldview, they overreached. This evolved into a proxy class war, with alcohol as its battlefield, in an effort to control American life. The surge in immigration hadn't helped; in the decade prior to the Great War more than 10 million people entered the United States, a nation with a population of just over eighty million. Generally poorer and less educated eastern or southern Europeans, they assimilated slowly and tended to live in cultural groupings within large American cities. The new arrivals clung to their non-Protestant religions and comforting traditions, which included drinking. Earlier immigrants, like the Germans and especially the Irish, came from a culture that had always incorporated alcohol, and the nearly 900 million gallons consumed by 1900 proved it. Big brewers like Pabst, Schlitz, Busch, and Miller were all German-American companies, founded by immigrants, and built around large, working-class, urban populations.

The nation's large distilleries were generally controlled by Jewish businessmen like Lee Levy and the Canadian Bronfman brothers. By 1916 Jewish companies made up some 80 percent of the National Liquor Dealers Association, including Max Hirsch, Pritz & Company, and Elias Hyman & Sons. The stage was set, then, for the showdown of white, rural Protestant teetotalers against city-dwelling alcoholic papists, Jews, and immigrants. Other issues, such as direct senatorial elections, income tax, and women's suffrage, were dragged into the fight whenever possible. As Philipp Blom wrote in *Fracture,* "The great campaign for renewed morality was old America fighting new America, rural America fighting urban life, the nineteenth century fighting the twentieth."

This thirteen-year feud unquestionably changed the fabric of life in the United States by altering how people thought. Because some 1,500 underpaid federal agents could never patrol the 5,525-mile Canada-U.S. border, nor blockade the 4,993 miles of American coastline,* disrespect for the law, at least silly laws, became commonplace. To take advantage of a $3 billion untaxed industry, organized crime also rose dramatically. Violent assaults and murders rose from 12 per 100,000 in 1920 to 16 per 100,000 by the time Prohibition was repealed. At least 30,000 "speakeasies," illegal drinking establishments, popped up in New York alone.

---

* Coastal shoreline only. Does not include tidal or freshwater coastlines.

Skirt hems rose to nine inches and girls rolled their stockings down to show some leg below the knee. Corsets were discarded. Wild young social ladies called flappers appeared in the
speakeasies, drinking in public in thin, sleeveless dresses. By
1927 their skirts were above the knee, though there's no indication Charles Lindbergh noticed—if he did, he was certainly too
shy to discuss it. Corsets and petticoats declined in use, with
cotton largely replaced by silk or rayon stockings. Bobbed hair
was no longer a sign of fashionable radicalism; it was simply
fashionable. The veneration of youth and beauty over age and
experience had begun and the trend has never waned, at least
in the United States.

The young medium of motion pictures reflected the times.
Lee de Forest had invented the triode detector tube, which essentially amplified sound, thus making long-distance communications possible. He also figured out how to imprint sound
onto movie film, and when Warner Bros. released Al Jolson's
The Jazz Singer, talking pictures became commercially viable.
As the *Spirit of St. Louis* flew east toward Europe, 80 percent
of the world's movies were made in Hollywood and film was
the fourth-largest industry in the country. More than eight hundred films per year were created, and some 100 million tickets
were sold each week, in 20,000 theaters. Some of these were
palaces, beautiful, ornate picture houses like the Roxy Theater
in New York, or Grauman's Chinese Theatre in Los Angeles.*
Toward the middle of the decade, as the recession ended and
prosperity increased, Americans often saw Rudolph Valentino,
Charlie Chaplin, and others on-screen several times a week.

The saxophone made its debut, heralding the fox-trot and

---

* The Roxy contained a 118-piece orchestra and boasted 6,200 seats. It was
air-conditioned and was among the first theaters with drinking fountains.

slow dancing in the dark. Cincinnati's *Catholic Telegraph* was among those expressing shock and indignation. "The music is sensuous, the embracing of partners—the female only half dressed—is absolutely indecent; and the motions—they are such as may not be described." The *New York American* decried jazz as "a pathological, nerve-irritating, sex-exciting music." People loved it nonetheless. "Petting parties" became a common indoor pastime, further shocking mothers and fathers across the country. "I've kissed dozens of men," Rosalind exclaims in Fitzgerald's *This Side of Paradise*. "I suppose I'll kiss dozens more." Yet this worldly, upper-class view was definitely at odds with most of rural, grassroots America. A city ordinance passed in Norphelt, Arkansas, read: "Section 1. Hereafter it shall be unlawful for any man and woman, male or female, to be guilty of committing the act of sexual intercourse between themselves at any place within the corporate limits of said town." This did not, of course, apply to married couples, unless the act was "of a grossly improper and lascivious nature," though who would police this and render a judgment was far from clear. But in cities, sex was truly out in the open, nearly as much an obsession as drinking.

Meanwhile the evangelicals, the Klan, and myriad groups of teetotalers fumed. They believed illicit alcohol was the root of all this decadence, and immigrants were providing it. They viewed immigrants as filthy masses from Eastern Europe or drunken Irish. Theodore Roosevelt once called his opponents "a stupid, sodden, vicious lot, most of them being equally deficient in brains and virtue." Immigrants were at the root of job shortages, crime, and, above all, the alcoholic evil causing moral decay, or so the various movements claimed. Frances Willard, national president of the WCTU, called immigrants the "scum of the old world" and joined the Klan in petitioning Congress to keep out "European riff-raff." This riffraff had put ground glass into Red Cross bandages, they claimed, and plotted to poison American reservoirs or blow up bridges. A sort of national paranoia spread and anyone who was European or a socialist or spoke against the government, the flag, or the president was a target. One immigrant, arrogant or unaware enough to shout "To hell with the United States," was shot and killed in Indiana. A jury took just two minutes to acquit the shooter.

Washington's answer was the Immigration Restriction Act of 1924, which created an annual limit on immigrants, capped at 2 percent of their countrymen already residing in the United States. Gaming the system further, the government based this total number on the 1890 census, not the more current 1920 census. There were 943,781 Poles in the United States as of the 1920 census, but the 1890 figure of 91,000 would be used, thereby reducing the number of incoming Poles from 18,876 to 1,890.

But the real concern was the Russians.

On November 7, 1917, Vladimir Lenin and his Bolsheviks stormed the Imperial Winter Palace in Petrograd. Early in March 1918, the new Soviet government made a separate peace with the Kaiser and pulled out of the Great War. This released an additional million German soldiers to fight the combined American, British, and French armies on the western front and prolonged the war. Surprisingly, communist and socialist ideology had enough of a following in the United States to cause concern and produce the "Red Scare."

In April 1919, a six-inch by three-inch brown paper package was delivered to the Atlanta home of Senator Thomas R. Hardwick, chairman of the Senate Immigration Committee and a vehement supporter of immigration restriction. Tragically, a female servant opened it and lost both hands as it blew up in her face. The next day a clerk in the New York Post Office parcel post division read about the Hardwick bomb and remembered that he had put sixteen such packages aside for insufficient postage. Returning to work, he informed the police, who examined them in a nearby fire station and found they all contained explosives. All were marked with a return address to Gimbel Brothers in New York and intended for prominent officials and businessmen: J. P. Morgan, John D. Rockefeller Jr., the commissioner of immigration, and a Supreme Court justice, to name a few.

In Washington, D.C., the attorney general of the United States, A. Mitchell Palmer, was going to bed on June 2 when he heard something hit the front door. An explosion followed, so powerful that the entire front of Palmer's house at 2132 R Street NW was peeled off and windows were shattered all over the neighborhood. Smoking rubble hung from trees and was scattered over lawns. So were bloody bits and pieces of the bomber; a leg was across the street on a neighbor's doorstep and part of his head wound up on S Street, two blocks away. He had likely stumbled on the Palmers' steps, fell against the door, and detonated the bomb prematurely.*

Bombs rocked seven other U.S. cities that night, all within ninety minutes of each other. As with modern concerns with terrorist groups, the anarchists caused a great deal of public unrest and distrust. Advocating violence as a means to effect change, they saw as their prime enemy a society based on law and the people who supported such a society through capitalist principles; in other words, the United States of America. Special Agent Todd Daniel of the Department of Justice Bureau

---

* He was later identified as Carlo Valdinoci, a twenty-four-year-old anarchist who enjoyed making bombs, though apparently without much success.

of Investigation characterized it as a "terrorist movement . . . national in scope." Indeed this was, and it further fragmented a populace already struggling with other issues.

Though such fanatics had always been present in small numbers, they had previously not attracted much of a following in the United States. With the successful Russian upheaval as a model, a wealth-based class system to fight against, and a faltering economy, the radicalization found fertile ground among the disillusioned and those who believed themselves disenfranchised. The immediate catalyst for this had been the 1918 armistice and subsequent widespread cancellation of government war contracts. Unemployment rose as plants shut down and thousands of men were laid off, while the artificially high cost of living from the war years remained high. Sirloin steak had increased from 27 to 42 cents a pound, milk from 9 to 15 cents per quart, and eggs from 34 to 62 cents a dozen. The price of coffee, sugar, and all other sorts of essentials rose with the wartime economy but did not correct when it ended.

For sectors that remained strong, shipbuilding in particular, companies refused to increase wages and shorten hours. Owners felt they had sacrificed profits for the war and they now wanted to get back to the business of making money. Anyone or anything hampering that return, particularly the American Federation of Labor and other such unions, was not to be tolerated. Fears of a Bolshevik-style revolution were very real in 1919, and to pour fuel on the flames the United Mine Workers struck in September, advocating the nationalization of the mining industry. That meant full government control over private ownership, essentially communism. These sentiments were echoed by the Industrial Workers of the World (IWW), nicknamed the "Wobblies." Emerging in 1905, the IWW was more radical than other unions. Their central platform was workplace democracy, a system by which workers elected their own immediate supervisors, or delegates, and in the most extreme cases advocated running their own factories.

With disturbing similarity to Russian groups, the Wobblies' ultimate goal was forming a separate social class composed of workers. Understandably, the idea of American industrial power at the mercy of a revolutionary working class was anathema to big corporate interests and there was considerable friction. Ordinary people, unnerved and frustrated, often acted on their own accord to combat the situation. One IWW member, Wesley Everest of Washington State, had his genitals cut off by an angry mob, then was hung from a bridge and eventually shot. His death was called a suicide and no one was ever charged with a crime.

It didn't help a volatile situation that large numbers of left-wing literati were also rebelling against traditional Americanism. Sinclair Lewis was among the many who rejected cultural attitudes of the time, and his novel *Main Street,* released in 1920, was an indictment of the very cornerstone of American life, the small town.* That Lewis felt this way was not surprising, but what was surprising was how his fictional nonfiction resonated with the reading public. Nearly 400,000 copies of *Main Street* were sold, and its satirical sequel, *Babbitt,* was equally well received, giving Lewis the very fame, fortune, and status that he railed against.

Like Charles Lindbergh, Lewis was a small-town Minnesota boy who had difficulty making friends or forming long-term relationships. Unhappy with his roots and unable to adapt to the outside world, he was a "homeless intellectual." As with

---

* *Main Street* was awarded the Pulitzer Prize for literature in 1921, but the decision was overturned.

Carl Sandburg, Willa Cather, Theodore Dreiser, and others, this lack of faith in anything, most of all in themselves, was a notable characteristic of those of age in the 1920s.

As Lewis himself once admitted, "in America most of us—not readers alone, but even writers—are still afraid of any literature which is not a glorification of everything American, a glorification of our faults as well as our virtues." These were people who desperately needed reaffirmation that there was still good in this country. In the wake of Prohibition, the Red Scare, and brewing government scandals, they were rapidly losing confidence in their leaders. Overbearing, vitriolic groups like the Methodist Board of Temperance, Prohibition, and Public Morals were similarly eroding their faith in organized religion, and people were looking for someone to believe in. They needed a hero and there wasn't one in sight.

Yet.

BY 1925 THE decade's social and cultural revolution was well under way. The threat from anarchists, labor unions, and radicals was still there but had diminished somewhat, at least in the public mind. Nicola Sacco and Bartolomeo Vanzetti, two Italian anarchists, had been arrested for the brutal murders of Frederick Parmenter and Alessandro Berardelli of the Slater & Morrill Shoe Company, outside Boston. Their trial was a showpiece of government force arrayed against paranoia and idealism. The pair was suspicious, true, having been arrested with weapons and anarchist literature. Both were Italian, a nationality widely regarded as uneducated and violent thanks in large part to the likes of Alphonse Capone and Luigi Galleani, with their ties to organized crime and anarchism, respectively.

There was scant, if any, evidence tying Vanzetti or Sacco to the murders, but they were declared guilty by virtue of being in the area, being subversive, and being Italian. The trial garnered a great deal of unfavorable domestic and international attention, but an example had to be made and they were it. Unfortunately, the government's obtuse handling of the case went a long way to undermine the very values that the average American had been raised to believe.*

Just as Prohibition was a long-running battle in the cultural proxy war, there was a short, sharp incident in 1925 that undeniably exemplified the struggle for the soul of America. In the wake of several sensationalistic events, a small group of men decided to try to put their town, Dayton, Tennessee, on the national center stage. This would help them all; the local economy would expand, businesses would grow, and everyone would know Dayton. George Rappelyea, a mining engineer, and a state prosecutor somewhat implausibly named Sue Kerr Hicks believed they'd found the perfect venue.

The 64th General Assembly of the Tennessee legislature had passed Senator George Washington Butler's House Bill 185 in March 1925. This act prohibited "the teaching of the Evolution Theory in all the Universities, Normals and all other public schools of Tennessee, which are supported in whole or in part by the public school funds of the State, and to provide penalties for the violations thereof."

Hicks was aware that the American Civil Liberties Union (ACLU) was seeking a way to constitutionally challenge the bill. He and the others, nicknamed the "drugstore conspirators" because they gathered in Robinson's Drugstore, figured a

---

* Massachusetts ultimately executed Sacco and Vanzetti by electrocution on August 23, 1927, as Charles Lindbergh flew the *Spirit of St. Louis* to Minneapolis during his tour of the United States.

way to help defeat the bill and draw a media circus to Dayton. They persuaded John Thomas Scopes, a biology teacher at Dayton's Central High School, to be caught teaching the evils of evolution. He agreed, later stating, "I do believe in the ethical teachings of Christ, and I believe there is a God. . . . But all biology and most other sciences are basically the story of the evolution of matter and of life. I was hired to teach science, and I went ahead and taught it."

A fourteen-year-old student named Howard Morgan was produced to confirm he had been instructed on the theory of evolution, and an arrest warrant was subsequently issued for Johnny Scopes. Hicks and Rappelyea were delighted, and per the agreement with Scopes they wired the ACLU in New York. With the trial set for July, high-powered legal counsel was retained, with Dudley Field Malone, Arthur Garfield Hays, and no less a personage than Clarence Darrow himself making their way to rural Tennessee.

Darrow was probably the most famous defense lawyer in America in 1925. A committed agnostic, as an ACLU board member he was also a firebrand for civil liberties. The year before he had successfully prevented the execution of Nathan Leopold and Richard Albert Loeb for their cold-blooded, premeditated murder of fourteen-year-old Bobby Franks in Chicago. Darrow was widely regarded as a consummate orator, and a gifted lawyer well versed in bending the law to his own ends.

Likewise, the prosecution spared no expense and the World's Christian Fundamentals Association retained William Jennings Bryan. A three-time presidential candidate and evangelical champion, Bryan had become extremely wealthy through speaking engagements and Florida real estate speculation. As secretary of state under Woodrow Wilson, Bryan had seen the Great War as the manifestation of European godlessness and had tried to keep the United States out of the conflict.

Commencing in July 1925, the trial was front-page news across the country. Almost immediately the actual matter of John Scopes was eclipsed by larger issues: creationism versus evolution, and to an equal degree, the allowable interference of government into the lives of its citizens. Reporters were numerous, but none was more influential than H. L. Mencken, the "Sage of Baltimore." Ruthless, but eccentric in his beliefs, he thought very little of Negros, Jews, or America's white middle class; the "Booboisie," he called them. A brilliant satirist nonetheless, it was Mencken who coined the "Monkey Trial" moniker.

Darrow was brilliant. He turned the issue into a First Amendment challenge against the establishment of religion and free speech. He argued that any infringement struck at the foundation of our basic American rights, and that it was intellectually stifling to not be taught all that science can offer. The state of Tennessee, he claimed, was violating its own constitution by forcing one explanation for life on its schoolchildren. "The modern world," he eloquently phrased it, "is the child of doubt and inquiry, as the ancient world was the child of fear and faith." In a single sentence he summarized the principal misgivings that Americans felt during the 1920s.

Fluently persuasive, Bryan's rebuttal argued for the right of the people to decide, however ridiculously, what would be taught in public schools funded by their tax money. A literalist, in a state whose legislature was dominated by fundamentalists, he framed the crux of his prosecution as simply, "The one beauty about the Word of God is, it does not take an expert to understand it." This, and the fact that Scopes had indeed broken the law, won the case for him. Judge John T. Raulston, no doubt wearied with posturing that had nothing to do with the law, expunged most of the peripheral arguments from the record.

Scopes was fined one hundred dollars according to the statute and released. He went on to graduate school at the University of Chicago, then became a geologist for the United Gas Corporation. Bryan returned to Dayton five days after the trial and passed away there in his sleep. Clarence Darrow continued to litigate, including in the racially charged Sweet Trial, and died in Chicago thirteen years later. On the face of it, fundamentalism had triumphed, but it was a Pyrrhic victory. On a technicality, Scopes's conviction was eventually overturned by the Tennessee Supreme Court and grassroots fundamentalism had been shown for what it was. Not the benevolent teachings of a gentle God, or a group of sincere practitioners dedicated to helping their fellow man, but rather an intolerant attempt to force a single, narrow-minded interpretation on everyone.

America, it seemed, was drifting more than ever.

THOUGH THE TWENTY-THREE-YEAR-OLD Charles Lindbergh undoubtedly followed the trial, as did everyone else, it was likely with more amusement than genuine concern. Of much greater interest to the young aviator was the second big event of 1925: the crash of the airship USS *Shenandoah* and the subsequent court-martial of Colonel William Lendrum Mitchell. A courageous tactical officer who had proven both his bravery and the potential of aircraft in combat, Mitchell was a visionary proponent of airpower. In 1923 he predicted the Japanese attack on Pearl Harbor, in great detail, and though primarily concerned with the fighting capabilities of aircraft he could see a time when commercial airliners would fly passengers to Europe in hours.* Lindbergh, who could also envision the vast potential of aircraft, agreed. But the similarity ended there.

A few months after the Scopes Monkey Trial, on September 2, 1925, the airship USS *Shenandoah* slipped away from her mooring mast and slowly eased upward above Lakehurst Naval Air Station in New Jersey. She was to proceed over the Allegheny Mountains, stopping in at events and fairs during a twenty-seven-city publicity tour. Fall weather over the Ohio Valley was notoriously unpredictable; thunderstorms were sudden and common, as they were over the plains farther west into Iowa.

But her captain, Navy lieutenant commander Zachary Lansdowne, had little choice but to follow the plan. The Army and Navy were in a desperate competition for scarce funding, and this trip had been directed by Rear Admiral William Moffett, chief of the Navy's Bureau of Aeronautics. Commander Lansdowne, a Naval Academy graduate who had earned the Navy Cross during *R34*'s transatlantic flight six years earlier, was arguably the most experienced airship captain in the service. He'd actually jumped from the British ship while it floated over Long Island and landed by parachute in order to moor the craft, since no one on Roosevelt Field knew the procedure.

Shenandoah and her forty-one crew members flew west all night, making good headway at 55 miles per hour. Running into a squall line approximately seventy-five miles east of Columbus, Ohio, the 682-foot long airship pitched up from 2,100 feet to 6,300 feet. Gas was vented, ballast was dumped, and she plunged back to 3,200 feet. Just two years old, *Shenandoah* was a rigid airship, not a bag of gas, and she had a keel with interior wire supports for strength and stability.

---

* Most professional military officers could see a reckoning with Japan; among others, Douglas MacArthur and George S. Patton Jr. also predicted the attack.

It wasn't enough.

Though *Shenandoah* was filled with helium, an inert gas that would not explode like hydrogen, the real danger was in the tremendous asymmetrical stresses on her support structure. Lansdowne tried to clear the storm but was caught in another violent updraft that pitched the airship up above 6,000 feet again. The hull broke in two pieces initially and the control car tore loose. Disappearing into the storm below, thirty-seven-year-old Lansdowne would die less than two hundred miles from his birthplace in Greenville, Ohio. Seven others went in with him, while the remaining thirty-three crew members clung to girders inside the shattered airship. Seven more would perish, bringing the total to fourteen deaths.

When Billy Mitchell heard about the disaster, he was based at Fort Sam Houston in San Antonio, Texas. He considered the post the end of the earth, a betrayal by the Army, and he was bitterly, fundamentally unhappy. Born in Nice, France, in December 1879 to a wealthy midwestern family, Mitchell had a paternal grandfather, a banker, who had made an enormous fortune in railroads and was known as the "Rothschild of Milwaukee." Mitchell's father, though no businessman, was a Civil War veteran and U.S. senator. Young William, or "Billy," as he was called, dropped out of college to enlist in the army at the outbreak of the Spanish-American War. His father saw to it that he was commissioned an officer and the young lieutenant was sent to Cuba. Technically minded and adept at solving problems in the field, Mitchell laid the first telegraph cables between Havana and Santiago de Cuba. He did it so well that he was sent to Alaska, where he laid nearly 1,500 miles of the Washington–Alaska Cable & Telegraph lines.

Fascinated with aircraft, at his own expense Major Mitchell learned to fly in 1916 and managed an appointment to the western front as the War Department's aeronautical observer. Seeing combat at St.-Mihiel and the Meuse-Argonne, he was widely regarded, especially by himself, as the most experienced American air combat leader in Europe. Despite his vanity, there was no denying his command prowess. It's one thing to be a superb fighter pilot, but another to be able to command such men, especially a combination of French, British, Italian, and American squadrons totaling 1,481 planes—yet he did just that.

At age thirty-nine, eighteen months after arriving in Europe, Billy Mitchell was a brigadier general, receiving the Distinguished Service Cross and the French Legion of Honor, among others. Yet despite his battlefield skills and unquestioned personal courage, he was also abrasive, dismissive of lesser intellects (everyone else in France), vain to the point of silliness, and insubordinate past the point expected of a thinking, experienced officer. It was this last trait that would land him before a court-martial and eventually cost him his career.

Upon learning of the *Shenandoah*'s crash, Mitchell penned a scathing 6,080-word, seventeen-page indictment of Army and Navy senior leadership. He wrote that the recent spate of accidents, including the airship, "are a direct result of incompetency, criminal negligence and almost treasonable administration by the War and Navy Departments. As far as aviation is concerned, the conduct by these departments has been so disgusting in the last few years as to make any self-respecting person ashamed of the clothes he wears. I doubt," he added, "if a real man would remain with the colors under existing conditions."

Four years earlier Mitchell had embarrassed a battleship-centric U.S. Navy by bending the rules during a joint exercise and sinking the German battleship *Ostfriesland*. By revealing the weaknesses of a seemingly impregnable battleship to air attack, he threatened the Navy's future, at least as far as the battleship admirals saw it. They never forgave him, which is one reason Mitchell found himself in the relative oblivion of San Antonio. Now, in the wake of the *Shenandoah* disaster, Mitchell was at it again. Only this time it was not just the Navy; he basically accused the entire War Department of treason and incompetence, embarrassing them and the president.

Mitchell made his first court appearance on October 28, 1925, and held the nation's attention for more than seven weeks. Ninety-nine witnesses were called and the drama from both sides was intense. At 6:35 P.M. on December 17, 1925, at least two-thirds of the ten court members hearing his case sentenced him to "be suspended from rank, command and duty with the forfeiture of all pay and allowances for five years." Mitchell could remain in the Army if he wished, but with no responsibilities, no command or rank, and no pay. It was, as Douglas Waller wrote in *A Question of Loyalty,* "five years of peonage." Understandably, and very likely as hoped by the military, he resigned.

As with Scopes, which was a proxy fight between science and organized religion, the court-martial of Billy Mitchell was more than a simple trial. It was the establishment versus the next generation; the resistance of old standards to new tactics and technology; the essential military need for discipline weighed against the timeless, reciprocal need for common sense among senior commanders.

Was it a decorated, gifted combat hero fighting the hidebound, politicized inertia of the government, or was Mitchell a discontented, passed-over prophet who didn't know when to keep his mouth shut? Or worse, one who didn't realize no one was listening because they couldn't separate his brilliance from his vitriol? The frustration from both sides was evident and, as

in the Monkey Trial, captured the 1920s in microcosm: idealism, reality, truth, lies, and, most of all, many who could not
tell the difference. The decade, in many ways, was one big gray
area, a contest between laws and lawlessness, conservatism and
daring, morals and independence. As historian Frederick Lewis
Allen succinctly phrased it, "They could not endure a life without values, and the only values they had been trained to understand were being undermined. If morality was dethroned, what
was to take its place? Honor? Their saints were sinners and
there were no icons."

So that Friday in May 1927, still eighteen months in the
future, took on an importance far beyond expectation, because
as Slim lifted off alone, seemingly unafraid, and turned the
Spirit of St. Louis toward the vast, empty ocean, people saw,
at last, something real. Here there was no duplicity, corruption,
or shades of the truth. This flight, and the young man's spirit
in accepting the challenge, were beyond doubt or question. At
last there was a way to reconcile older values of courage, determination, and skill with an unequivocal symbol of a promising
future. In Lindbergh, America and the age got its hero.

SIX

THE EMPIRE OF THE NIGHT

THE LAST GATE is closing behind me.

I've reached the point where real navigation must begin.

For the first eleven hours Slim had held the very real reassurance that he was never too far from land. Over the Gulf of Maine, even along the Atlantic between Nova Scotia and Newfoundland he'd seen boats, shipping lanes, and people below. But no more. From now until Ireland, nearly 2,000 miles distant, there is nothing but ocean. His route lies over waters made too hazardous by weather or ice to be used as shipping lanes. As with an alpinist whose only safe path is up over the summit, not back, Lindbergh's commitment would be total. A naval officer who reviewed his plan in San Diego had suggested he move the route farther south. Even though this would increase the distance, time in flight, and fuel required, the weather was milder so if something went wrong there was a much better chance of rescue. "You ought to carry a navigator on a flight like that," he had added, concerned about the complexity and planned distance.

But Lindbergh had opted for the shortest route and least amount of weight—everything that could be sacrificed for more fuel on board and the most direct route. He knew, just as Coli and Nungesser had understood, that following the shortest distance meant less time, less fuel, and theoretically less risk. Still, the odds were long and the list of dangers nearly endless. Any one of a dozen calamities could have doomed the Frenchmen—and could still get him.

Slowly climbing up to 800 feet, away from the tea-colored waves, Slim runs an eye over the instruments then sets the throttle at 1,625 revolutions, which produces a 90 mph airspeed. Craning forward left and right, Lindbergh stares from both windows, but it is too dark to gauge the wind. He knows he should still be able to see whitecaps but, squinting now, all he can see is opaque darkness, fuzzy and thickening by the minute.

Fog.

Glancing at the altimeter he wonders whether the *Spirit* will be able to climb over it. Tilting his head back, Slim looks up through the skylight and is reassured by the stars. Maybe this is just surface fog—a mere nuisance since there are no landmarks out here to see anyway. *We are children of the land, not of air or of water,* Lindbergh thinks, realizing he is now both, but caught squarely between the two most dangerous environments on earth. Slim peers at the instruments.

The magnetic compass reads 087 degrees and the earth inductor is centered. Fuel pressure is good. Oil pressure reads 59 pounds and that's fine. Best to check the magnetos now and make certain they're both still generating the millions of sparks that keep the cylinders firing and *Spirit* flying. He reaches to the dial just below the periscope, grasping a two-inch lever between his thumb and forefinger. Moving it from BOTH to LEFT, Slim holds the switch in place and watches the tachometer. The needle barely drops, meaning the other magneto is carrying the full load.

Switching back to BOTH, then to RIGHT, he again sees no significant movement and is satisfied but not surprised. No big drop in engine revolutions and no roughness. All is as it should be.

Not that the engine is a big concern. In Lindbergh's opinion, and that of the other two teams trying to fly to Paris, the Wright Whirlwind is the finest aviation motor available. All the way from San Diego to New York he had been concerned about the details: how the engine would get serviced, where he would stay in New York, the new instruments he needed installed, and where the *Spirit* would be hangared until departure. They seem a trivial set of worries, but as Slim's mind drifts he finds the past a welcome diversion from what lies ahead tonight.

AFTER THE SEVEN-HOUR flight from St. Louis to New York, Slim had circled overhead trying to figure out where to land. There was Mineola, the train tracks, and several surfaced east–west running roads. The whole area had been the Hempstead Plains Aerodrome until America joined the war in Europe during the spring of 1917, when it was renamed Hazelhurst Field.*

There had been two main airfields. Hazelhurst Number One would split into an East Field and West Field. The east side subsequently became Roosevelt, and the only facility with a paved runway. After the military relinquished control in 1920, three hundred acres of the old West Field were purchased by Glenn Curtiss and renamed Curtiss Field. Slim had craned left and right from the side windows, finally sighting the southernmost

---

* Named in honor of Lieutenant Leighton Wilson Hazelhurst, the third U.S. Army pilot killed in an aviation accident. The Hempstead Plain is also home to Belmont Park, the longest Thoroughbred racetrack in the world.

landing strip by the railroad tracks. This had to be Hazelhurst Number Two, now the U.S. Army's Mitchel Field.* Yes . . . as he banked around, Slim had seen orderly lines of olive-drab painted aircraft, definitely military.

Landing at Curtiss Field on May 12, 1927, Lindbergh needn't have worried about his reception. He'd taxied up to Hangar 16, somewhat taken aback by the crowd of several hundred and wondering what they were all there to see. In fact, they'd come to see him. He didn't know it then, but newspapers had made much of his record-breaking 14-hour, 25-minute flight from San Diego to St. Louis, so public interest was intense. Lindbergh was the last of three pilots to arrive in New York, and certainly the least well known, but that was changing rapidly. In fact, it would be fair to say that he was *unknown* until word circulated about his night solo flight out from the West Coast.

The May 13, 1927 *New York Times* ran the following headline:

LINDBERGH ARRIVES AFTER RECORD HOPS
Air Mail Pilot Sets the Fastest Time of 21 Hours 20 Minutes From the Pacific Coast. FLEW 2,550 MILES ALONE With Aid of Compasses Only—Curtiss Field Crowds Cheer Daring Youth as He Lands. AIRPLANES AND PILOTS WHO ARE NEARLY READY FOR TRANSATLANTIC FLIGHTS.
While the Bellanca monoplane was receiving her last grooming in a closed hangar, before the door of which a guard was seated, a slim gray monoplane appeared in

---

* Named for former New York City mayor John Purroy Mitchel, killed during pilot training in 1918.

the sky yesterday and circled rapidly and with the grace
of a bird over Curtiss Field, Long Island.

That feat alone made it impossible to dismiss the young mail
pilot, who was immediately surrounded by photographers after
landing. The newsreel cameras were swinging heavily back
and forth on their tripods when Charles "Casey" Jones, Great
War fighter pilot, air racer, and aviation legend, astounded the
young pilot by pushing through the crowd and personally wel-
coming him to Long Island. Jones had become Curtiss-Wright's
chief pilot in 1926 and now also managed the airfield.

"We've got one of the hangars ready for you." He gave
the cockpit a quick, professional glance. "You've made a fast
flight."

Mechanics gathered around the *Spirit*. They left the big
hangar doors open but strung a rope across the entrance to keep
onlookers out, shielding the plane from the milling throng before
carefully rolling it back into the hangar. Most of the rickety buildings on the field had obviously been built by the government and
were left over from the war. A decade ago this whole area had
belonged to the Army Signal Corps as Aviation Station Mineola.

A slender, balding man with a dark mustache approached,
stuck out his hand, and said, "I'm Dick Blythe. I represent the
Wright Aeronautical Corporation. They've instructed me to
offer you all the help they can give."

They did, too.

Ken Boedecker was a field rep appointed to ascertain Lindbergh's needs and see to them. The *Spirit* had a dedicated mechanic, Ed Mulligan, assigned to check and recheck everything
from the tires to the tail. When Slim returned from dinner that
evening, Mulligan had the engine cowling and propeller off.
He had found a crack in the spinner, the protective cone over
the end of the propeller, and was replacing it free of charge.

Brice Goldsborough from the Pioneer company was also there checking each instrument and installing the new earth inductor compass. In the morning Mulligan would lead lines from a pair of engine cylinders into the carburetor intake, thus heating it with hot exhaust gases.

More surprising to Lindbergh than the thorough work-up was the warm reception he got from his competitors for the Orteig. Commander Richard Evelyn Byrd, an exceedingly polite Virginia aristocrat, had, just over a year ago, reached the North Pole by air. On May 9, 1926, he and Floyd Bennett had taken off from Spitsbergen, Norway, and returned nearly sixteen hours later.* Instant national heroes, the pair was awarded Medals of Honor from President Calvin Coolidge on March 5, 1927, while Lindbergh was in San Diego.

But Byrd had his eyes on a greater prize. A highly experienced aviator, he was a 1908 U.S. Naval Academy graduate and had planned the transatlantic flying boat operation that NC-4 completed in 1919. By the spring of 1927 he'd attracted the sponsorship of John D. Rockefeller Jr., the National Geographic Society, Dwight D. Morrow, and department store magnate Rodman Wanamaker†—resulting in a budget of at least $500,000 and a slick, professional organization. Through Wanamaker he leased Roosevelt Field, improved buildings, and graded the runway. A true gentleman, Commander Byrd was adamant that his competitors be granted use of any of the facilities and services at his disposal.

Nonetheless, he felt nearly ready, and on April 16, 1927, his team took off in their big Fokker trimotor, named *America,* for a series of flight tests. Tony Fokker himself was at the controls

---

* There are various opinions as to whether Byrd and Bennett actually reached the Pole.
† Ironically, Lindbergh would marry Morrow's daughter Ann on May 27, 1929.

when the plane crashed on landing, flipping over, then sliding to a halt. Floyd Bennett got a piece of propeller through his chest and Byrd broke his left arm. Fokker and navigator George Noville were unharmed, but the aircraft required at least a month's worth of repairs.

The other contender, Clarence Chamberlin's *Miss Columbia*, was in a hangar only yards away, which was ironic since Slim had tried to buy that very plane back in February. The Wright Corporation owned the aircraft, a Bellanca WB-2, and decided the aircraft was more useful as a publicity showcase for its outstanding engines, so they refused to part with it. Not until Chamberlin and his copilot, Bert Acosta, set the world endurance record on April 12, 1927, did Wright sell the plane to entrepreneur Charles Levine.*

Levine, who had made his fortune by recycling surplus shell casings for their brass, was quarrelsome, domineering, and, like many of his generation, fascinated with flight. He had partnered with Giuseppe Bellanca, the brilliant Italian-born designer who built the first enclosed cabin monoplane five years earlier, to form the Columbia Aircraft Corporation. Levine had the money but was not a pilot, while Bellanca had the ability but no money or business acumen. His WB-2 design was so capable that Lindbergh, convinced that it represented his best choice, made two trips to New York in an attempt to purchase the aircraft. During Slim's last visit in February 1927, Levine had agreed to sell it for $15,000, then added, astoundingly, "We will sell our plane, but of course we reserve the right to select the crew that flies it. You understand," he continued smugly, "we cannot let just anybody pilot our airplane across the ocean."

Recalling the moment years later, Lindbergh wrote that he was "dumbfounded," and who could blame him? "If we buy

---

* Fifty-one hours, 11 minutes, and 25 seconds.

a plane," he had replied, "we're going to control it, and we'll pick our own crew. As far as I can see, we'd be paying $15,000 for the privilege of painting the name *Spirit of St. Louis* on the side."

Understandably upset about wasting time and another two-thousand-mile train ride, Lindbergh retrieved his check and spent the rest of the day window-shopping along Fifth Avenue in an angry haze. He'd now been refused by Columbia, Wright, Fokker, and Travel Air. Slim was well aware of the competition and that time was running out. The Army Air Corps had purchased a trimotor Huff-Daland bomber for Wooster and Davis; René Fonck was building another Sikorsky for his reattempt at the prize; and Levine's odd capriciousness was the only thing preventing *Miss Columbia* from making the Paris flight. In fact, the plane could have departed at any time in May.

Clarence Chamberlin, who was among the first to amble into Hangar 16 and greet Slim, had been ready to go since the April 12 endurance flight, but Levine was the problem. Confronting his team, Levine informed them that he couldn't make up his mind who would fly *Columbia* to Paris, so it would be decided with a coin toss. Bert Acosta, a former Army aviator and Pulitzer Race winner, gave him a hard look and simply walked out. Levine, who didn't care much for the mild-mannered Chamberlin, wanted to replace him as chief pilot with Lloyd Bertaud, but Bellanca, the co-partner and aircraft designer, refused to let the plane depart without Chamberlin. To further complicate matters, Levine had promised both pilots 50 percent of the Orteig winnings, plus life insurance policies for the flight, yet when he handed them their contracts neither was mentioned.

Instead, the forms granted Levine a one-year monopoly on all royalties from endorsements, appearances, and any other monies *Columbia* generated. The two pilots were to each receive $150 per month for the year following the flight, and could do *nothing* without Levine's approval. Bertaud, who didn't want to share the limelight with Chamberlin and refused to be coerced into a bad contract, hired a lawyer who promptly filed an injunction against the flight. Sheriff's deputies were posted around the aircraft and *Miss Columbia* could not leave the ground until the matter was settled.

The court date was May 20, 1927—the day Charles Lindbergh lifted off for Paris.

NOW, EIGHT DAYS later as Slim stares out at the lonely black Atlantic, New York seems another world: chatting with the mechanics in the drafty hangar, eating a hot meal, writing letters. Right now it's after 8 P.M. back in New York and there are folks dressed for dinner, or off to see a Broadway show, as he had done the night before takeoff. Others would be visiting with family, as he had the prior week. Arriving from Detroit, Lindbergh's mother, Evangeline, had spent May 14 on Long Island, then left, satisfied that her son knew what he was doing. How strange was the fate that had put him here. Now he was alone in this frail cotton-and-steel cocoon over a dark ocean while millions of others around the world were warm and safe. People were doing all those mundane tasks that constitute most of life, and are so seldom appreciated unless one realizes it can all be lost. In his case, very quickly. Would anyone remember him? His whole life summed up in a few lines of newsprint to be read, then forgotten.

Shifting and stretching, Slim checks the gauges again. He'd left St. John's on time with plenty of fuel and, while not on the planned course, he knew exactly where he was. It's very dark outside, not that it matters. Seeing the ocean isn't necessary and flying by instruments the whole night will certainly keep him awake. *I'm giving up both land and day,* he realizes. *Now*

I'm heading eastward across two oceans, one of night and one of water. It will be a long night, but . . . Eyes narrowing, Slim catches something white moving on the surface below. Leaning farther left he squints at the ocean, trying to make it out. Whatever it is, it's definitely white. The sail of a ship? No, of course not, this is 1927.

Iceberg.

There are several of them, like pale jagged teeth against blackened gums, and tendrils swirl around the tips. Fog again: floating gray wisps hanging over the dark water. Slim tilts his head back and looks up through the skylight. Plenty of stars above, though he knows nothing about celestial navigation. Besides, how would one fly while using a sextant, especially at night? He can find the North Star well enough, though. Straight up from the corner of the Big Dipper to the handle of the Little Dipper: Polaris. Since the star is directly over the pole, the earth rotates beneath it and the star never seems to move. But judging a cardinal direction, at night, by peering through the skylight of an aircraft at a star millions of miles away is hardly accurate. Still, Europe is a continent; how can he miss it if the *Spirit* flies east long enough?

Slim decides to use only the nose and fuselage tanks for the 100 gallons he ought to consume tonight. If the fuel pump were to malfunction then gravity would feed gas from the wings, and more weight above should help stabilize the plane in the event of turbulence. Of course if ice forms, the wings will be that much heavier, but he would have other problems then anyway. Lindbergh has used seventy-five gallons from each of the three wing tanks. That leaves at least 300 gallons between the other two tanks. *I won't run out of fuel over the ocean tonight. It was measured too carefully.*

Settling down, Slim stretches his shoulders then leans back in the seat. The engine sounds smoother than at the beginning of the flight, he notices, and that's good; it's simply the smoothness of a well-cared-for engine during the early hours of its life. The *Spirit*'s Whirlwind Number 7331 was assembled by Wright's youngest builder, Tom Rutledge, at their manufacturing facility in New Jersey, with a zero error tolerance from the specifications. Designed in 1925 by Charles Lawrance, Wright Aeronautical Corporation's president, the engine measures forty-five inches in diameter and weighs 508 pounds.* The Whirlwind J-5C operates on a four-stroke cycle; pistons draw fuel and air into the nine cast-aluminum cylinders during the intake stroke, then compress it, combust the mixture, and finally expel the exhaust. The valves, which must operate flawlessly for millions of cycles, are made of tungsten steel and activated by rocker arms with enclosed push rods. Lindbergh had insisted on this point—exposed rods were easier to damage. L. B. Umlauf of Vacuum Oil, which supplied *Spirit*'s consumable fluids, stated that over the thirty-six-hour flight "[t]he engine had to make 14,472,000 explosions perfectly and smoothly."

The Whirlwind draws in, or displaces, 788 cubic inches of fuel and air during each complete cycle, roughly equivalent to a late-model Great War fighter. Combustion, or exploding the fuel-air mixture in each cylinder, is what drives the engine. A motor's efficiency is expressed as a ratio between the compressed volume in a cylinder and the empty volume. For the Whirlwind this is 5.2:1, greater than that in Eddie Rickenbacker's Nieuport 28 fighter.† Wright's mechanical perfection pro-

---

* Lawrance had been a racing car motor designer until World War I. His Lawrance Aero Engine Corporation produced the only air-cooled aircraft engine in the United States by the end of the war.
† The Nieuport 28 generally used a Gnome 9N rotary engine with a compression ratio of 4.85:1.

duced an engine that was averaging nine thousand operating hours between failures, more than a year of continuous use.

All Slim needed was forty hours.

The fog is now a thick gray ramp, sloping upward and forcing him into a gradual climb. He is passing 2,000 feet with the throttle set at 1,625 revolutions, and it is dark. No—*black*. Fog swirls a hundred feet beneath his wheels and he wonders how high it goes. Can he continue to get above the stuff, or will *Spirit* be forced to fly through it the rest of the night? The U.S. Weather Bureau's Daily Weather Map showed a low-pressure area extending east from Newfoundland to the mid-Atlantic area. High pressure from the south was supposed to be pushing the front north, but what if it stalled? It could be a weaker weather system than forecasted and that would put him in the middle of it.

Or at best on the fringe.

Passing 5,000 feet Slim glances at his eight-day clock: 8:35 P.M. New York time. The ocean has disappeared and now the horizon is gone too. All that remains to Slim are the instruments and stars, those hard, silver specks sparkling against a velvety night sky. *I wonder if man ever escapes from worldly bonds so completely as when he flies alone above clouds at night,* he thinks, staring through the skylight. It's a lonely feeling, especially solo over the vast ocean. He'd known all day that there was land close by, even if he couldn't see it, and contact with the earth, with his own kind, was possible. But not here. Not now. Even though the oceans belong to the earth they are so foreign, so mysterious, that they are a different world entirely.

You fly by the sky on a black night, and on such a night only the sky matters. The Army always taught him to avoid clouds; however, when flying the mail, delivery schedules did not account for bad weather. Clearly nature had to be conquered, or at least subdued, if aviation was to ever progress. Many tried "blind" flying, using very primitive instruments, only to die, deceived by their senses.

An Army pilot named William Ocker had successfully used a turn indicator back in 1918, and there was a similar instrument mounted in Slim's black panel now.* Officially named a Pioneer #54 Speed and Drift Meter, this was gyroscopically mounted so it always remained horizontal. The instrument displayed the rate of heading change, or yaw, that it detected and revealed this to the pilot by a black ball floating in a horizontal window. As long as the ball stayed within a few degrees of center the aircraft wasn't turning appreciably. Slim's main source of attitude information was the T-shaped Riecker P-1057 Inclinometer. Both glass arms of the T were fluid filled and functioned just like a surveyor's level. Each arm was a tube graduated in 10-degree increments up to 30 degrees, with a bubble displaying horizontal slip and vertical pitch. By using these instruments with the compass it was possible to fly without visual references, and Slim felt that time was fast approaching.

Why try to hold on to those stars? he asked himself. Why not start in now on instruments? After all, the cockpit was a cozy, safe little world and what else was needed? His body had conformed to the seat and through the stick and throttle he could *feel* the aircraft. The throbbing power of the engine, the wings had become an extension of his own fingers, with the slightest touch lifting or dropping an aileron. Gauges glowed faintly from the Radiolite paint and everything worked in harmony. He and the *Spirit* were connected through a bond only pilots share with aircraft. *But if I start flying blind, God only knows how many hours of it lie ahead. It might go on through the entire night.*

---

* Essentially a turn indicator is a wheel that remains balanced regardless of the position or movement of the frame. *Spirit*'s instruments mounted the gyro inside gimbal rings that isolated it, but allowed for the measurement of exterior forces, which were then displayed to the pilot.

•   •   •

WHAT ABOUT GOD?

Slim's mind drifted to the thought. Is there an existence after life? Is there something within one's body that doesn't age with years? It's hard to be an agnostic up here in the *Spirit of St. Louis,* aware of man's frailty, that he is a speck in the universe between earth and stars. When one confronts nature, either by a storm, on the sea, or especially in the air, it becomes painfully obvious that humans are just guests here. We think we control the planet and all that is on it, but that arrogance is a farce. *If one dies, all this goes on existing in a plan so perfectly balanced, so wonderfully simple, so incredibly complex that it's far beyond our comprehension.* There's the infinite magnitude of the universe and man conscious of it all . . . a worldly audience to what, if not to God?

As the time nears 9 P.M. Slim is still climbing.

Passing 9,300 feet with the throttle set to maintain 1,700 revolutions the *Spirit* is holding 85 miles per hour. Playing the beam of his electric flashlight slowly around the panel, Lindbergh confirms that oil and fuel pressure are both fine. The compass heading is about the same, 089 degrees, and he is still correcting left, or to the north, for winds. At 10,000 feet the clouds change from soaring peaks to rolling plateaus, misty and gray in the moonlight. Leveling off, Slim flicks the light around again and leans the mixture out. Air is thinner up here so less fuel is needed for combustion, and he's very pleased with the *Spirit*'s performance. There are still more than 300 gallons of fuel in the tanks, and he doesn't need to open the throttle all the way to climb. Lindbergh is also relieved to see that the stars are brighter, with no ominous black smudges blotting them out. *That means I'm gaining on the storm,* he thinks hopefully.

But it's cold, too. The temperature has noticeably dropped

above 5,000 feet, and he knows the decrease will continue as he rises: 3.5 degrees for each 1,000 feet gained in altitude. Zipping the flying suit back across his chest, Slim pulls on the wool-lined helmet and tugs leather mittens over his fingers. Under standard conditions the air temperature is approximately 55 degrees at 1,000 feet, so that means now, at 10,000, it ought to be right around 23 degrees. Well below freezing, and he feels it. Slim considers slipping into his warm, oversized flying boots but decides to wait. The cold is endurable for now, and too much warmth would make him want to sleep, and the bracing air is helping to keep him awake.

His neck is cramping from staring up through the skylight, so Slim shifts, wriggles, and lowers his chin. Slowly moving his head to flex the muscles, he alternates glances between glowing dots on the instrument panel a few feet in front of him and focusing on the distant stars. *How high should I climb tonight*, he wonders, gazing at the billions of hard, little lights. There is no way to get above a storm, and if one lies ahead he can either deviate around it or fly through it. Both have their risks, but with no way of ascertaining the size of the storm he could be forced hundreds of miles off course with no guarantee of better conditions. In effect, this would be tossing his carefully planned navigation out the window. Going through the storm, especially at night, isn't an appealing option, either. Turbulence could rip the wings off, he could be struck by lightning, or ice could form. Lindbergh is hoping for the best, but his instincts tell him that nature hasn't finished with him yet.

Even at this altitude, shredded bits of cloud seem to cling to the whirling propeller like halos in the faint silver light. Thinking about ice, Slim is glad to have chosen an all-metal propeller. Wood is still the most common material in 1927, yet it can pose problems. Wooden blades are not a single slab of timber, but rather five to nine laminated layers: usually mahogany, sugar maple, black walnut, yellow birch, or black cherry. With a powerful engine like the Whirlwind, wood can delaminate, lose its bond, and come apart with prolonged use. Ice can also accumulate, and wood is comparatively easy to damage. Up through and after the Great War, propellers were designed to operate with specific engines and their blades were mounted at a fixed angle.

Advances in metallurgy and a deeper grasp of aerodynamics made the *Spirit*'s two-bladed, ground-adjustable pitch prop possible. Manufactured by the Standard Steel Propeller Company of Pittsburgh, the blades measured eight feet, nine inches in diameter and were cast from duralumin. This was a new aluminum alloy with 3.5 percent copper, subjected to a rapid cooling process known as "quenching," and hardened over the course of several days.* The end product was a lower-density, lighter metal that was extremely malleable, inherently corrosion resistant, and easy to cut.

Everything in *Spirit*'s design, from the airfoils to the Wright Whirlwind engine, was dependent upon the propeller's capacity to translate aerodynamic form and mechanical power into efficient flight; the props were literally and figuratively the point of the spear. Beyond materials and construction, this was a matter of pitch angle: the angle the blades cut into the air. Slim's props could be adjusted on the ground by loosening them in the hub. This entailed physically turning the blades to either a "fine" or "coarse" angular setting, then tightening it all up again. A fine pitch, or lower angle, worked like low gear in an automobile. It bit heavily into the air and was good for takeoff, climb-out, or any type of low-speed acceleration. But a fine pitch resulted in

---

* The alloy also contains 1.25 percent iron, manganese, and silicon, respectively.

much higher drag, as more of the prop was facing the wind, so fuel efficiency suffered. Slim had opted for a coarse prop setting of 16.25 degrees, which would maximize his long-range cruise capability. The higher pitch angle meant less drag and lower engine revolutions, so fuel could be conserved. This had made it harder to take off, but that is now a moot point.

The clouds suddenly wrapping about him are not.

It is like flying through a narrow, dark mountain pass, cliffs rising on both sides with nothing visible ahead. Unlike in the open air with no references, Lindbergh can feel *Spirit*'s speed as they slide along the shifting walls of cloud. And what walls! Charcoal towers only slightly less black than the night, they soar upward to seemingly immeasurable heights, blotting out the stars above and yawning open far below. There is no doubt now that a storm area lies ahead. The weather has tricked him, those gently rolling plateaus merely an illusion to draw the *Spirit* in close before springing the trap.

It's time.

It's time to transition to instruments, and "flying blind." Anything he sees outside at this point will just be a distraction, and there's comfort in the cocoon of the cockpit, with the familiar dials and the mental precision of blind flying. The body's reflexes must be largely ignored so the mind can take complete control. The mind must operate mechanically just as the gyroscope that guides it. Slim knows this is the hardest part—to disregard the senses and his instincts, to put all his faith in a few dials.

Suddenly everything beyond the windows vanishes. He's completely in the clouds now with no outside references. Even the stars are gone. At least the cloud plateau and towers had a surface, something *to see*. Now there is nothing but blackness. Except . . . a yellow-white flash catches his eye, then another and another. The exhaust! It's just the exhaust glaring off the mist, he realizes with relief. So that is visible to keep him company, and the glow from his dials. *Nothing else exists now,* he tells himself; *my world and my life are compressed within these fabric walls.* Flying blind is a constant, grinding chore and Slim begins a systematic cross-check, glancing at the altimeter, then down to the airspeed indicator. His eyes flicker to the mirror at the panel's top center, reading backwards the magnetic compass heading in the reflection, then his gaze drops straight down to the inclinometer. The wings rock and the little bubbles bounce, but he fights an impulse to instantly correct. Let it settle out . . . small movements. *When a single one strays off, the rest go chasing after it like so many sheep.*

Flying tense is never good so he flexes his right hand, opening it and letting the stick rest lightly against his fingers. The stabilizer and throttle are set so Slim can switch hands when he wishes, to ease the fatigue. Focusing on the turn and bank indicator he is relieved to see the little ball centered. The tachometer is steady at 1,650 revolutions. Lindbergh checks the oil temperature and fuel pressure last, two little gauges at the bottom of the panel. Why are they so small? Then the scan begins again, slowly and methodically.

Time passes. Ten minutes or thirty, he's not quite sure. *Spirit* is at 10,500 feet now and it is cold! Suddenly a thought occurs: there are things to be considered outside the cockpit. Slim pulls off his left mitten, sticks his arm out of the window, then instantly snatches it back as sharp pinpricks shoot through his hand. No . . . no, not that! He fumbles for the flashlight, switches it on, and aims the beam outside. Shining it out along the double struts, he squints at the bottom of the wing, then plays the beam forward. The leading edges of the strut are bright with ice, and a knot twists in his gut, heavy and tight. Particles fly through the light and Lindbergh hunches forward, playing the beam along the wing.

More ice.

Fighting the hollow, rising fear, Slim knows that this can kill him; ice can disfigure the wing, disrupting the airflow and causing a stall. Or it can overcome the carburetor heater and choke the engine as it did over Arizona. Eyes wide, he stares at the instrument panel. The airspeed indicator depends on a wandlike pitot tube mounted on the leading edge of the left wing, while the altimeter receives air pressure from static ports, exterior flush-mounted openings shielded from the wind stream. If either clog with ice, the cockpit instruments won't function. Nor will the earth inductor compass if the little windmill mounted behind him on the fuselage freezes up, too. The cups rotate in the wind and generate power for the inductor's generator.

He knows he must get back into clear air—quickly. But as his hands and feet begin to move, Slim is conscious of something dark hanging overhead. Heavier and thicker than the surrounding night, it droops across the sky like a huge mushroom. A thunderstorm. Ominous, unpredictable, and extremely dangerous, it's something you can't outrun or outclimb. A pilot must either get around it or go straight through.

"Kick rudder hard . . . no time to lose," he mutters anxiously. "The turn indicator's icing up right now . . . there's no time . . . only a few seconds . . . quick."

But if he rushes through the turn, the plane could spin out of control. At night, in a thunderstorm, over open water, this would certainly kill him. Slim watches the instruments and with the concentrated discipline of a trained pilot slowly forces everything else from his mind. He must fly carefully and deliberately despite knots in his stomach, a lurching, skidding aircraft, and the bitter cold. If he panics, he dies.

"No," he says aloud, comforted by the sound of his own voice in the tiny cockpit. "No, faster; turn the right amount."

Left boot forward against the pedal . . . Lindbergh can feel the rudder strain against the wind and he locks his eyes to the turn indicator. The little black ball creeps in the opposite direction just beyond the two parallel center lines. As he nudges the stick forward and left, his eyes flick down to the inclinometer. The ball is high, above level, and the plane is rocking in turbulence. Airspeed is 10 miles per hour too low—if he doesn't correct then the *Spirit* will stall and spin into the dark, cold water below.

"Turn faster! You see the airspeed's dropping. It's ice doing that! Quick, or it'll be too late!"

Eyes wide open, he fights for calm. Slow movements. Deliberate and steady. With his left hand he shoves the throttle forward until the tachometer rises by 50 revolutions.

"No," Slim argues with himself. "It's not ice . . . at least not very likely. It's probably just the normal slowing down in a bank."

Spirit bobbles its way through the turn and Slim has no way of knowing how far he's come. He's at 10,500 feet, then 10,200 feet, as the airspeed needle hits 100 miles per hour. Descending in the turn . . . skidding . . . can't keep the plane level. The pitch indicator is an entire bubble low so *Spirit*'s nose is down. Add power . . . pull back on the stick! *I ought to be turned around by now,* Slim thinks, rolling the wings level and shining the flashlight on his instruments. At 10,300 feet the airspeed is steady, but the earth inductor compass is moving backward and the magnetic compass is swinging wildly. Rough air. It always takes a few moments for the heading card to stabilize.

But what's that?

Slim's eyes shift outside, and he realizes *Spirit* isn't wrapped in gray. Stars! Bright, hard, and glittering. The air around the plane is still hazy, but the cloud's drooping wet fingers have released the *Spirit* temporarily, and it's clear above. He looks at the clock . . . ten minutes. That's all he spent in the thunderstorm, but it seemed like all night. Picturing the weather chart in his mind, Slim thinks south is the best bet. If he is truly on

the southern edge of the storm and high pressure is pushing it
north, as Doc Kimball reported, then he must try to get around
it to the south. Stick and rudder left, he holds the turn indicator
steady, feet and hands working to keep the *Spirit* coming back
around to 089 degrees. If it were daytime, Slim could navigate
from cloud tower to tower, sighting off in the distance like one
would do with mountain peaks. But at night he can only try to
hold the heading and, if another thunderstorm blocks the way
east, bank up around it again to the south. Always to the south.

But then he has a nasty thought. What if the Weather
Bureau was wrong and the whole ocean is like this? Slim leans
back in the seat and again cross-checks his instruments. If he
climbed up higher maybe the clouds would break up and the
shifting canyons far below would widen. Maybe not. But he
cannot go back through them. Ice, turbulence, or disorientation
would surely get him eventually, sending him stalling, diving,
and spinning into the ocean.

For the first time since takeoff he seriously considers turning back. But to where? Where would he land? Or would he
try to fly 1,400 miles back to New York and Roosevelt Field's
muddy runway? But the weather may have closed in behind him
and the American coast might be worse than this. How would
that be anyway, to fly thirty hours and end up back in Long
Island? No, if he can keep heading eastward he'll strike Ireland,
or at least Europe.

Lindbergh is shaken but determined. *What I can do depends largely on what I have to do.*

SEVEN

PHANTOMS IN THE MIST

LAST NIGHT I couldn't go to sleep . . . tonight I can barely stay awake. I cup my hand into the slipstream, diverting a strong current of air against my face. I let my eyelids fall shut for five seconds, then raise them against tons of weight. . . . protesting they won't open wide until I force them with my thumb. Sixteen hours and 1,500 miles into the flight. So 300 till the halfway point and 2,100 miles more till Paris.

Lindbergh shifts in the wicker seat, flexes his aching back muscles, and shrugs his shoulders. With the windows out, at least the cold air and noise help keep him awake. His feet are cold through the leather boots, and Slim thinks again of the big, warm flying boots he made himself, but decides not to use them yet. He'd have to unbuckle the safety belt and twist around in the little cockpit while flying with one hand. There had been enough confusion for a few minutes so why add more? Then there were the instruments. His compasses have both gone crazy and the earth inductor is hopeless. The needle's wobbling back and forth from peg to peg, not that he trusted it much anyway. Too new, too experimental, too unproven. So that leaves visual navigation and the liquid magnetic compass. But even it is swinging wildly, 60 to 90 degrees off course. Why? He's never seen one do this before. It could be precession, the normal drifting associated with maneuvering, but that should stabilize quickly, and these needles have been swinging awhile.

Is it possible that I'm entering a magnetic storm?

He's not sure, but it's possible. If earth's magnetic field is horizontal enough for the inductor to function, then might not it be disturbed by a storm at sea? After all, a ring of electrical current surrounds the planet, and since electricity is used to magnify metal, like his compass needle, why wouldn't weather that generated electricity disrupt the magnetic field? Science has always interested him and he knows that a massive energy release like lightning accelerates atomic particles, so isn't it reasonable that this would interfere with magnetic instruments?

Maybe.

As for visual navigation . . . Slim realizes he no longer needs the skylight to see stars. They are lower in the sky and visible from the windows since the weather ahead is breaking up somewhat. Frowning, he notices the clouds' bright outlines, sharp against the heavy, dark sky. How is that possible? It's much too early for dawn.

The moon!

I'd almost forgotten the moon. He stares out and up. *Now, like a neglected ally, it's coming to my aid.* The clear night sky can seem two-dimensional—so deep, so infinite, as to erase any point of reference. But with moonlight touching the cloud formations there are shadows, and Slim can again see the world around him: massive gray arches brushed with silver curve between vast vertical colonnades. A temple in the air. Chasms yawn open beneath *Spirit*'s wheels, liquid darkness that shifts in all directions. Like pale brushstrokes on black glass, shades of gray streak the sky against a backdrop of cold stars.

Being able to see around him, even the unreal, shapeshifting world of weather and sky, makes a tremendous difference. The threats are visible, the cloud formations less frightening. They assume personalities and seem to come to life: one a dragon, another a mountaintop, a springing tiger off to the side. They can be avoided now and maybe seem a bit less hostile that way. Who could blame them? *Spirit* is penetrating them, disturbing their existence, not the other way around. Perhaps this is a truce that will last till morning.

Till morning.

His eyelids drop and there's nothing he can do to stop them. For a full five seconds Slim feels that warm bliss, that overwhelming relief that strikes just before sleep. *No! I can't let anything as trifling as sleep ruin the flight I spent so many months in planning.* Against every fiber in his body Lindbergh wills his eyes open again. He knows he must do something, and cups a hand outside the window, directing a blast of cold air into his face. Sucking in a lungful, he draws it in, hoping to wake himself from the inside out.

I've never understood the meaning of temptation or how powerful one's desires can become. Slim violently shakes his head, then his whole body. But it makes sense now, and he's ashamed of his inability to overcome the desire to sleep. Growing up as he had, Charles Lindbergh developed an iron determination and tangible ability to overcome adversity. Combined with his native stubbornness, perseverance, and innate contrariness Slim has always believed that nothing is impossible if he wants it bad enough.

But this is different.

•   •   •

ASIDE FROM FIGHTING off sleep, navigation is an urgent challenge: all that turning and backtracking with malfunctioning instruments. Yet there's no way to compensate or even check his position until day comes again. *I've got to do a better job of navigation,* Lindbergh thinks angrily. This isn't a school exam with nothing but a grade in the balance. The entire flight, the Orteig Prize, the millions following his progress, and his very life all depend on his position over the ocean. Hopefully this puzzle, Slim thinks as he spreads the chart on his lap, can keep him awake. Pressing the stick between his knees he shines the flashlight on the map and realizes he's already flown off its edge. Pulling the next section out, he tries to hold it down with a forearm, but it doesn't work and one end flutters about. The stick bumps back, *Spirit*'s nose rises, and the airspeed drops to 80 miles per hour. As it hits 70 miles per hour Slim feels the sluggishness, switches off the flashlight, and levels off quickly to avoid a stall.

For the next hour he just flies, concentrating on his course and the instruments. According to the Mercator chart for the eastern half of the North Atlantic Ocean, his compass and magnetic courses are both 103 degrees. Minus out 10 degrees left for drift, so he holds 093 as a compass heading. There's no way to know about the wind, but his gut feeling is that *Spirit* is south of course, so angling northward ought to put him close to the great circle plot: but for how long? The eight-day clock reads midnight in New York so what time is it here?* Five hours out of St. John's at 90 miles per hour is 450 miles. Glancing at

---

* So named as it contained a tightly coiled spring that only required winding once every eight days.

the Mercator, he eyeballs a position about 1,000 miles south of Greenland. That should put him two hours ahead of the U.S. East Coast and four hours behind Paris. If, that is, he's in the right spot. *If* his calculations are correct.

Well, why not?

The moonlight is brilliant and he can see well enough to avoid the big cloud masses, and both compasses are enjoying a welcome steady period. It's warmer in the cockpit, too, almost pleasant. Slim tugs off a mitten and sticks his left arm outside into the wind stream. No ice. It feels tropical compared to the earlier Canadian air. Returning to the map, Lindbergh figures if his distance calculations are nearly correct then he might have crossed into the warmer waters of the Gulf Stream. If that's so, the freezing Labrador Current is behind him for good and so are the icebergs. Craning forward, he sees nothing but a cloud deck well below *Spirit*'s wheels. Warmer water is down there somewhere, and a man could live a long time in a rubber boat on the Gulf Stream . . . especially if it rained a little.

Spirit wings on eastward through the night at 10,000 feet, a tiny man-made speck invisible in the vast space over the North Atlantic. But in the eighteenth hour a change occurs, something so subtle that Slim's senses fail to detect it at first. There is depth to the sky, more than just shades of gray, or black, and silver. There is color: a faint streak of pink across the cloud bellies. Very, very high, tens of thousands of feet above him, but Slim can see a splash of lightness in the east.

Dawn.

Could it be dawn? Night surrendering to morning at last, and this long night finally ending? It is just 1 A.M. in New York so it would be 3 A.M. here locally, wherever "here" happens to be. Locally. Local for whom? Fish . . . and the *Spirit of St. Louis*. So it would be 6 A.M. in London, and according to his weather brief, sunrise there occurred two hours ago. Slim is suddenly excited. I've waited for morning the whole night through, and now it's coming! We will see the same sun on Europe today. Not as guests, but as part of the same continent. *I've burned the last bridge behind me,* he thinks, straightening, stretching, gazing from both windows.

All through the storm and the darkest period of the night, his instincts were anchored to the continent of North America. If the weather had been too bad, or something mechanical had gone wrong, Slim was always thinking of turning back to the west. In the back of his mind it was there: an anchor, a place of safety. *Now my anchor is in Europe.* He stares past the propeller hopefully. *On a continent I've never seen.* Lindbergh feels good. The dread of the first night, a great dark wall he had to fly toward and pierce for survival, had always loomed over the flight. Aside from the heavyweight takeoff on Long Island, it had preyed most upon his mind. Relief washes through him, a warm, relaxing flood spreading out from his chest, flowing through the aching muscles in his back, and melting down through each cramped leg.

Tension and fear can keep a pilot alive and alert in life-or-death situations that would kill most people, and frequently kill pilots as well. Sheer willpower wires the senses, keeps the hands and feet moving and the mind active, but this lasts only so long. With dawn and the freedom from night's crushing burden comes an unquenchable urge to sleep. Muscles go soft and the spine molds itself to the seat; fingers and toes tingle pleasantly as the body dreamily shuts down. With every bit of physical and mental strength he possesses, Charles Lindbergh fights back. Holding the stick between his knees, Slim pumps his arms as if running, pounding his boots on the floorboard. Shoulders ache again, knotty and painful, and his back stiffens.

Then he rocks the *Spirit* back and forth, slipping sideways to blow fresh air through the open windows. He uses every trick at his disposal: rubbing his cheeks hard, shaking his head until his temples throb, and pulling the cotton wadding from his ears to hear the noise.

But it's the third morning since he's last slept, and Slim has begun to lose control of his eyes. They close involuntarily, then stick together. His forehead lifts and his cheeks stretch as he pulls the lids apart a fraction of an inch at a time. Sleep ... *sleep* ... his whole body screams for it. To throw himself down, to lie flat and completely stretch every muscle. Would there be anything better than this? Yanking the leather helmet from his head, Lindbergh runs stiff fingers through his flat hair and scratches the scalp. Maybe some water would help. Pulling the canteen off the seat back he takes a big swallow, tasting the metal and smelling the canvas holder. It occurs to him that he's had no food since yesterday.

Possibly if I eat a sandwich.

The paper bag is next to him, spotted with grease. Ham, or beef, or egg? But no, he's not hungry, and eating may make him more sleepy, if that is possible. *Should I have taken along a thermos of coffee?* Would that keep me awake? No. At this point it wouldn't help. Nothing internal will do it. If he's to beat this then the stimuli must come from outside. Leaning far forward he peers at the ocean two miles below. *If I could get down through the clouds and fly close to the waves, maybe that would help me stay awake.* But the slight gray of dawn he can see up here hasn't penetrated to the surface yet. Maybe it won't, either. These clouds could go all the way to the waves, and it's still much too dark to see water.

Shoving the stick forward, he dives through a cloud, then pulls up sharply into clear air on the other side. Physically flying helps; doing something more than simply maintaining a course got the blood flowing again. This is good. It proves that outside influences have the greatest effect on his alertness, but he can't do aerobatics all the way to Ireland. There are still more than eighteen hours left in the air, and at least twelve of them are over water. This is the key. Flying. Once again Slim is grateful that the *Spirit* isn't an easy or comfortable plane to pilot. The slightest relaxation of pressure on either stick or rudder starts a climbing or diving turn. The very instability that makes it difficult to fly blind or hold an accurate course at night now guards him against excessive errors. He breathes deeply and glances at the clock. Two A.M. in New York.

The routine of switching tanks and making notes is a good one: visible progress, and the marks on the instrument panel and in his log are slowly filling up. As long as he can stay awake Slim can fly the plane without conscious thought. Hands and feet become extensions of the charts, of the geography, and of where you want the aircraft to be. The problem is what to do with your mind while your body is working. So at the top of every hour Slim lays the log sheet on his chart and dutifully inscribes the numbers. The *Spirit* is holding 87 miles per hour at 9,000 feet. Oil temperature and pressure are fine, and so is the mixture. Reaching down to the Lukenheimer he opens the valve to the NOSE tank, waits a few seconds, then deliberately puts his fingers on the FUSELAGE valve before closing it. Shutting off the wrong fuel supply had happened before to others, and he has no intention of beginning this day with that sort of excitement.

Setting the throttle to hold 1,625 revolutions, Slim again focuses on the clock. Something about that . . . of course! This is the eighteenth hour. He's officially halfway to Paris. Eighteen hundred miles to go, which doesn't seem so bad. The window's rectangle neatly frames the sky, and he's thrilled to see that the visibility is clearing with the sunrise. There are still clouds out here, though, and he can't make out the horizon ahead, so Slim decides to remain at this altitude for a while. Businesslike, he straightens up, blinks his eyes, and shrugs his shoulders. Another milestone passed, so he should update the heading now, too. But a few degrees . . . how is that going to make much of a difference when *Spirit*'s nose is pitching back and forth like an angry horse? Another hour, he tells himself. *I can work it all out then.* Let the sunrise come first; with it, new life will spring. After all, how many sunrises does one see in a lifetime?

SUNLIGHT!

It suddenly surrounds the *Spirit,* washing the silver wings in bright light and flooding the cockpit. Slim blinks and stares out into a huge gap of deep blue air. He is overjoyed, as any pilot would be, at being able to see again, but his relief is tempered by what lies on the other side. Another towering heavy wall of clouds. Slim is humbled; man can put a plane together, even fly it blind through bad weather, but he still eventually needs to see. Even now the next line of thick, gray air doesn't seem so bad because he can *see* it. Sight: the sense that ties all the others together, at least those related to flying. Lindbergh is certain that someday pilots will be less reliant upon sight; after all, he just flew all night without it. He savors the sight of valleys and peaks, the shifting, craggy summits and shadow-filled precipices. During the night one's eyes are fixed on the heavens, yet at the first hint of dawn they're drawn earthward to the barely perceptible pale world below. The sky before him is an immense canvas being painted as he watches. Clouds change from dark to light gray, then melt into bronze, gold, and red, spreading down the sky like stains.

Dawn's flag.

Night has passed and this is morning, Slim realizes, the time to descend and again make contact with the ocean. But he's reluctant; despite the dazzling whiteness up here at 8,000 feet there's no telling what lies closer to the water. *Suppose I start down through these clouds, blind, where should I stop?* His altimeter measures the pressure difference between ambient air at his current altitude and a reference setting on the ground. This ground calibration setting—New York measured 29.90 inches of mercury—was dialed into the instrument before take-off. Higher-pressure air has more mass than that of lower pressure so the number of inches displaced by the weight of earth's atmosphere rises, and the altimeter needle moves accordingly.* Unfortunately, all he has is the Weather Bureau's chart from May 18, nearly sixty hours old now, and the barometric pressure here could be anywhere from 29.80 to 30.00 inches. This could translate into an error of a hundred feet or more, and is too big a risk to take.

Slim knows he should also update his course, but continues to hold the 096-degree heading he's flown for the past several hours. There are already too many variables and it's best not to introduce another now. Staring from the window, he decides that course correction can wait until the water is visible again, and he has some idea of the winds.

Suddenly he leans forward, squinting down through the clouds. The ocean! He's flown out into another gigantic sunlit

---

* Mercury was used because it remains liquid under standard temperature and pressure conditions: 273.15 degrees Kelvin and 14.504 pounds per square inch of pressure.

valley in the clouds, only this one dips all the way down to the blue-gray waves. The surface is smeared with whitecaps and ripples, and if he can see ripples at eight thousand feet that means there's a very heavy sea down there. A lot of wind.

Excited, Slim pushes the stick forward and noses the *Spirit* over. A little light in the seat, he watches the airspeed needle rotate clockwise past 100 miles per hour . . . then 110. Reaching forward, Lindbergh wraps his left hand around the big wooden knob under the window, pulling it out and moving it forward a notch to reset the stabilizer. One hundred twenty miles per hour. Letting go of the knob, he reaches up and slides the mixture control all the way to RICH, then tugs the throttle back. The valley wall looms ahead so Slim boots the left rudder while bringing the stick left against his leg. Spiraling down is the only way to stay in clear air, and as long as the ocean is visible that's exactly what he'll do down to the wavetops. If this is only a hole, Slim figures, he can just spiral back upward.

At 4,000 feet, he feels his ears pop with the pressure. The engine is roaring, noticeably loud after all those hours with no change. Sunlight washes through the throbbing cockpit, then a shadow, then sun again as *Spirit* rotates and the spiral deepens. Working his jaws to keep his ears clearing, Slim's eyes dart back and forth between the ocean and cockpit gauges. The tachometer is steady and that's good; the last thing he needs is to lose the engine at this altitude.

Two thousand feet now . . . He's dipped under the lowest layer of cloud and can see the ocean fairly writhing beneath its saltwater skin. Air rushes over the *Spirit,* rasping along the cotton-covered fuselage, and the rudder pedals tap against his boots. Stiff in his hand, the stick feels heavy against the faster air, and for the first time in hours Lindbergh is completely awake. A thousand feet . . . then five hundred. The air down here is thicker, humid, and tinged with brine. *It's like stepping through the door of a greenhouse full of plants,* he muses, startled by the contrast.

The waves!

They're enormous. Breakers rather than waves. Deep, white-flecked rollers rippling towards him. Leveling out fifty feet over the dangerous water, Slim pushes the throttle up to hold 95 miles per hour but keeps the mixture at RICH. *Spirit* is rocking and pitching and he might need to power his way out of here. Looking through both windows, Slim realizes the descent might be a bad idea. As far as he can see the ocean's surface is beaten white from the wind. Foam spray whirls, climbs, and vanishes like pale blowing hair. Why, it must be blowing 50 or 60 miles per hour, he thinks. It would have to blow with great force to build up a sea like that. That sea would do fearful damage to a ship, even a liner, so what would it do to the *Spirit*'s puny steel tubes and cotton fabric?

Back in the warmth and safety of San Diego it had seemed logical to tether his life raft to the plane in the event he ditched over water, but he hadn't imagined waves like this. *I feel naked above it,* he thinks, looking down, wide eyed. The plane would sink in seconds, dragging him down, too. Best to ride it out, he knows now, and hope to float southeast into the sea-lanes.

But the wind!

Fighting to stay level against the winds, Slim has both hands on the stick now and his feet are playing the rudder bars like pedals on a bike. Suddenly the sun vanishes and he risks a look back past the tail. He's flown out of the valley now and is beneath a low ceiling; a wide, dark roof with hanging sheets of rain connecting sky to water. Fog, too. The horizon ahead vanishes, and he must decide to turn around and try to ascend again, or go on ahead at low altitude. If he turns back, there's no guarantee the valley will still be there. It could close up and swallow him. But going on at fifty feet is too risky, and so he pushes the throttle up to climb back to a thousand feet and some safety. At least a wave can't reach up this high to grab him, pulling the *Spirit* into the ferocious deep sea.

What is the depth here anyway? He's well past the Flemish Cap, a relatively shallow plateau some 500 miles east of St. John's, so that puts *Spirit* somewhere between the Newfoundland Basin and Mid-Atlantic Ridge. Slim knows that farther south near the equator the Atlantic plunges to more than 25,000 feet. But here the largest little black number on his chart reads 2,070 fathoms; at six feet per fathom that's over 12,000 feet. Deep enough.

But he can't dwell on that. Navigation. He *must* figure out a rough position. Alternating glances between the altimeter and the furious, boiling sea below he lets his mind work on the problem. Assuming the winds were coming from the northwest all night and he was holding a northeasterly heading, then a quartering tailwind has been pushing the *Spirit* since yesterday. Winds aloft are usually greater than those close to the surface—but had they been blowing with such velocity all through the night? If so, he certainly hadn't corrected enough to prevent being blown far to the south. This could explain the warmth of the air.

He looks at the compass. *I have a strong feeling that I'm too far south to strike Ireland unless I change my heading.* But change it to what? Without knowing a starting position how many degrees to the north would it take to get *Spirit* back on course? Perhaps the best thing to do is hold the same course as a baseline, then sort it out when the fog lifts. Slumping back in the wicker seat he marvels at how easy it is to fly on instruments now. *I've done almost as much on this single trip as on all my flights before put together,* he realizes. His eyes move from the turn indicator to the tachometer, then back to the ball in the middle of the turn indicator. It begins to rock rhythmically back and forth so his eyes follow it.

Tick, tock . . . like a clock. It looks funny. Almost fuzzy. Maybe the gauge is wet. They should all be wiped off. Tick, tock . . . in a minute. In a minute. Now the whitecaps are clouds and clouds are whitecaps. That's odd. So is the sky . . . it looks like the water now, gray-green and angry. Water?

Slim jerks awake and his heart thumps against his chest, frantically pumping blood as panic shoots through every muscle in his body. In a split second his mind registers the picture before him, and his hands and feet react instantly. Jamming the stick into his left thigh, he stomps the left rudder to pull the *Spirit* out of its death spiral. Too much . . . too much! He's climbing now, nose up in the opposite direction. The airspeed falls off and the turn indictor is pegged left. Stall . . . he's going to stall and spin in! Centering the stick and rudder, Slim shoves the nose back down to regain some flying speed. The mottled, fierce ocean fills his vision for a few agonizing seconds before he feels *Spirit*'s controls bite into the heavy, wet air. Stomach in his throat, Lindbergh smoothly pulls the stick back.

Level flight.

Staring at the gauges, Slim pants a bit as the pedals smack his boots, and one wing dips as he struggles to hold altitude. Adrenaline is marvelous; it has snapped him completely awake and coherent in a matter of seconds, muscles poised and skin tingling. He waits, listening and feeling the plane until everything is back to normal. *I should climb to 1,500 feet,* he thinks. But flying higher means he might miss any clear air down low. Still, if he flies lower, more than half-asleep, there'll be too much chance of crashing into water.

Squirming in the seat, Lindbergh goes through the shoulder shrugs, neck stretches, and back twists that have become routine. Inhaling deeply, he smells the gasoline from the Lukenheimer trap, salt air, and his own stale sweat. His ears are dulled by the engine's continuous roar. The cotton wadding helps, of course, but it also makes his head feel full. Does all that stuff jammed into his ears interfere with balance or the ability to fly blind? Apparently not, since he did it all night. He's removed his mittens so the stick trembles against his hand, tickling the bare skin. With the throttle and mixture set Lindbergh can return to alternating hands so his wrists don't cramp too badly. The seat is hard, and he can feel the wicker pattern through his flying suit. Unfortunately the air cushion is still flat, deflated from his descent, and there's no way to blow it up again without the *Spirit* wandering all over the sky. Slim's throat is dry and he decides to reward himself next hour with a cool drink.

Next hour.

Will he be in the clear by then or still trapped in the shifting gray fog?

"It's clear up above," he tells himself.

"But you've been there all night long."

"It's better than this fog."

The sky is mesmerizing; it is daylight, but there's nothing to see except mist. Like trying to see through a smoky glass window. With the increasing warmth and the engine's steady vibration Slim's mind begins to wander. Scenes from his Minnesota childhood appear as he stares from the window. Wahgoosh, his dog, and the beautiful family home on the Mississippi River burning to the ground. It's as vivid as a motion picture: life on the farm, hunting for Easter eggs on the White House lawn, and watching his father from the gallery above the House floor.

Twelve degrees off course.

He blinks and the images fade as he corrects his heading. Slim tries to concentrate, but each time his mind wanders the *Spirit* strays. Once 7 degrees . . . then a full 20 degrees. Always left, to the north. Using his thumbs, he pries his eyelids open again and focuses on problems. Just how big is the storm that he could spend nine hours in it, at least 900 miles, with only very brief patches of clear sky? Of course, there's never a guarantee with weather, and Doc Kimball only reported high pressure moving in along the route of flight. He never said it would be clear. Pulling out the Weather Bureau chart, Slim studies it between glances at the compass. The isobars, or lines of constant pressure, begin compressing where low and high pressure areas collide: exactly along his route from Newfoundland to Ireland.

Maybe this fog is the ragged edge of all that. Higher-pressure air beating down the lower-pressure air, and like casualties in a battle the mist is all that remains. By that logic he should deviate south toward the better weather, but then he might miss Ireland altogether. England too. *Spirit* could end up in the Bay of Biscay, adding another 300 flying miles before the French coast. Was there even fuel for that?

Fuel.

Slim gropes around for his pencil and forces himself to catch up on the calculations. He scratches one more hash mark into the upper right corner of the black plywood instrument panel. The performance figures he and Don Hall worked out gave a range of consumption between 7.2 and 14.4 gallons per hour, depending on weight, throttle, and mixture setting. Slim feels sharper now; the mental exercise is keeping him awake. Given all the corrections and altitude changes made during the night, consuming an average of 12 gallons an hour seems reasonable. That's not factoring in wind, which very likely helped out for much of the flight, though there's no way to tell for certain. Best to ignore it and be conservative.

He's used the nose tank, which he is feeding from now, for a total of seven and a quarter hours, so at 12 gallons per hour that would be . . . 87 gallons. It had been designed to hold eighty but was slightly oversized. Even so, it should be nearly empty, and that is precisely what Slim intended to prevent a "nose heavy" aircraft. The main fuselage tank has eleven tally marks against it, meaning 132 of its 200 gallons are gone. This tank has additional capacity too, maybe an extra five or ten gallons, but even by the official numbers there are still 68 gallons remaining.

Each of the three wing tanks held 48 gallons, though they were also slightly larger. He's used 14 gallons from both outer tanks, and several from the center. Therefore the total fuel remaining in all five tanks is about 182 gallons; subtracting this from the 425 official capacity means he should've used 243 gallons by the end of the twenty-second hour. Subtract a few extra gallons for takeoff and climb-out and there still should be a minimum of 175 gallons left.

But if the boys at Roosevelt Field had actually squeezed another 25 gallons into the tanks then Slim has closer to 200 gallons remaining. Even at 12 gallons per hour this gives the *Spirit* at least another sixteen hours of flying time. Actual consumption is less, he knows, based on the continuously lightening fuel load, but there is no way to calculate exactly how much less. The winds would've helped a great deal, but being over conservative with gas is safer.*

So there is no shortage of fuel and mechanically the *Spirit*

---

* In fact, his actual fuel state was much better. By this point in the flight Lindbergh had approximately 265 gallons remaining, but with no fuel gauge (which he considered unreliable) there was no way for him to know that.

is performing perfectly. Of course navigation and the threat of bad weather are always risks, but the greatest danger remains himself. No sleep for twenty-three hours before takeoff had been a ridiculous risk, he knows now. He shouldn't have gone into New York to see the Broadway show; he ought to have slept someplace quiet and secluded. The need and desire for rest is nearly overwhelming now, and his mind seems oddly detached.

He's low . . . too low. Maybe five feet between the rolling gray waves and his wheels. Salt spray blows up over the *Spirit*, through the window, and he tastes it on his lips. It's time to climb. Sleeping with eyes open at wavetop height in the fog is no place to be. Again lifting the mixture lever up to RICH, he opens the throttle, and pulls back on the stick. Leveling at 1,000 feet Slim resets the stabilizer and throttle.

He is not alone.

There are human shapes in front of him, beside him, and in the back! The fuselage is filled with them. These phantoms speak with human voices . . . friendly, vaporlike shapes that are familiar and somehow comforting. They lean forward over his shoulder, speaking above the engine's roar, then press back into the crowd behind. They're talking about navigation and the flight, muted and hollow as if from a tremendous distance or beyond some barrier. In fact, these emissaries from a spirit world are quite in keeping with the night and day. They're neither intruders nor strangers.

Spirit breaks into the clear again and it is a much larger space. Tilting his head back, Slim sees blue sky through broken clouds above. A brief reprieve from blind flying is just what he needs to take a drink from his half-full canteen and stretch aching muscles. There's another wall of fog ahead, so he pulls out the flattened air cushion, leans forward to grip the stick between his knees, then quickly blows it up and jams it back under him as the shifting, misty walls close in from all sides. He decides to stay low since there seems to be a better chance of open air down here. Rain patters on the skylight and floats past the windows in translucent sheets. That's good, he thinks. Rain may be an indication of better weather ahead.

Who are the spirits?

They seem to come only with the mist. Are they here to keep him awake, to give encouragement and revive him? Perhaps they're long-dead aviators, or instructors from his past who are permitted to come back to advise and reassure him: to inspire. Is it coincidence that they came now at this worst of times? Did they save him? Somehow Slim isn't surprised and, startlingly, wonders if he's already dead. *Am I crossing the bridge which one sees only in last, departing moments?* Am I already beyond the point from which I can bring my vision back to earth and men? Death no longer seems the final end it used to be, but rather the entrance to a new and free existence that includes all space, all time.

No.

Spirit's pitching and slipping is too real. So is the feel of the stick and the rudder straining against his boot heels, and the smell of the sea. Suddenly the mist lightens, looking almost like snow, and in an instant the gray veil tears away leaving Slim blinking furiously in the sun. Warm light fills the cockpit; washing away the dials and numbers, flooding the sky and sea with beautiful brightness. Waves still roll, but they're much smaller and the wind has slackened. Whitecaps seem fewer and less angry, almost friendly. The plane bobbles as Lindbergh's eyes adjust, then it straightens out, level and steady at 200 feet over the ocean.

Excited, he noses over toward the waves and is heartened

to see *Spirit*'s shadow leaping from green crest to green crest; the black shape shrinks and expands in the waves. He's not alone, and this shadow is real! Would there even be a shadow if he'd passed on to the other world? No, this is life. Maybe the phantoms were sent to keep him awake, to save him and to give hope.

Hope, that greatest of things. Pilots cling to it when all else has faded, just as he's done through this dark, deadly night. The clear patches he'd seen before were just teasers but this is daylight, and morning. Clouds are still everywhere, including a magnificent north–south arch that he now flies through. *Spirit* is surrounded by clouds but they're widely spaced and he can see past them. With blue sky above and no ceiling, Slim pushes the throttle forward then eases back on the stick. Leveling at 500 feet he playfully banks left and right, threading around several gigantic columns, enjoying the freedom of flying with no bleary eyes fixed on instruments, no careful stick and rudder movements, and no fear.

A pilot likes nothing more than clear air, plenty of fuel, and knowing exactly where he is. Slim has two out of three, at least. More than ten hours has passed since he left St. John's so land of some kind is only eight hours away. Eight hours! The figure seems inconsequential after twenty-three in the air. After Ireland, there are six more to Paris so, in fourteen hours, with any luck, the flight will be done. Slim sits straighter, feeling refreshed and alive as he gazes out at the ocean, a friend again.

Suddenly he stiffens, eyes wide with shock.

It can't be.

It is.

Land!

But . . . but I'm in mid-Atlantic, nearly a thousand miles from land. His mind races. Are the compasses completely wrong? Am I hopelessly lost? Slim's eyes dart over the gauges and his chart. Impossible. He knows it's impossible. Leaning from the window, Lindbergh pulls down his goggles and peers at a haze-covered coastline about five miles away. It's purple and rocky . . . with scattered clumps of trees. Sleep. He must be still asleep! Slim shakes his head until it hurts, shoves up the goggles and rubs his dry eyes, then blinks them clear.

It's still there.

I know there's no land out here in midocean . . . nothing between Greenland and Iceland to the north, and the Azores to the south. What if the compasses were malfunctioning? What if the storm scrambled them and he'd been flying north all night? Doubt is a deadly, formidable enemy to any pilot, and Lindbergh feels it, clawing at his stomach lining. Reason and calm thought can beat it back down so he forces himself to *think*. Say he'd covered 1,000 miles from Newfoundland during the night. Greenland was about that distance to the north. Could it be? Lindbergh gropes for the chart, but finds no answers.

It's easy enough to check. Slim banks up left, bringing the *Spirit* around to the north, then abruptly changes his mind. Booting the right rudder, he nudges the stick right and comes back to his northeasterly course. *It's nonsense, pure nonsense* to be lured off course by fog islands in the middle of an ocean flight. *I'll waste no time and gasoline on fanciful excursions which can only end in disillusionment and fatigue.* But minutes later another island appears off the nose. As implausible as it seems, it looks like land, too: rolling hills and more trees with a beach. Skidding the plane slightly, he stares from the window, bewildered and curious. But even as he watches, colors fade to green and the hard outlines become fuzzy. The "beach" is nothing more than lighter mist against the darker wave troughs. Rocks and trees are merely shadows, and in an instant the mirage completely yields its illusion and only the sea remains.*

Slim knows he must take stock of his situation. Eight hours till Ireland, he hopes, but what part of Ireland? It's a 300-mile-long island and Scotland, well to the north, has a similar coastline. He could make landfall anywhere from Mizen Head in South Ireland to the Orkney Islands up past Scotland. Navigation can't be neglected any longer. *If I keep putting it off for fifteen minutes at a time, the entire day will pass.*

He knows he must do it . . . but simply cannot. Nearly two days without sleep, plus the physical and mental stress of survival, are overcoming his last vestiges of strength. Even with a good wind Paris is more than ten hours away. *How can I pass through such ordeals if I can't wake my mind and stir my body?* Europe is still far away, and if the weather gets bad again, *can I even reach the Irish coast?* Hopelessness gnaws at him again; the alternative is death and failure. The cockpit mists over and control of his muscles slips away. Despair wells up, and he tries to shake himself awake, but this time it's not working. The waves below are gone! Where are the wings? Are they level or not? He doesn't know. There's no horizon up ahead.

I'm passing out.

God give me strength. . . .

---

* Lindbergh wasn't the first to encounter "land" so far out to sea. From the years 1325 to 1865 an island named Bracile, or Brasil, was erroneously depicted hundreds of miles west of Ireland. However, Rockall Islet does exist, a tiny granite tooth emerging from the North Atlantic, but it is considerably northeast of Lindbergh's position.

PART THREE

By day, or on a cloudless night, a pilot may drink the wine of the gods.

—CHARLES LINDBERGH

EIGHT

CROSSING THE BRIDGE

I'VE FINALLY BROKEN the spell of sleep.

Sun beams through the skylight, heating the cabin and reflecting off the gauges, but he doesn't mind. Maybe this is a second wind, or perhaps the sight of death has drawn out the last reserves of strength. The clock reads 7:49 A.M. New York time, so he's been airborne now for nearly twenty-four hours. Others have been up longer; France's Maurice Drouhin and Jules Landry's 1925 record of 45 hours stood until Chamberlin and Acosta remained aloft for more than 50 hours just last month.* But Lindbergh is solo and no one else has flown alone for so long.

The sun is bright, the sky is clear, and he figures the wind is dead astern at about 30 miles per hour. Now is the time to figure out where the *Spirit* actually is, or as close as he can anyway. Slim believes he's far off course to the south. Backtracking to

---

* Forty-five hours, 11 minutes, and 25 seconds.

avoid the thunderheads didn't help, and he figures the cumulative effect of all those 10- and 20-degree deviations probably added up to, what, 50 miles? Slim has also been using the stars, when they are visible, and because in this hemisphere they rotate counterclockwise around the pole this naturally draws a navigator south. How far south? Maybe 20 miles? What about the heading? Departing St. John's he'd offset 5 degrees north to correct back to the plotted course, but that should have happened a thousand miles later.

Spirit left Newfoundland more than twelve hours ago, and if he had updated his course as planned then Ireland should be 600 to 700 miles ahead. Yet he hadn't flown the plotted course, nor had there been any navigation updates for at least seven hours, so is *Spirit* too far north? Several degrees every hour would add up to . . . 50 miles north? Wouldn't that pretty well offset the errors to the south caused by his flying?

The real wild card is the wind.

If it had remained off his left quarter all night the *Spirit* would have been pushed to the right, or southeast, and he would still be south of course. But suppose it had been from the other side of the tail and was blowing him north? Combined with his northeast heading the *Spirit* might be hundreds of miles off to the north. Or vice versa: he could be hundreds of miles south and miss Ireland or England altogether. Certainly, though, a tailwind had pushed him along through the night, so at least *Spirit* was that much closer to land.

But which land?

Supposing that at 10,000 feet, the wind had been stronger and more constant than he'd anticipated? Working his mind again felt good, so with the engine set for 1,575 revolutions and the compass steady on 120 degrees he is free to concentrate. The airspeed has remained fairly constant at 90 miles per hour, but that is *indicated* airspeed, displayed on his cockpit gauge, not his actual speed over the water. The pitot tube on the left wing's leading edge measures ram air pressure, which is just as it sounds: air ramming itself into the tube. So as the plane's speed through the air increases the pressure also increases, and this difference is shown on the airspeed indicator.

Ground speed is the aircraft's horizontal speed over the earth, corrected mainly for wind. A tailwind, as the name suggests, is any wind meeting a plane between the tail and the wing. If this was 180 degrees behind the *Spirit* then the number could theoretically be added directly to his airspeed. This means a 50 mph tailwind would give a 100 mph aircraft a 150 mph ground speed. Conversely, a headwind of the same velocity would give the aircraft only 50 miles per hour over the ground. Of course, unless the wind was hitting precisely on the nose or tail the actual amount added or subtracted would be a vector sum of the total. This is all guesswork anyway since he has no idea of the exact direction or velocity.

Like any pilot, Slim is well aware that wind can make or break a flight in terms of fuel consumption and time elapsed. Navigation is also impacted as wind rarely strikes at convenient, calculable angles. A good pilot can recognize and admit his or her errors in flight, then compensate accordingly. And strong intuition, which Slim has, transforms a fine pilot into an exceptional one. At dawn the wind was off his left shoulder so he'll assume it had been that way all night. He'd give himself a component of 30 out of a 50 mph velocity so a fair ground speed estimate is 120 miles per hour. After twelve hours, including the deviations, he would be 1,440 miles from St. John's.*

---

* His actual ground speed was faster than this; approximately 135 miles per hour, and his position was much closer to Ireland—about 250 miles. Lindbergh was quite correct in being conservative here, especially given all the variables at this point in his flight.

Walking off the distances with his fingers on the Mercator chart, he fixes his position about 420 miles to the west of
the Irish coast. At this point the updated magnetic course is
120 degrees; subtracting a 5-degree correction left into the
wind gives him a 115-degree heading. Switching the stick to his
left hand, Slim reaches down to set the earth inductor compass
by his right leg. *But that's almost exactly the heading I've been
following!* Hope again floods through him like the sunlight.
If he is too far south then he'll surely see ships, and if too far
north then it ought to get much colder. In any event, Slim figures he should see land by sunset and that is reason enough to
relax a bit.

Running an eye over the instruments he realizes that he could
fly a little faster. He has plenty of gas and each minute brings
him closer to land, so why not? Easing the throttle forward to
hold 1,650 revolutions, he moves the elevator trim a notch and
feels it click into place as the airspeed settles on 100 miles per
hour. The extra 7 miles per hour for the seven hours till sunset
would get him 50 miles farther east. How satisfying it is, Slim
thinks, to sit still and fly eastward toward Europe. Everything
seems resolved; the gnawing concern over navigation has been
somewhat resolved, the Whirlwind is throbbing away as if it
will never stop, and the weather is gorgeous. *Whatever may
come later, these sun-filled hours are mine.*

Time for a reward.

Little things can be vital to a pilot's mental state: a cool
drink, a photograph, the luxury of a dry handkerchief to wipe
a sweaty face. Something clean that doesn't smell like gas,
metal, or stale man. Reaching down Slim unsnaps the flying
suit's right leg pocket and pushes his hand inside. Pencils and
his knife . . . but what's this? Something thin attached to a
chain. Pulling it out, he cups the hard, round coin in his palm

and blinks. A medal of St. Christopher, the patron saint of travelers and sailors. Bachelors, too, so it's fitting all around. He wonders how it got in there: a mechanic maybe, or someone in the crowd. A person who asked for no thanks, who cared for no credit. *It was sent with me like a silent prayer,* he realizes, deeply touched, and carefully replaces the medal in his pocket. Shifting on the cushion for a better position, Slim automatically checks the instruments, then looks outside. What . . .

He freezes.

Movement. There is something below on the waves. A shadow? *Spirit*'s shadow? No, it's too small for that and this is moving through the water, not skimming along the surface. From 1,000 feet he can see it clearly behind the struts! It's a porpoise, *the first living thing I've seen since Newfoundland.* After all those lonely, solitary hours Slim's tense muscles relax, and suddenly everything feels different. *I feel that I've safely crossed the bridge to life.* He sits back and enjoys the moment.

When a pilot is uncertain, or worried, everything seems hostile: a twitch of the stick or tiny change in the sound of the motor. But now, *why do I find such joy, such encouragement, in the sight of a porpoise?* It is contact with something that lives as he does, breathing air, using muscles, and entering, if briefly, the world above the waves. A companion, and unlike a shadow, this is life! *This ocean,* Slim reflects, *which for me marks the borderland of death, is filled with life* . . . life which welcomes me back from the universe of spirits and makes me part of the earth again.

Being a pilot is a transitory, contradictory existence. You live in the sky, flying a piece of man-made machinery through the air—these are foreign experiences. The bird is intended to fly, but humans are not; they overcome this handicap through the skills of engineers, builders, and themselves. Slim knows that there is no better evidence of man's innovative capacity than mastery of the air. Well, perhaps not mastery, but at least to tame it for temporary use. Is it real, this mastery, or an illusion? Against the immeasurable emptiness below him, the sense of control feels illusory. For if man is the master, why does a pilot naturally retreat into the safe, familiar confines of the cockpit, the dials and gauges that measure his life? The smells, too. The tang of gasoline and metal is preferred over salt air or the freshness of rain simply because they are of the earth, not the sky.

Surrounded by danger and uncertainty, Slim takes comfort by focusing on the manufactured details around him: heel marks from his boots, stitching in the fabric along the fuselage, the shining glass of his gauges and especially of the clock. By now it is 10:22 A.M. in New York—three or four hours later here depending on exactly where he is. Sleep is still catching up, but not fast and sharp like before. Now it creeps under his lids, slowly and irresistibly. Leaning forward, Slim sticks his face into the wind stream, blinking fast and breathing deep. Pulling back into the cockpit he shifts hands on the stick, noticing that his left hand feels numb as it drops to the side of his wicker seat. Almost by itself, his hand wanders into the chart bag and shifts through the contents: pencils, maps, first-aid kid.

Sunglasses.

Given to him by a Long Island doctor, he'd completely forgotten the sunglasses. Still using his left hand, Slim opens the tan case and holds the glasses up. The thick, circular dark green lenses were in a silver frame, with an unpadded, fixed bridge and wraparound earpieces. Tilting his head sideways, Lindbergh hooks the curved metal around both ears and stares out at the ocean. With the tint of the glasses, the sky again looks overcast, and that brings back bad memories. He's too happy to see the sun and the glasses are too comfortable. *They make it seem like evening,* he thinks, and sleep. Sleep.

There's a constant burning deep behind his eyes and no position is comfortable for his neck. Slim's head droops, then rises, almost involuntarily, pulling his frozen shoulder muscles with it. He's well past the stage where anything physical seems to help and he is afraid he's reaching the end of his reserves. Got to do something, he realizes, and removes the glasses. Fumbling in the chart bag again, he pulls out the shiny red first-aid kit. Balancing it on his left leg Slim snaps the metal case open. Smelling salts. Silk-wrapped ammonium carbonate capsules used to revive athletes and fainting women. They ought to be a weapon against sleep for an exhausted pilot, he decides, crushing one between his thumb and forefinger. Flying with his right hand, Lindbergh lifts the silk mush to his nose and cautiously sniffs.

Nothing.

No burning eyes and no stinging nostrils. Slim tosses the capsule from the window and realizes how detached his senses must have become to be so unaffected. Focusing on problems has helped thus far, as have the sheer mechanics of flight. It's easy to get more complacent at higher altitudes since there is less of a sensation of speed, and more time to recover from mistakes. But it's different down low. Flexing his right forearm slightly, Lindbergh lowers the nose and drops down toward the ocean surface. Leveling just ten feet over the water, he nudges the throttle back a bit and leaves the mixture as it was.

Spirit glides, comfortably riding on a cushion of air just above the dappled waves. Called "ground effect," this phenomenon occurs when a plane is very low to the surface, usually within one wingspan. The deflection of wingtip and airfoil vortices against the nearby surface mean the disturbed air has no place to disperse, creating extra pressure beneath the wings and generating greater lift. Ground effect reduces drag so less power is needed to hold the same forward airspeed. It can be very effective in saving fuel, but the trade-offs are physical stress from low-altitude flying, little margin for error, and turbulence.

But flying low is nothing new for Lindbergh.

Barnstorming pilots did it all the time, skimming over fields and towns to attract attention for shows. One time, he'd flown the last forty miles between Colorado Springs and Burlington, Colorado, at a scant two feet above the ground.

After the Lincoln Flying School was sold in 1922, he'd found himself with eight hours of cockpit time to his name but not the solo flight that marked a true pilot. Erold Bahl, who had purchased the school's Tourabout biplane, went barnstorming through Nebraska and took Lindbergh along to clean the aircraft. Slim figured they could draw bigger crowds if he stood on the wing, and so for a month or so he was a wing walker until returning to Lincoln.

By then Ray Page, who'd sold the Lincoln Flying School to Bahl, had created his own "Aerial Pageant." He had hired a parachutist named Charles Hardin, who delighted crowds by tumbling from planes and then floating gently to the ground. Deciding another skill could only help further his plans, Slim asked Hardin to show him the ropes. Lindbergh's first drop was a "double," designed to give the audience a thrill by mimicking a parachute malfunction. Slim opened one parachute, then released it and fell again before opening a second chute. The "Aerial Daredevil Lindbergh," as he was billed, spent the summer falling out of aircraft throughout Colorado, Kansas, and Montana.

Barnstorming ended each October due to weather, so Slim went to be with his father for a few months during the winter of 1922. Spring found the young pilot in Americus, Georgia,

Charles Augustus Lindbergh, the "Lone Eagle."
(New York Public Library)

(*left*) Congressman and lawyer Charles August "C. A." Lindbergh, with young Charles, circa 1910. (*right*) "Old Swede" Lindbergh, as Charles was known during his Army Air Service days: 1924–1925. *(United States Air Force)*

Billed as the "Daredevil Lindbergh" on the barnstorming circuit, Charles would perform wild stunts, fall off a wing, and parachute to earth in order to attract paying customers. *(San Diego Air and Space Museum Archives)*

Charles Lindbergh adjusting his parachute before a flight test of an experimental plane. Lambert Field, St. Louis, Missouri, 1925. *(Library of Congress)*

THE RAYMOND ORTEIG $25,000 PRIZE

PARIS-NEW YORK - NEW YORK-PARIS

Trans-Atlantic Flight

(Under the Competition Rules of the National Aeronautic Association of the United States of America, and the Federation Aeronautique Internationale of Paris, France.)

A prize of $25,000 has been offered by Mr. Raymond Orteig of New York, to be awarded to the aviator who shall cross the Atlantic in a land or water aircraft (heavier-than-air) from France to the shores of France to New York, or from New York to Paris or the shores of France, without stop, within five years from June 1, 1925. The flight may be made either way across the Atlantic.

QUALIFICATION OF COMPETITORS:- The Competition is open to aviators of any allied nationality holding an F.A.I. certificate (Land plane or seaplane) and annual sporting license issued by a National Federation affiliated with the Federation Aeronautique Internationale and duly entered on the competitors' Register of the National Aeronautic Association.

ENTRIES:- The Entry Form for each attempt, which must be accompanied by the Entrance Fee of $250.00, must be sent to the Contest Committee of the National Aeronautic Association at Washington, D. C., and notice thereof sent immediately to the Secretary of the Trustees of the Raymond Orteig $25,000 Prize at the Army and Navy Club of America, No. 112 West 59th Street, New York City.

No part of the Entrance Fees is to be received by Mr. Raymond Orteig, the donor. All amounts received will be applied toward payment of the expenses of conducting the competition.

STARTING PLACE: - Competitors must advise the National Aeronautic Association of the starting place selected and should indicate as nearly as possible the proposed landing place.

The start or landing may be made from land or water. If a land plane is used the point of starting or landing must be within fifty miles of Paris or New York. If a seaplane or flying boat be used, the start or landing must be made from a point within fifty miles of New York and the start or landing may be from or on any point on the Coast of France. The time will be taken from the moment of leaving the selected starting place, in the case of the land machines. In the case of starts made from the water, the time of start and finish will be taken from the moment of leaving or reaching land, or crossing the coast line. In each case the pilot must report in person to the Trustees of the Raymond Orteig $25,000 Prize or the National Aeronautic Association of the United States of America, at the Army and Navy

Cover page from the Orteig Prize official rules pamphlet. *(Author photograph at the Missouri History Museum Library and Research Center)*

French aviation legends and Great War combat veterans, Charles Nungesser and Francois Coli attempted the Atlantic crossing from Paris to New York on May 8, 1927. They disappeared in the *White Bird* and were never seen again.

NUNGESSER et COLI - Les Héros du raid "Paris-New-York"
et l'avion marin P. Levasseur, moteur Lorraine-Diétrich

Lindbergh in his *Spirit of St. Louis*. Note the magnetic compass mounted above his head. It was read backward in a mirror mounted on the instrument panel. *(Agence Rol/Gallica)*

RYAN AIRLINES, INC.

BUILDERS OF AIRCRAFT
OPERATORS
LOS ANGELES - SAN DIEGO AIRLINE

SOLD TO
CHAS. LINDBERG,
ST. LOUIS, MO.

SAN DIEGO, CALIF., February 25 1927.

1	Special Ryan Monoplane with Wright J-5 Motor	$10580.00
	Payment with order $1000.00	
	" March 1st/27 6580.00	
	" April 28/27 3000.00	
	Total Pay't	$10580.00

Received payment in full for the above
RYAN AIRLINES.

LINDBERGH COLL.
BOX 291 #45
ST. LOUIS

The original receipt for the *Spirit of St. Louis*. *(Author photograph at the Missouri History Museum Library and Research Center)*

Installation of the nine-cylinder Wright Whirlwind J-5C. Assembled by hand, the engine performed at least 14,472,000 perfectly timed explosions during the New York-to-Paris flight. *(Library of Congress)*

Cockpit of the *Spirit of St. Louis*. Forward visibility was only possible through a periscope viewed through the rectangular cutout left of center. Note the scratched hash marks on the upper right where Lindbergh kept a running tally of fuel consumed.

The man and his aircraft. Note the fuselage-mounted vane aft of the wing. This connected to the generator that powered the earth inductor compass. *(Library of Congress)*

Even with side windows installed, the Spalding flying suit was usually necessary as the temperature normally fell below freezing around 8,000 feet. The wood plank beneath the fuselage is to keep the tailskid from sinking into the mud. *(Library of Congress)*

Spirit of St. Louis waiting to make history. Lined up facing east on Roosevelt Field, May 20, 1927.

Check and recheck! Knowing his life hung in the balance, Lindbergh was meticulous and precise in caring for the *Spirit*. Aided by tech reps Karl Boedecker, Ed Mulligan, and Brice Goldsborough, nothing was left to chance.

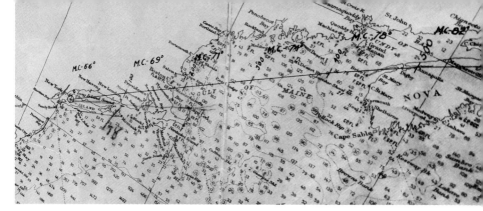

The Mercator projection chart showing the first phase of Lindbergh's planned route. *(Author photograph at the Missouri History Museum Library and Research Center)*

National Weather Bureau forecast given to Lindbergh by James "Doc" Kimball. *(Author photograph at the Missouri History Museum Library and Research Center)*

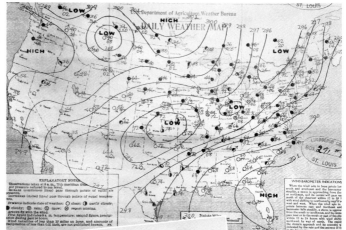

In-flight photo of the *Spirit*. The poor visibility from the cockpit is obvious. Lindbergh's face is barely discernible through the port window.

The final phase of Lindbergh's planned route. Note the lack of detail on the European mainland. *(Author photograph at the Missouri History Museum Library and Research Center)*

Lindbergh's position log. Striving to keep this updated was one of many self-imposed tasks he used to remain awake. *(Author photograph at the Missouri History Museum Library and Research Center)*

Dist.	Lat.	Long. W	True C.	Hrs D.Long	Degrees D.Long	Lat	Meridinal Parts	M Diff	Log M
0	40°45'	73°37'	51°05'	5-43.8	72°51'	55	2665	72	
100	41°40'	72°07'	54°57'	4-57.8	74°21'	50	2739.3	74.8	1.86213
200	42°30'	70°31'	56°03'	4-51.4	72°51'	48	2806.4	67.1	1.82672
300	43°18'	68°54'	57°09'	4-41.4	71°14'	47	2871.7	65.3	1.81491
400	44°05'	67°14'	58°12'	4-38.3	69°34'	46	2935.5	63.8	1.81157
500	44°51'	65°40'	59°24'	4-31.3	67°50'	49	3000.7	64.2	1.80734
600	45°35'	63°44'	60°51'	4-24.2	66°04'	42	3063.0	62.3	1.79449
700	46°17'	61°56'	62°08'	4-17.0	64°16'	41	3122.2	60.2	1.77960
800	46°58'	60°03'	63°54'	4-00.5	62°23'	39	3182.7	59.5	1.77452
900	47°37'	58°08'	64°57'	4-01.4	60°28'	37	3240.0	57.3	1.75815
1000	48°14'	56°10'	66°25'	3-54.0	58°30'	35	3295.0	55.0	1.74436
1100	48°49'	54°09'	68°00'	3-45.9	56°29'	33	3347.7	52.7	1.72181
1200	49°22'	52°05'	69°33'	3-37.7	54°25'	30	3398.0	50.3	1.70157
1300	49°51'	50°01'	71°12'	3-29.4	52°21'	28	3444.1	46.1	1.66630
1400	50°20'	47°53'	72°08'	3-21.9	50°13'	26	3487.7	43.6	1.63949
1500	50°45'	45°44'	74°33'	3-12.3	48°04'	23	3526.9	39.2	1.59329
1600	51°08'	43°32'	76°16'	3-01.5	45°52'	21	3563.3	36.4	1.56110
1700	51°29'	41°15'	78°06'	2-54.3	43°35'	18	3596.8	33.5	1.52504
1800	51°47'	38°58'	79°31'	2-45.2	41°18'	15	3625.7	28.9	1.46090
1900	52°02'	36°41'	81°44'	2-36.1	39°01'	12	3650.0	24.3	1.33561
2000	52°14'	34°27'	83°34'	2-27.1	36°47'	10	3669.5	19.5	1.29003
2100	52°24'	32°03'	85°31'	2-17.5	34°25'	7	3688.8	16.3	1.21219
2200	52°31'	29°36'	87°34'	2-07.7	31°56'	4	3697.3	11.5	1.06070
2300	52°35'	27°03'	89°38'	1-57.5	29°23'	0	3701.8	6.5	0.81291
2400	52°38'	24°27'	91°47'	1-47.1	26°47'	3	3708.8		0.0

Rare in-flight shot with the skylight clearly visible over the cockpit. As of 1926, registration numbers were required by the Department of Commerce. The *Spirit of St. Louis* was North American, Experimental, number 211, and remains so today. *(Agence Rol/Gallica)*

10:22 p.m, May 21, 1927. After more than thirty-three hours in the air, Lindbergh and the *Spirit* come in over the hangers at Le Bourget to land. The spotlight, and several others like it, were the only source of lighting for the tired pilot. *(Alamy)*

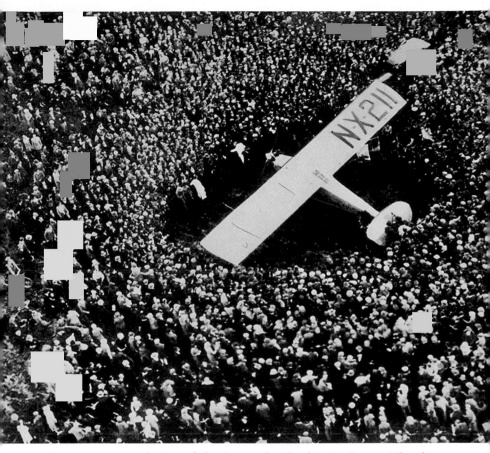

An amazing aerial view of the *Spirit* after landing in France. The sheer mass of people gives a good idea of the hysterical enthusiasm generated by Lindbergh's feat. *(National Geographic collection)*

(facing page) Rescued from the mob, the *Spirit* is surrounded by a protective cordon as it is wheeled into Hanger Five at Le Bourget. *(Gallica)*

The world gone wild! In the United States alone, an extra 25,000 tons of newspapers were delivered heralding Lindbergh's arrival in Paris. *(From The Spirit of St. Louis by Charles Lindbergh)*

(below left) Man of the hour: Lindbergh's quiet nature and modest, unassuming demeanor were a tonic to a nation in the midst of tremendous, often disconcerting changes. *(New York Public Library)*

The Parisians loved Charles Lindbergh. His impromptu visit to Charles Nungesser's mother and his donation of a 150,000-franc prize to fallen French aviators forever endeared him to the French people. *(Gallica)*

Welcome home for the newest national hero. 500,000 congratulatory airmail letters were received in Washington, D.C., alone. *(From* The Spirit of St. Louis*)*

Celebrated with banquets, speeches, and award ceremonies, America could never get enough of Charles Lindbergh in 1927, fueling a wave of souvenirs and memorabilia.

Time magazine's first "Man of the Year."

New York City welcomes the nation's hero, June 13, 1927. Estimating crowds at four million, the *New York Times* called the ticker-tape parade along lower Broadway "the greatest reception the city has ever accorded a private citizen."

Lindbergh and Raymond Orteig, 1927. Though technically Slim didn't qualify for the prize due to the timing of his application, no one considered denying him the honor. At left, an invitation to the presentation of the Orteig Prize. (*New York Public Library; Alan R. Hawley*)

(right) Lindbergh meeting with President Coolidge in Washington. (*Library of Congress*)

(below) Lindbergh Air Mail stamp, issued less than a month after *Spirit* landed in Paris. As hoped, the flight proved the viability of commercial aviation.

After returning to the United States, Lindbergh and the *Spirit of St. Louis* visited eighty-two cities in all forty-eight states. Spirit's last flight was to Bolling Field near Washington, D.C., and it was placed in the Smithsonian Institution, where it remains today.

The circle closes: Charles Lindbergh *(above, left)* at the White House with Apollo 7 and 8 astronauts, December 1968. Paying homage to Lindbergh's 1927 flight, NASA's Wernher von Braun said of the Apollo program: "The moon is our Paris."

After 489 hours, 28 minutes in flight, the *Spirit of St. Louis* forever remains airborne in the National Air and Space Museum, Washington, D.C. *(Library of Congress)*

New worlds: A 2015 image from NASA's Mars Exploration Rover (MER) *Opportunity* of the "Spirit of St. Louis Crater" and the "Lindbergh Mound," the dramatic rock spire within the 3–4-billion-year-old Martian crater. "The MER team stands on the shoulders of many giants of exploration and discovery and we were delighted to shift into a naming convention based on one of the great adventurers who proceeded us, Charles Lindbergh, and the flight of the *Spirit of Saint Louis* aircraft— what a great tribute to an amazing feat," said Ray Arvidson, MER deputy principal investigator. *(NASA/JPL/Cornell/Ken Kremer/Marco Di Lorenzo)*

scouting out war surplus aircraft owned by an entrepreneur named John Wyche. Wyche had purchased 116 Great War relics at $16 per plane, a rock-bottom price, then spent a few hundred dollars fixing each one up to resell them for $1,000 each. Slim managed to bargain him down to $500 for a reconditioned JN-4D, the redoubtable "Jenny," and finally soloed in early May 1923. Lindbergh, feeling like a pilot at last, kept the Jenny until the fall. He'd applied to the Army Air Service and received a letter ordering him to Chanute Field, Illinois, in January 1924 for the flying cadet examinations.

Those were good days.

Sticking his face outside again, Slim fills his lungs with heavy salt air and flies formation with *Spirit*'s darting, shifting shadow. Watching the elusive, dark shape with one eye, he lets his peripheral vision take in the huge rollers, the feathery whitecaps, and the distant horizon. Anticipating the shadow's crests and dips, Slim twitches the stick forward, sideways, then back to follow it. Boots against the pedals, he presses left and right as needed, feeling the rudder bite into the ocean breeze as the plane skids along on the wavetops. It's exhilarating and it is certainly waking him up.

But it is also extremely perilous.

A freak wave could rise up in an instant, or a gust of wind could slam him down into a trough. *No*, he tells himself, *I won't clip the top of a whitecap here, hundreds of miles from shore.* There are enough unpreventable disasters that might befall him; a cracked fuel line, a broken rocker arm, or a stuck valve could all bring the plane down quickly. He won't add another, especially when it can be avoided by flying slightly higher. Pulling the stick back, Lindbergh brings the *Spirit* up to a safer 50-foot height, then slumps back into the wicker seat. His eyes, now long accustomed to the cockpit scan pattern, touch each gauge on the instrument panel. Oil, one of his principal concerns, is stable; pressure is 59 pounds and the temperature a cool 35 degrees. Altitude is fine, low enough to keep him alert but not so close to the whitecaps for concern. Nearly twenty-seven hours into the flight at 12 gallons per hour would mean 324 gallons consumed, two-thirds of *Spirit*'s total fuel load, and he would burn a little over 100 gallons to fly another nine hours.

Good. Everything feels and looks well, except for a layer of clouds forming off to the northeast. Another storm maybe, but after last night no daytime threat seems so bad. Weather had always been a problem when Slim flew the mail. Bill Hopson, one of the early U.S. Post Office Department Air Mail Service pilots, famously wrote, "The best system of flying in bad weather is not so much to go rip roaring through nasty weather, but to use your head for something else besides a hat-rack, and fly where bad weather aint [*sic*]."

Airmail wasn't a new idea. The British had implemented the first regularly scheduled system in September 1911 between London and the city of Windsor. Two weeks later, on September 23, American pilot Earle L. Ovington flew 1,280 postcards and 640 letters between the Aero Club of New York, in Garden City, Long Island, and the Mineola post office, six miles away. Despite the promising start, Congress failed to appropriate the $50,000 required to fund the program and American airmail languished until after the Great War.

Lindbergh, like all boys fascinated with aviation, had enthusiastically followed the establishment of the U.S. Air Mail Service in May 1918. This time Congress appropriated $100,000 to get the program started correctly. Six military Air Service "Jenny" biplanes under the command of an army major began flights from the Washington, D.C., Polo Grounds, through Philadelphia, to Long Island's Belmont Park. Domestic transcontinental air carriers, working in conjunction with trains, initially operated eight planes per day, and for twenty-four cents could get a letter to its destination 22 hours faster than by the existing rail service. In 1924, a letter leaving New York traveled through a series of fourteen airmail relay stops to arrive in San Francisco less than 35 hours later.

By the time Slim, or "Old Swede" Lindbergh as he was known in Army flight school, signed on with the Robertson Aircraft Corporation (RAC) in October 1925, the fledgling Air Mail Service was expanding rapidly. For seven years after the program's 1918 inception, government pilots had flown the mail in government aircraft. But in February 1925, Congress passed a piece of legislation labeled H.R. 7064, or the Contract Air Bill. Also known as the Kelly Act, this was intended to "encourage commercial aviation and authorized the Postmaster General to contract for Air Mail service."

Based on a bid of $2.53 per pound, Robertson Aircraft was awarded Contract Air Mail (CAM) Route 2, flying five round-trips per week from Chicago to St. Louis. Company president Major Bill Robertson, who also commanded the Missouri National Guard's 35th Division Aviation Section, appointed one of his young, bright lieutenants as his new chief pilot: Charles Lindbergh.

Those days seemed a lifetime away from this lonely patch of the North Atlantic. It was no exaggeration, though, that Slim had discovered himself during that year spent in San Antonio. He'd arrived on March 15, 1924, along with 103 other flying cadets. With more than three hundred flight hours logged already, Slim wasn't overly concerned about the flying, but his university failure made him leery of academics. Ignoring the drinking and girl chasing that are a normal part of flight school, Lindbergh buckled down and studied the required aerodynamics, meteorology, and navigation harder than he'd believed possible. What made the difference was the purpose behind it all. Unlike college, this time he was emotionally involved with his subject in a way not possible before. He loved flying and truly believed it was his best future, a future he had decided wholeheartedly to undertake.

This singled-minded purpose changed everything.

Thirty-three cadets, including Slim, beat the 50 percent attrition rate and continued on to the Advanced Flying School, across town at Kelly Field. The margin of error in using a high-performance aircraft for fighting other aircraft was infinitesimal compared to barnstorming, and he reveled in the precise discipline of military flying. Remembering that year, he would recall, "The Army schools taught me what I had never learned before . . . how to study, even subjects in which I had no interest." Slim constantly carried a dictionary to expand his vocabulary while tightening up his grammar, and especially his writing.

It was a year mixed with sorrow, however, as his sixty-five-year-old father passed away in March, 1924. The elder Lindbergh never managed to reverse his fortunes and lost a final bid for a Senate seat. Tragically, he was then diagnosed with an inoperable brain tumor and passed away quietly in his sleep. Nevertheless, on March 14, 1925, a day short of one year since his arrival, Charles Lindbergh and eighteen other survivors were awarded their wings, then commissioned as Army Air Service Reserve lieutenants. Slim had finished second academically with a 93.36 grade point average, but due to his flying skills and instructor evaluations he passed out first in his class overall.

Unfortunately this made little difference, because the Army Air Service was so small that new pilots were barely needed. Reservists like Slim thus had to find other work. That, he reflected, was how he found himself back in St. Louis flying the mail, and it was during one of those flights he had begun planning this very trip.

SOMETHING CATCHES HIS eye again and Slim leans forward, peering past the struts at the ocean below. A second sign of life! A gull, wheeling low over the waves. And another. He hunches over the stick, staring at the big gray birds. If he can see them from this distance he figures their wingspan must be four to five feet. They float, pirouette, and dive magnificently. *They are really children of ocean and air,* Slim muses, while I am an intruder where I don't belong. Gulls fly by nature, by God's design; I stay aloft by man's witchcraft. He wonders how long gulls fly, because these must be terribly far from land. If *Spirit* is at least three hours from Ireland then these birds are 300 miles away. Unless . . . unless he's too far south and has drifted into the shipping lanes. Gulls follow boats—he knows that—so this is a definite possibility. The ocean looks different as well: flatter, less windswept, and much bluer.* *Well,* he decides, *in three hours, if I haven't sighted land, I'll turn thirty degrees to the north.*

Looking northeast from his left window, Slim notices that darker patches of gray dot a horizon already fuzzy with mist. Now that is a faint worry. More storms, probably. If so, how far do they extend? Hopefully not a thousand miles like the last one. Lindbergh is more concerned about fog when making landfall in Europe, because without seeing the ground he can't be sure where he is.

---

* Lindbergh didn't know it at the time but he was over the Porcupine Banks, only 100 miles or so west of Ireland. The water looked bluer here because it was shallow relative to the deeper mid-Atlantic.

Airmail pilots used all sorts of tricks to land in the fog, including following cracks on the surface of an icy river, or trailing car lights along a road at night. Slim frequently dropped a parachute flare through fog and used the vague light to land on some pasture, hoping for the best. One foggy twilight near Springfield, Illinois, he'd used a "beacon," a hundred-watt light that a farm boy rigged in his yard, in order to land. "Your mail planes fly over my house every day," the boy had written to them, "so I have fixed up an electric light in our yard. Maybe it will help you when the weather is bad this winter. I will keep it lit every night."

Thank goodness he had, Slim recalled. But there would be no farm boys with beacons along the Irish coast waiting to help him. If he could see the ground, then it was possible to compare coastlines or cities to the contours on his map. *The greatest test of my navigation will come if I make a landfall in darkness,* he knows, when hills merge into valleys and railroad intersections are impossible to see. If the *Spirit* is too far north, but he can find his way to Dublin, then Slim is sure he can locate London and from there, Paris. But if he strayed south and missed Ireland altogether, well . . .

Putting it all out of his head, Lindbergh tries to relax, but his muscles are now at that miserable stage when no position is comfortable. In a way he's glad because shifting every few seconds makes it impossible to fall asleep. To be drowsy and craving sleep, yet physically unable to let go—is there anything worse than that? The instruments are mesmerizing: too constant and too man-made, with perfect circles, precise lines, and straight needles. The variety of waves and clouds is better, and Slim forces himself to look outside again.

For a long moment he sits perfectly still.

Blinking, Slim struggles to process what he sees, but after

so many desolate hours it refuses to register. There, several miles away off the right wing: a bobbing dark speck on the waves. Lindbergh squeezes his dry eyes shut, wincing as red-orange lights explode across the inside of his lids. Slowly he opens them, focusing again on the same spot of ocean, and his eyes widen.

A boat.

A small boat! Several small boats, in fact. Suddenly Slim's weariness, his aches, all fall away like leaves in a gust of wind. Almost involuntarily his right wrist and foot move together, bringing the *Spirit* southeast toward the little vessels. The ocean is no longer a dangerous wilderness and Slim is exuberant. *I feel as secure as though I were circling Lambert Field back home.* Nosing over, he brings the throttle back slightly, pushes the mixture to RICH, and stares down at a changed world. He's not alone. These aren't porpoises or gulls, these are men! Men like him, who breathe and see and talk.

He's a mile away from the boats now, close enough to see masts and a cabin. They are real. They *must* be real. Leveling off at 50 feet, Slim banks up, kicks the bottom rudder, and skids the plane sideways for a better view. These aren't lake boats or day sailors, these are fishermen. The nearest craft is some sort of yawl, no doubt, about thirty feet long. Far too small to be hundreds of miles out to sea . . . so where is he? *The coast, the European coast, can't be far away!* But which coast Scottish, or Irish, or . . . even French? He could be anywhere from the northern Scottish Isles to the Bay of Biscay. But these are men, and after fifteen hours of solitude over a dangerous ocean that's all that matters.

Rolling out, Lindbergh heads to the next fishing smack and circles. Again there is no one visible on the deck, and he wonders if the noise has frightened them. After all, who would expect an aircraft to just drop in from the sky so far out to sea? As he leans from the window, a blast of thick, salty air ruffles Slim's hair and he squints at the boat. Suddenly a dark ball appears from the cabin porthole. Not a ball, a head. It turns and a very pale face peers up at the plane. Stick forward . . . throttle back . . . left wing down.

Slim leans far out of the window and shouts excitedly, "WHICH WAY IS IRELAND?"

No response.

Flying solely by feel for a few seconds, he is fixated on the boat until his instincts kick in. So low, so close to the water, and in the excitement of the moment he's suddenly in a very dangerous situation. Water fills his vision, the horizon disappears, and Slim instantly shoves the throttle forward while bringing the stick back to his lap. *Spirit* pitches like an angry horse, and as he rolls out, power throbs through his boot heels as the plane claws upwards to safety. The nose is up too far. *Spirit* could stall. It's the distraction, the novelty of actually seeing other humans. He's forgotten the most basic rule in aviation: fly the aircraft.

Releasing pressure on the stick, Slim lets the nose drop, and the down wing falls to the horizon. Roaring fills his ears as the Whirlwind's powerful cylinders breathe, combust, and expel at full throttle. Rolling out, heart thumping, Slim stares at the airspeed indicator to the right of the stick, relieved to see the needle swinging up as the *Spirit* surges ahead to normal flying speed. That particular shot of adrenaline shattered all vestiges of sleep, and he's fully alert now. This is the third circle he's made around the boat and still the face hasn't moved.

It looks like a severed head in that porthole, as though a guillotine had dropped behind it. *Why don't they pay attention to my circling and shouting?* Lindbergh guns the motor but it makes no difference. He wants to remain close, to see more men or at least get a warmer welcome than this, but it's not possible. Rolling out a hundred feet above the waves, Slim glances at the Mercator chart and sets 120 degrees for a new course. He'll hold this for a few more hours, then correct north if there's no land. But what about that? Thirty-foot smacks don't anchor in the middle of the ocean, so land must be close. It must be!

But how is that possible unless gale-force winds blew him much, much farther eastward during the night? He gazes northward to the darkening horizon. *Well, only time will tell.* And the time is . . . 10:52 in the morning along Fifth Avenue, according to his clock. He's certainly passed the 20-degree West line of longitude, so regardless of *Spirit*'s distance from the coast he's four hours later than in New York, so it must be nearly 3 P.M. here. Rain squalls sweep across on all sides, random gray curtains that drum onto the wings and wreath his propeller with mist. The struts gleam. Looking northeast from his left window, Slim notes that the horizon has darkened ominously with low clouds.

Or maybe fog.

Or . . .

Slim's eyebrows slowly knit together. Incredulous, he hunches forward, gaping from the window. *Can it possibly be land?* He blinks, looks away, and carefully stares again to his left. Pillars of rain to the north and south perfectly frame a hard coastline, not fifteen miles away. Flat and purple below with a jagged blue-green band of hills above. Lindbergh is instantly relieved, confused, and relieved again. It is definitely land, but where? St. John's is just sixteen hours behind him and if he's averaged 100 miles per hour then *Spirit* ought to be—must be—300 miles from Ireland. What land is within 1,700 miles of Newfoundland? Iceland . . . but surely it would be much colder that far north. No, that just isn't possible. The Azores? No, those are about 1,600 miles southeast of Newfoundland, but he can't be *that* far off course.

Ireland?

But . . . but he'd figured at least eighteen hours to reach Ireland, so if that's where he is then *Spirit* is three hours ahead of schedule. He wonders if it could be a mirage, like the "land" he saw earlier. Well, there's an easy way to find out. His other islands disappeared when he got close, so Slim banks up to the left, angling toward the "coast" and staring hard. It doesn't vanish. In fact, details grow sharper. Adding power he begins a gentle climb while looking down the left wing.

It is definitely real.

Slim's excitement mounts. Awake and fully alert he levels the *Spirit* off at 2,000 feet heading southeast parallel to the coast. Islands, true islands, jut up from the sea like green, broken teeth weathered by centuries of wind, rain, and sea.* He can see at least three of them guarding the entrance to a bay that is so long it looks like a fjord. Wedging the stick in the crook of his right elbow to hold it steady, Slim crouches forward and spreads the Mercator chart across his lap. Assuming this is Ireland, what contours on his map match what he can see?

Galway.

Galway is a huge bay with some outlying islands. No . . . his tired eyes and the engine vibrations make the map fuzzy. But the Aran Islands, they lie smack in the middle of that bay on his chart, and there are none here like those. Craning his neck left then right, Lindbergh can see a big island on the south side of the bay hugging the coast. Mostly flat, with startling blue waves

---

* These are the Blasket Islands. During Spain's ill-fated invasion of England in 1588, nearly 20 percent of the 130-ship Spanish Armada was lost on the Irish coast, many of them among the Blaskets.

breaking against charcoal-colored cliffs. Gray granite covers the worn, inland hills like old frosting on a cake. By walking the rudder pedals, Slim manages to hold the plane steady while his eyes flicker over the chart. Studying his chart again, he sees that the River Shannon estuary is too narrow, and Loop Head, near its mouth, is sharper than this spit of land. It also doesn't fit Bantry Bay, or Cape Clear far to the south of Ireland.

Well, what's in the middle?

Stick back in his right hand, Slim begins a slow, shallow circle over the funnel-shaped opening. There are small farms inland, and crooked lines of chalk-colored fences. Kenmare Bay has islands at its mouth, he sees on the chart, and a curved bite mark along its southern shore just like this one. He takes a mental picture of it before peering outside again. No, this island is much bigger. Holding the chart flat with his left hand, Slim squints at the next series of contours. A long, tapering bay with scattered islands at its mouth to the north, a curving bite mark on the south shore that's practically filled with a much larger island. *Yes, there's a place on the chart where it all fits* . . . lines of ink on lines of shore.

Dingle Bay and the island of Valencia.*

It all fits.

But it can't be southern Ireland.

But it is.

I CAN HARDLY believe it's true. Lindbergh is astounded. Three thousand miles and twenty-seven hours of flying, and his landfall in Europe is just 25 miles north of the planned route! All of those long hours bent over a drafting table in San Diego

---

* More commonly spelled "Valentia," on the 1927 Mercator chart used by Lindbergh it was labeled "Valencia."

plotting this out, and to hit it so close. After all the wild compass swings from the storm and his deviations during the night,
and of course, the wind. How powerful had the wind been to
blow him here, over southern Ireland, hours early? The fishing
boats he'd seen made perfect sense now; they weren't hundreds
of miles from home, more like twenty. They may have even
been from the port *Spirit* is now circling.

Tugging the throttle back, Lindbergh drops the nose, kicks
the left rudder, and spirals down over the little town. There
are boats, of course, and wagons on the road, and—people.
Townspeople are running out in the streets and waving. With
joy and relief bubbling up from his chest, Slim levels off at a
hundred feet, stretches as far from the window as he can, and
waves back. *I've never seen such beauty before*, he grins from
ear to ear, *here's a human welcome!* Stone forms the jetty and
the houses are painted in reds and yellows, like St. John's.* Is
it the bleakness of towns like that in winter that feeds the love
of color, or maybe the inhabitants just want a break from all
the green?

And Ireland is *green*.

All shades and variations of it can be seen with a single
sweep of the eyes. A sage ring surrounds the blue waters of the
bay, though beyond the foothills darken to jade as they rise.
Fields cover the upper slopes like dragon scales, their mints
and emeralds laced with gray stone fences. Colors fade at the
top into a dull olive fringe that hangs from the crown of each
hill.

*During my entire life I've accepted these gifts of God to
man and not known what was mine until this moment*, Slim

---

* This is Knightstown, the largest populated area on Valentia Island, though
Lindbergh didn't know the name at the time, and most likely didn't care.

muses. He is relaxed and reflective after crossing the ocean, and why not? *I know how the dead would feel to live again.* Beginning his third circle, Slim spreads his map out. It had once seemed an enemy, presenting an endless number of segments to conquer, challenges yet to be met. Not anymore. Now it's a lifeline.

Continuing southeast he figures to cross counties Kerry and Cork, then fly across the St. George's Channel to Plymouth, England. That's about 300 miles from Dingle Bay, and then another 300 to Le Bourget. *Only six more segments to fly, only six hundred miles to Paris.* Slim is so excited he can barely sit still. It's just after 3 P.M., so most of the next six hours will be done this afternoon, and then the long summer twilight ought to get him close. With any luck, *Spirit* should touch down a little after 10 P.M., Paris time. Six hours is a shorter flight than most of the airmail runs he'd made, and all the big water is behind him now. After Plymouth there is only the English Channel . . . about 80 miles between Start Point Lighthouse and Cape La Hague on France's Cherbourg Peninsula.

The wicker seat doesn't seem so hard anymore and minor compass deviations have lost the grave importance they had carried over sea. The Whirlwind's throbbing is comforting now, and every variation in sound doesn't send him upright, eyes fastened to the tachometer. Slim is grinning and cheerful now; there is nothing like absolutely knowing your position and being certain of what lies ahead. Now if only the weather will hold. The smile freezes, then slides off his face.

There is no coast ahead!

All the excitement, all of his hope, drains straight down through his boots. Slim's cheeks sag and his eyes widen in shock. Another mirage . . . another cruel trick of nature. It's not possible. His mind reels and the muscles in his back knit together tightly. *Have I lost ability to distinguish fact from fancy? Is this perfect landfall also an illusion?*

Or a nightmare?

He blinks, shakes his head, and slowly focuses on the curtains of rain breaking up the desolate horizon far beyond *Spirit*'s propeller.

There is nothing ahead but open ocean.

NINE

DREAMS

HE COULD NOT have imagined it.

Cliffs, beaches, and people waving. It just wasn't possible. But what about the misty islands and the phantoms in his cockpit? Or the boats and haunted fishermen. Was he that exhausted and detached? There *must* be an answer. *All Ireland couldn't disappear!* Slim shakes his head and cranes forward to look down each wing, right and left, then right again. His belly is hollow, and more from desperation than anything else, he looks back toward the tail.

And freezes again.

There. Valencia Island is less than a mile behind him.

Somehow he had rolled out of his circle and inadvertently headed out back to sea. Like the incident over the boats, this is another example of how dangerous it is for a pilot to become fixated. He'd stared at the chart too long, and his body didn't recognize that *Spirit* was no longer spiraling around the island.

Enormously relieved, Slim tilts the plane on its left wing and pulls around to the southeast. He's north of his course so about a 5-degree correction should do. Leveling off at fifty feet, heading 126 degrees, he figures it's a good time to check the magnetos again. When was the last time? Just after leaving St. John's and heading into the darkness of last night, some seventeen hours ago. Seventeen *hours*. Each minute seemed so slow at the time, yet now the entire night is a blur. And why not? The sky is clear and he is skimming over the hunter-green fields of County Kerry at 90 miles per hour. Rock walls careen haphazardly across the hills, carts creep along dirt roads, and clumps of sheep break apart at the roar of his engine.

Switching between magnetos he sees all is well and the Whirlwind is performing flawlessly. Sleep is the furthest thing from his mind now, so all the energy he had devoted to remaining awake can now be used for navigation. Gazing through the right window, then glancing to the map, Lindbergh confirms the heading is correct. *Spirit* will cut across the tops of Kenmare and Bantry Bays, then ought to cross the Irish coast over County Cork west of Cape Clear. After that, it's barely two hours across St. George's Channel to the southern tip of England. *One more island to cross.*

Slim's eyes wander out over the landscape, and he thinks of how Nungesser and Coli saw these same barnyards and hills just thirteen days ago.* Twisting to look back past the tail he sees the western horizon is already fading, and he turns around, settling in the seat. *It's as though a curtain has fallen behind me,* Slim thinks. Like a theater performance where the play carries you along in time and place. Life is real, he knows; it always was real. The stage, of course, was the dream. But his

---

* Lindbergh's landfall was within fifty miles of Carrigaholt, where *L'Oiseau Blanc* was last seen heading out to sea.

flight must be both: a definite reality, yet part dream as well. He also knows that the two brave Frenchmen vanished somewhere in that curtain and that he, Charles Lindbergh, is profoundly fortunate to have emerged back into life.

There were those who said this flight was impossible. Major A. S. Shearer, a well-known Canadian pilot, was quoted in the *New York Times* saying such an attempt was "a physical impossibility for one man to pilot an airplane across the Atlantic for forty hours." Shearer had been speaking about Nungesser, but many "experts" said it applied to any flyer making the attempt. When Lindbergh had told his plans to Major Bill Robertson, a friend and mentor, the other pilot had whistled softly and replied, "That's some flight, Slim. Do you really think it can be done?"

Now he has done it—and the implications for reliable, nonstop Atlantic crossings are enormous. What limitless possibilities aviation holds when planes can fly nonstop between New York and Paris! Slim can see that the time will surely come when passengers and mail fly every day from America to Europe. Planes may even replace automobiles someday, he thinks, just as automobiles replaced horses. Though the idea of millions of planes flying around doesn't thrill him.

Still, he's not to Paris yet.

SLIM HAS BEEN flying too long to take anything for granted, but at least he feels normal again, and that's something. The tight little cockpit is comfortable, and his muscles have ceased to ache. Much of this is mental, he knows, and just being certain of one's location removes a huge weight. There may be more trouble ahead, a mechanical fault or difficult weather, but it won't compare to what he's been through already.

The rippling hills stretch far off to the northeast, an amazing green patchwork fading into the mist hanging between every dip and valley. From the air, Ireland is a land of ghosts. Slim thinks of his own phantoms—*the voices that spoke with such authority and clearness*—and wonders if they arrived in those dark hours just to guide him here. To safety after the ocean and the storm; here, barely a hundred miles off *Spirit*'s left wing is where his mother's family once lived.

Just before noon, less than an hour after leaving Valencia Island, Slim crosses the Cork shoreline above southeast Ireland. Fuel is fine, oil temperature is good, and on this heading he should merge with the plotted route about twenty-five miles into the St. George's Channel. The coast is scalloped as far as he can see, and from the window Slim watches a beach emerge from the line of sheer cliffs. It parallels his course before running off into a spit of land shaped like a rabbit's foot. A small horseshoe inlet appears on the other side, but it's the little lighthouse that catches his eye. A startling white tower perched on a rocky pinnacle, easy to see against the grassy plateau. Breaking waves throw spray high into the air, splattering the slate-colored rocks. Tonight, he muses, its beam will guide me back to Ireland if England should be blanketed with fog.*

Cork and Waterford slide away past the right wing as *Spirit* roars over the cliffs, heading out to the next stretch of water. Slim takes a last deep breath of earthy Irish air, then stares ahead at the channel. Puffy, white cloud towers cast black shadows on the water, but he's unconcerned. It's daylight and the crossing should take less than two hours. Pulling his head in, Lindbergh lets his eyes adjust and focus on the instrument panel. He takes the stick in his left hand and adds another tally mark for fuel, the

---

* Galley Head lighthouse, County Cork.

twenty-seventh. Twisting the stubborn valve, he opens the nose tank and shuts off fuel flow from the fuselage. None of the tanks is dry yet, but Slim decides to run out the nose tank.

Switching hands again, Lindbergh rests his left wrist, and eyeballs the water. Somewhere off to the left, maybe fifty miles or so, is an imaginary line dividing St. George's Channel from the Atlantic. The Irish call it the Celtic Sea, and whichever name one calls it, it is strikingly beautiful. From this altitude he can almost see Cornwall, on the southwest coast of England.

Spirit is level at 1,000 feet and Slim can see by the waves that there is still a tailwind. Undoubtedly that makes him faster than the 100 mph indicated airspeed. He's also corrected back to course, so the 123-degree heading should lead straight to Plymouth, and then from there Paris is just three hours away. Out ahead, past the blur of the propeller, the eastern horizon is darkening slightly. This is land—not bad weather—and with no real issues at the moment his mind wanders back to the future of aviation.

Just imagining what his crossing will do for airmail and commercial flying is exciting. For instance, if a plane like the *Spirit* were to stop in Newfoundland, and again in Ireland for refueling, some 1,700 miles in fuel could be saved. At ten gallons per 100 miles that would reduce the load by 170 gallons, or about 1,040 pounds. The domestic rate used by Robertson and the other commercial mail carriers had been set the previous year at three dollars per pound for the first 1,000 miles. After that it dropped to thirty cents per pound for each 1,000 miles.

Slim automatically scans the instruments, then the sea under both wings as numbers spin around in his head. For the weight in fuel saved, not even counting the weight of the tanks, that would mean $3,900 for each one-way trip, just at the domestic rate. Surely they could charge more for international airmail.

An increase of a dollar more for the first 1,000 miles, plus ten cents extra per thousand miles after that, would bring a gross profit of $5,200-one way. Even accounting for operating expenses, this plane would pay for itself in just two round-trips. And yet the consequences of his achievement still trouble him. *I feel like the western pioneer when he saw barbed-wire fence lines encroaching on his open plains,* Slim thinks. The success of his venture brought the end of the life he loved. Still, it's a beautiful afternoon, so why be—

Suddenly the engine coughs, the plane jerks, and the nose falls toward the sea.

HEART INSTANTLY IN his throat, Lindbergh shoves the stick and throttle forward. *Spirit* lurches, yawing left as the motor slows down, and for the first time in twenty-nine hours the Whirlwind isn't roaring in his ears. Blue-gray water fills his peripheral vision as the plane drops toward the channel, and his eyes lock on to the tachometer. The needle is jumping, steadily rising on the right side of the gauge as the revolutions decrease. Because he dumped the nose, *Spirit*'s airspeed is hovering at the dial's upper left near 85 miles per hour. Stomach hollow, his eyes dart to the altimeter; *Spirit* had been at 1,000 feet but is at least one hundred feet lower now. Oil pressure is okay and Slim looks outside again, his gut in knots. No ships—wait. He squints and leans forward. Yes, there is one—no, several, but too far away to see him. His eyes bounce back into the cockpit. Altitude 800 feet, airspeed good for now. Fuel pressure is . . .

Near zero.

But of course! Relief washes over him. The nose tank simply ran dry, *as I intended it to.* Left hand on the stick, Slim reaches down to the center wing tank petcock, the middle of three valves along the top right of the manifold, and turns it horizontally to open the flow. Then grasping the far left petcock, he twists it straight up and shuts off whatever remains from the nose fuel tank. Changing hands again, he slaps the mixture lever all the way up to RICH, then wraps his fingers around the wooden throttle knob. There's no land to turn toward and Slim knows he'll glide longer straight ahead. Pulling the nose up slightly, he slows *Spirit*'s descent to give the engine more time.

As the airspeed needle falls below 70 miles per hour Slim gently nudges the stick forward. He doesn't dare drop below 60 for fear the plane will stall. He'd gotten all the way down to 49 miles per hour at Dutch Flats back in California, but that wasn't at half weight over water as he is now.* Time slows. For a few long seconds he is acutely aware of details: the altitude, airspeed, even the grain of the plywood instrument panel. Wind rushes through the open windows and scrapes along the cotton fabric. If he does go in, at least Slim knows where land is. If this had happened a few hours ago . . .

Suddenly the Whirlwind's weak coughing speeds up into sharp, staccato bursts. Slim eyeballs the approaching water and his tachometer. Spluttering, the engine catches, then roars back to life. Biting hard into damp, heavy air, the prop spins up and *Spirit* lurches hard to the right. Booting his left rudder, Slim neutralizes the yaw but keeps the nose pointed at the waves. A long second passes, then another. Fingers wrapped around the wooden knob, he eases the throttle forward and smoothly pulls back on the stick. The propeller's spinning silver plate rises through the horizon and again points at the blue sky. Leaving the mixture set he climbs back to 1,500 feet and levels off.

---

* During his flight tests in San Diego, Lindbergh calculated a stall range of 49 to 71 miles per hour depending upon gross weight.

Relieved, Lindbergh slumps backward in the wicker seat. Running an eye over the gauges, he throttles back to hold 100 miles per hour, lines up a 123-degree heading, and sets the stabilizer trim. Two hours ago Slim figured there were a minimum of 175 gallons remaining, and probably more. The tally marks for the nose tank bear that out: eight and a quarter hours ran it dry, so if *Spirit* is using ten to twelve gallons per hour that tank had to hold nearly 90 gallons. Even with a conservative estimate of 150 gallons left in his other four tanks, he still has well over ten hours of flying time available. If the weather worsens he could circle all night over some lighted city and try for Le Bourget at dawn, or even turn back to Ireland and find a clear spot to land. But with each passing minute the idea of turning back becomes more repulsive, and Lindbergh considers his options.

I have enough fuel to reach Rome, he realizes, pulling out his map of Europe and unfolding it. *How surprised people back home would be if I cabled them from Rome instead of Paris!* He runs a finger along the map: it was only 700 miles farther, and that seems trivial after the 3,200 miles behind him. New York to Rome wouldn't beat the endurance record set by Chamberlin and Acosta back in April, but it would certainly be the longest solo flight on record. With a 4:45 A.M. sunrise in Rome there would be no worry about a night landing if he went on to the Italian capital, and Slim isn't the slightest bit sleepy. At least not right now, but what about after another seven hours? And what if his fuel calculations are off? The tailwind should have helped with gas by pushing *Spirit* across the Atlantic so quickly, but what if it didn't? Or what if an extra twenty-five gallons hadn't been squeezed into the tanks back at Roosevelt? Running out of fuel over the Swiss Alps wouldn't be like Indiana or Ohio. Too many unknowns.

No, he decides, this flight is from New York to Paris. *I planned and organized it with the intention of landing at Paris. If Paris is covered with fog, that's different, then I can go on with a clear conscience.* But this is no time to make unnecessary changes, and if he speeds up a bit Slim can reach France before darkness. Then only fog or violent storms can hold him back at Le Bourget. He has plenty of fuel and likes the idea of covering as much of the remaining distance while there is still some light. Nudging the throttle forward, Slim sets 1,725 revolutions, which increases the airspeed to 110 miles per hour. The maximum airspeed he tested in California was 124.5, but due to the tailwind he's realized that *Spirit* likely exceeded this number all night with no ill effects.

Lifting his legs one at a time above the rudder pedals, Lindbergh stretches, then drops his boot heels to the floor. Holding the stick loosely in his right hand, he hunches forward and left in a now-familiar position to gaze through the window. The sky is clear, with a half-dozen ships visible in the channel, and after so many solitary hours, there is comfort in that. Up ahead a pale outline looms from the haze. The pilot squints and, like watching a drawing slowly fill in, the outline materializes into a line of cliffs rising up from the sea.

Cornwall! He's reached England.

WAVES SLAM INTO a line of offshore rocks, white froth outlining them against the deep blue channel. A hand-shaped spit of land juts from the coast, black rocky fingers splayed toward him in the surf and Slim is excited again at the sight of solid earth.* Running a finger along the Mercator chart he estimates

---

* Trevose Head. The rocks appear black due to millions of attached mussels.

this landfall on the rugged southwest tip of England puts him 3,250 miles out of Long Island, and within 350 miles of Paris. If he maintains 110 miles per hour, plus 5 more for a tailwind, that would mean a little over three hours remains to Le Bourget. As the haze drops away along the coast Lindbergh can see lonely houses along the cliff tops with waves breaking below. Nosing over, he pulls the throttle back a knob width and glides down to 500 feet. The clock reads 2 P.M. for New York, so it's 6 P.M. here and one hour later in Paris.

As the *Spirit* approaches the haze fades and tidy little farms appear on the rounded headland, neatly partitioned with rock walls and joined by narrow roads. The golden afternoon sun touches everything, softening the ridgelines and hard cliffs. Cornwall, with its clusters of homes and farmland, seems less wild than Ireland. Not quite the bottle-green shade of County Cork, southwest England is more of a jade color, tinged with yellow, though that could be sun. St. George's Channel runs into a line of bays, and as Slim peers ahead he sees a fair-sized estuary off to the left.* It would be fun to dip down and fly lower over several of the beaches, but he decides to stay at 1,500 feet and see more of the countryside.

Cutting across the larger bay, Lindbergh passes south of the estuary and leans out for a better look. The farms still amaze him. How, he wonders, can a farmer make a living from fields so small? A hundred of them would fit in a single Kansas wheat ranch. Passing over the hamlets, he can't help but think that many of the original American colonists came from places like this.

His forebears on his mother's side came from Kent, on the southeast channel coast, and Slim recalls reading in his great-great-grandmother's diary that American men are "far from

---

* Trevone, Mother Ivey's, and Harlyn Bays. The Camel Estuary is farther east, opening into St. George's Channel near Padstow.

being so good looking or gentlemanly as the English." She
didn't think very much of American women, either, writing,
"They are small women without hips, lanky, scraggy, pale, and
Lantern Jaw'd and rather prudish looking. At any rate they
look very modest." The Lodge family always enjoyed laughing
at those entries, and Slim decides to get his first impression of
the English by dropping a bit lower.

Paralleling the river for five or six miles, he gets a closer
look at the countryside. As in Ireland, the fields are irregu-
lar, bracketed by fences, and from the air they look reptilian:
scales of green, tan, and brown sweeping out in all directions.
Clumps of dark trees remain, as this area would have been all
forest once. The roads are bordered by sod walls and many
of the little houses, at least by the coast, have slate tile roofs.
Faces everywhere turn upward at *Spirit*'s growl, and Slim
guesses the locals think him just another British pilot. Even if
they'd heard a radio broadcast about his flight, how could they
know this is the plane that just crossed from the New World to
the Old in thirty hours?

Unknown to Lindbergh, the spectators below *did* know
about his flight. He would have been amazed to learn that the
entire world was now aware that he'd crossed the Atlantic,
overflown Ireland and was within range of the English Channel. Reporting from London, the May 20 Associated Press
banner read:

LONDON THRILLS TO FLIGHT
"Captain Charles Lindbergh's New York-Paris flight
has aroused interest here unequaled by any such undertaking recently. The novel flight is generally pronounced foolhardy, but elaborate arrangements have
been made by the press to keep watch tomorrow along
the coast."

The landscape to the north has changed.

From his left window a wide, scabby spot sprawls across the landscape. The lively greens from the surrounding farms have faded to dull olives and dingy browns. In fact, there are no farms here but Slim catches a gleam of dark water from several low spots. Blotchy, rolling hills rise and fall, almost like gentle waves, and it seems the troughs are filling with fog. Stunted patches of trees cling to life and, astonishingly, several fanglike white hills stick up like pyramids from the fields.* He can see animals running, sheep perhaps, or ponies.

Continuing southeast, Lindbergh stares ahead to the right and is surprised to see the familiar blue haze of water just above the horizon. The English Channel. *I've crossed England so quickly,* he marvels, *it seems so small.* For the next eleven minutes he flies southeast along the Cornish coastline as it gently curves into a hook pointing out to sea.† His map shows Eddystone Lighthouse somewhere off that spit of land, but it's not visible from here. However, past the left wing the tip of a blue-green river can be seen against dimpled hills. Meandering generally east, it opens into a bay on the other side of the hook and Slim can see buildings squatting right against the water.

Plymouth.

It has to be Plymouth. The harbor is filled with ships, and gray smoke from thousands of chimneys drifts across the sky. The pilot's wrist moves slightly and the *Spirit* comes right to a 123-degree heading. Leaving the throttle set for 1,725 revolutions, he scans the other instruments then looks out under the left wing at the famous port. Sir Francis Drake sailed from here to attack the Spanish Armada, the remnants of which

---

* Bodmin Moor.
† Rame Head.

were smashed onto the Blasket Islands, which he flew over a
few hours earlier. Man's ability to conquer the air is truly a
wonder, as Commander Read proved when he landed NC-4 in
this very harbor eight years ago. Old paradigms are irrelevant,
and yesterday's obstacles are vanquished. *Why, yesterday I flew
almost over Plymouth Rock,* on the coast of Massachusetts,
and now, right here, is the very port from which the *Mayflower*
embarked. What took the Pilgrim Fathers sixty-seven days the
Spirit has accomplished in thirty hours!

The Pilgrims had departed from these same chalk-colored,
limestone cliffs. Seen from his vantage point, that part of the
city is shaped like an enormous M with a tower perched near the
edge. Strikingly obvious with red and white bands, the tower is
easy to see against a bright green lawn.* Unlike the American
Plymouth, this harbor has no natural shelter from the sea, but
there is a man-made breakwater about a third of the way into
the sound with a circular fort built directly behind it.

Pushing the throttle forward with his left hand, Slim pulls
the stick back at 1,800 revolutions to climb and watches Plymouth fall away. The Devon shoreline slides along under his left
wing, and even in the dim light its beauty is obvious. Not so
scalloped as Ireland, it is nonetheless gray, weathered, and ancient. Grass and trees disappear close to the edges, but the cliffs
seem stained with green and red lichen. To his right dozens of
ships carve through the offshore waters, including a few liners.
Maybe bound for Southampton, or even Brest, he thinks. How
safe the people on those ships have been, but how little they
know the air and ocean.

---

* Plymouth Hoe and Smeaton's Tower. The breakwater was a marvelous engineering feat for its time, using more than four million tons of stone and
completed in 1814.

Leveling at 2,000 feet, Slim brings the throttle back to hold 110 miles per hour and clicks the stabilizer trim into place. From this altitude he has a spectacular view of Devon's undulating hills and mottled green fields, much larger and less rugged than those of Cornwall. The cliffs, with their long vertical cracks, smooth out and bend 90 degrees north into a long, pebbled beach on the shore of a bay. To the north the coast shrinks into a tail-shaped promontory with a plain, white lighthouse perched on the end. Like a giant finger, it seems to be England saying goodbye, pointing east across the last body of water before France.*

THE ENGLISH CHANNEL is a 350-mile long pathway to the British Isles, and for a long list of invaders, it has been a road to conquest. Julius Caesar and his Roman legions; Germanic Angles, Saxons, and Jutes; Viking raiders who pillaged, raped, and burned before settling in northern England themselves. William the Conqueror, who mounted the last successful invasion of Britain by a Frenchman, created modern England, and laid the foundation of the greatest empire the world has ever known. At its zenith, the British Empire controlled nearly a quarter of the world's surface, and through the channel it became the undisputed master of the seas. Others tried to end this global hegemony and failed; Napoleon himself would stand at Calais staring impotently across twenty miles of water at Dover's white cliffs, unable to defeat the English Channel.

But where military conquest failed, more peaceful means succeeded. Captain Matthew Webb, a British naval offi-

---

* The promontory is Start Point, from Anglo-Saxon *steort*, meaning "tail." The pebbled beach on Lyme Bay is Slapton Sands, future site of practice landings for the 1944 invasion of Normandy.

cer, completed the first unassisted channel swim in 21 hours, 45 minutes, on August 25, 1875. Just nine months before Lindbergh found himself over the channel, New Yorker Gertrude "Trudy" Ederle became the first woman to swim the channel, from Cap Gris-Nez to Kingsdown, Kent, in 14 hours, 34 minutes. She was met by a British immigration officer who politely asked to see her passport. Jean Blanchard, a Frenchman, and John Jeffries, an American physician, made the first successful air crossing in 1875, flying a hydrogen balloon from Dover to Calais in two and a half hours. On July 25, 1909, Louis Blériot took off from Calais and landed safely thirty-six minutes later near Dover Castle.

Now, barely forty minutes after leaving the Devon shore, Charles Lindbergh peers into the fading light and spots a dark mass looming up from the water. Ten miles off *Spirit*'s nose Slim sees what he hopes is Cape La Hague, the western tip of France's Cotentin Peninsula. Behind him the sun touches the horizon and a few final golden rays shoot out into the darkening sky. *The coast of France!*

SLIM LEANS FORWARD, excited. *It comes like an outstretched hand to meet me*, he thinks, glowing in the light of sunset. Again he considers Nungesser and Coli, how easily their fate could have been his. What was it, he wonders. Ice? Perhaps they lost a wing in the turbulence of a storm. *Could they have flown off through starlit passageways and lost the thread of earth entirely? They too rode on a magic carpet, but somehow the magic was lost.* It doesn't take much error or bad luck to bring a pilot to a lonely and often unknown death. A welder's mistake, a freak wind, or a bit of ice clogging a carburetor. It is far too easy to die in the air.

But up ahead the white V shapes of wakes are visible along the coastline. Cherbourg! Just over 3,400 miles from Long Island by 3:52 P.M. New York time—he has to think about the time—on May 21. Relief and a sort of numb amazement flow through him. Lindbergh tries to process what this means but cannot, so he concentrates again on navigation. As Dover is the key to the English Channel coast, so is this port to La Manche, the "Sleeve," as the French call the English Channel.

Peering from the left window, Slim watches the gray twilight cover the harbor. *Titanic* made a stop here on April 10, 1912, just five days before the unsinkable liner struck an iceberg and sank, never to complete her maiden voyage to New York. As the Normandy coastline disappears beneath his feet Slim leans far out to look down. *I'm over the country of my destination,* he realizes. *I've made the first nonstop airplane flight between the continents of America and Europe. No matter what happens now,* he thinks, *I'll land in France. There'll not be another night above the clouds.*

This part of Normandy is flatter than Cornwall or Devon, with large woodlands interspersed among the farms. Lindbergh folds up the Mercator chart for the last time and slips it into his leg pocket. Now for the map of France; there's Barfleur, off the left wing, and up ahead another harbor with an island at its mouth called St.-Vaast-la-Hougue. It's about ten miles off the nose, and the *Spirit* passes overhead six minutes later. Slim stares to the right, trying to pick out landmarks in the waning light. From both directions the coast bends into a giant funnel, an estuary labeled on his map as Carentan. The French names are tricky. *I don't speak a word of French,* Slim laments sheepishly. The map shows ten miles of beaches along the Norman coast; Calvados, it's called, and though there are some cliffs, they're more sheltered from the wind and waves than those seen earlier today.* He figures to cut across the Baie de Seine to parallel the coastline past Bayeux and Caen. This should take him to another estuary between Deauville and Le Havre: the mouth of the Seine. From there he plans to simply follow the great river all the way to Paris.

He overflew Cherbourg at 3:52 New York time, and it's sixty-two miles from *Spirit*'s nose to Le Havre, so he ought to reach the mouth of the Seine in forty minutes, about 9:30 P.M. local time. At 2,000 feet he is just beyond gliding range of the coast, but that no longer troubles him after last night. Slim settles back and tries to relax, but thoughts spin wildly through his head. *I didn't get a visa before I took off. . . .* I wonder how much trouble that will cause? Still, there's a letter of introduction in his pocket from Theodore Roosevelt Jr. for the U.S. ambassador to France, Myron Herrick. Surely that will help. *I'm so far ahead of schedule,* he also worries, *that I may not find anybody waiting for me on the field.*

Nearly three hours early, he notes. The original plan had *Spirit* landing after 1 A.M., but if nothing else strange happens he ought to touch down at Le Bourget by 10:30 Paris time. *I'll have to buy a new suit of clothes,* Slim realizes. *I haven't brought even a toothbrush, or an extra shirt with me.* To the west, toward England and the Atlantic, the last oranges and reds are washed with gray, like a thin watercolor, as the sun disappears below the horizon. To his right France is darkening and lights begin to twinkle below. It's not an ominous dusk, like last night, but a friendly one now, especially since he knows exactly where *Spirit* is, and that his life is no longer in imminent peril.

Two brightly lit areas, Le Havre and Deauville, show up off

---

* Lindbergh passed within five miles of Ver-sur-Mer where, in forty-one days, Commander Richard Byrd's *America* would crash offshore. Nearly seventeen years later, during June 1944, these same beaches would be the scene of the greatest seaborne invasion in history.

his nose and he flys toward the hazy spot between them. White wakes appear below obviously aiming toward the same place, and it's comforting to be near his fellow men again. Reaching for the Lukenheimer manifold, Slim twists the far right petcock to feed fuel from the right wing, then shuts off the fuselage tank. Out the left window, the sun is gone, and a deep red band stains the far-off horizon.

The mouth of this river is also very close to the prime meridian: zero degrees of longitude. That was measured from the British Royal Observatory at Greenwich, England, though the French still measured their meridian from Paris. He had now crossed over 73 degrees of longitude, and was 3,500 miles from New York.* *I've broken the world's distance record for a nonstop airplane flight,* he realizes with a start.

Directly off the nose is Deauville, and Lindbergh decides to drop low and see a bit of France before darkness covers it completely. Sliding the mixture up to RICH, he eases the throttle back, then pulls the stabilizer trim out to neutral. Right hand forward now, and *Spirit* drops toward the little seaside town. Wind whistles through the open windows and Slim sticks his head out to the right. Booting the right rudder, he skids the aircraft sideways to get a better view. The beach is wide and looks like pure sand, no rocks. There is just enough light to see rows of colored umbrellas above the waterline, and a boardwalk at least a thousand feet long just beyond.† As the airspeed hits 120 miles

---

* Most of the world's nations originally established meridians through their large cities, though this was theoretically resolved during the 1884 International Meridian Conference. France abstained, refusing to abandon her own meridian until 1914. Incidentally, the French liner *La Touraine* sent ice field warnings to the *Titanic* using longitudes based on the Paris Meridian, so they were of no use.

† The famous Promenade des Planches. Deauville had long been a glitzy vacation spot and was well known for its horse culture. F. Scott Fitzgerald specifi-

per hour Lindbergh pulls the stick back and brings the nose up. No sense taking foolish risks this close to the end. Roaring across the beach, he angles off left toward the Seine as a big racetrack passes beneath the right wing. Eyeballing the clock he does the math: 9:20 P.M. Paris time means he should be over the French capital in less than an hour.

Heading east, Slim is cutting across country at rooftop height and edging closer to the river. Below him people are running out of their homes to see what is making this great noise; he can see yellow squares of light from windows, a pale flash from a dress, and faces. Faces everywhere turned up to the sky. He feels good: completely alert, and the clinging sleepiness has vanished. *Why, it's past suppertime.* Slim is surprised to feel a hunger pang. It's been . . . how long since he ate? Dinner on the way back from seeing *Rio Rita* in New York the night before he left. Taking some water, Lindbergh finally eats a sandwich, and is thoroughly unimpressed with the taste. *One sandwich is enough,* he decides, crumpling the wrapper and leaning toward the window. *No.* He stops himself. *These fields are so clean and fresh it's a shame to scatter them with paper.*

The earth below his wheels has darkened noticeably in the past few minutes, and there is no color left on the fields. Shoving the throttle forward, Slim pulls back on the stick and *Spirit* climbs away from the shadows. He checks the mixture, oil, and fuel pressure, then glances at the heading. Southeast. Not that a compass is needed. Passing 1,000 feet he looks left and can see the smooth black ribbon of the Seine angling directly at him. Easing the pull to hold 100 miles per hour, Lindbergh continues to climb. Settling back again, he scans the instruments and

---

cally mentions the resort in *The Great Gatsby* and Lindbergh would move his family to France in 1938, to Île Illiec, off the Breton coast.

gauges, then decides to give up looking for checkpoints. If he holds this heading and keeps the river on his north side, the Seine will guide him all the way in. Slim wants to see Paris, and what better way to navigate than fly toward the glow of a city of three million people?

A sudden flash catches his eye, then another, up ahead on the left. Passing 3,000 feet, he focuses on the area and sees it again. It might be . . . he counts the interval between flashes. Eleven seconds. It is. Yes, it's an air beacon! There are others, he notices, at least two more blinking off in the darkness. The London–Paris Airway . . . *nobody told me it had lights.* But why wouldn't it? American airmail pilots had been using beacons for years. In 1925, the 2,665-mile route between New York and San Francisco had more than five hundred such towers, one every three to five miles.* Their acetylene-powered beacons could be seen for dozens of miles if the visibility was good, as it was tonight.

Slim leans into the wicker seat and stares around the cockpit with the satisfaction of any pilot who has completed a dangerous flight. Or nearly completed it. There's still Le Bourget and, he reminds himself, he's never brought the *Spirit* in at night before. But he's made many night landings in other aircraft and this is a magnificent plane. A sudden surge of affection for the *Spirit of St. Louis* shoots through him. They have shared this experience together. He looks around the cockpit, under each wing, and at the spinning, silver propeller. Each feeling beauty, life, and death as keenly as the other . . . *we* have made this flight across the ocean, not *I*, or *it*. All pilots are loyal to their aircraft, at least those planes that see them through dire times and bring them back to earth and to life.

---

* Constructed by the Bureau of Air Commerce, large concrete arrows were also erected next to the towers showing the direction to the next beacon, though their usefulness at night was somewhat doubtful.

But Lindbergh feels a special sense of loyalty and gratitude toward the *Spirit*, to Don Hall for his astounding design, to B. F. Mahoney and all the men at Ryan Airlines who painstakingly crafted such a magnificent piece of machinery. Wright's Whirlwind has been incomparable. At least 7,000 precisely timed explosions in each of his nearly 2,000 minutes of flight. *It's truly a magic carpet,* he marvels.

Slim levels at 4,000 feet, trims the stabilizer, and leans the mixture ever so slightly. His eyes, dry but no longer tired, roam over the instruments and gauges: all normal. Lindbergh leaves the throttle up since there's no need to conserve fuel on such a fine, clear night, so close to his destination. The sky is crisp and clear under a dark velvet blanket; bright pinpricks from innumerable stars show through, and a glow rises over the horizon.

Moon?

No, it's much too early for the moon. Slim slips the goggles down over his eyes and cranes forward out of the window.

Paris.

I see it.

That scarcely perceptible glow is the City of Light. Thirty-three hours of flying, and now the dot on his map is a real place. As real as St. Mary's Bay, St. John's, Dingle Bay, and Plymouth. The bone-chilling fear of that thousand-mile storm and the desperation of his mirages all drop away before Paris's yellow haze.* Every second he flies closer widens the glow; it now stretches from wingtip to wingtip, arcing above the city like a golden fan. Tiny, hard points begin to emerge and form distinct shapes. Alternating squares of light and darkness, long, straight lines of major thoroughfares, and curves. As the *Spirit*

---

* In 1828 Paris installed gas lamps along the Champs-Élysées, the first city in Europe to do so.

approaches from the northwest, boats on the dark, twisting Seine become visible.

He can see at least three bridges across the river, each dotted with headlights. Just past the Seine is a huge black area, bordered on the north by a long, extremely bright thorough-fare, and on the east by more of the French capital. No one at home could tell him the actual location of Le Bourget, and all he knows is that it lies some ten miles northeast of Paris. Not knowing the city, Lindbergh has to find a known point to start from, so he pulls the throttle back, slowing down and gain-ing some time. Sliding the stabilizer trim aft, he holds 4,000 feet and searches for the one landmark that ought to be impos-sible to miss. That big road must be something . . . and it runs directly into a big circle, like a wheel, that radiates spokes in all directions.* Clamping the stick between his knees again, Slim shines the flashlight over his map, then peers outside to the right.

Yes. Far below, a little offset from the center, is an unmis-takable column of lights stabbing upward.

The Eiffel Tower!

It's on the east side of the Seine, opposite a bridge, and well lit. With his left hand Lindbergh holds 90 miles per hour and with his right he banks up around the famous landmark. Even at 4,000 feet the air is bumpy from the heat below; the cool-ing of concrete, water, and trees after sunset can create turbu-lence. But with a little right rudder he hardly notices, and Slim watches the cityscape shift as *Spirit* comes around through the south. Crossing over the Seine again, he spots a wide bridge.

---

* The dark area is the Bois de Boulogne, bordered to the north by the Champs-Élysées. The unmistakable, brightly lit wheel is the Arc de Triomphe, just north of the Eiffel Tower.

Directly across from the Eiffel Tower, it joins a lighted rectangle with a circle on its west end.* Spokes fan out, disappearing into the dark area he'd flown over on the way in, and others
join the first wheel he had observed.

But where is Le Bourget?

THERE SHOULD BE some type of beacon for such an important
airport, he thinks, a big one. An American airport would have
one—"Ford" beacons they were called, after the car headlights.†
Rotating up to six times per minute, a 5,000-candlepower
beacon could be seen for forty miles in clear weather. Though
sometimes, Slim reminds himself, they only turned on when
aircraft were due—and he is three hours early.

But at this altitude he might also be above the narrow
5-degree beam. After all, most lights are angled to be visible
to low-flying aircraft searching for a field, not one as high as
he is. Stick and rudder left, Slim rolls level as the Eiffel Tower
slides past the right wing, then disappears beyond the tail. *I
shouldn't be hunting for a beacon,* he realizes and leans from
the left window. Lights sprawl out everywhere below. Yellow or
gold along the streets and buildings, then thousands of white,
moving specks of automobile headlights. Le Bourget is probably a big patch of dark ground, like the one he flew over near
the river.

Looking at the panel he sees about 90 miles per hour and
4,000 feet, so Slim nudges the *Spirit* farther right to the northeast. That's where to look: northeast of the Eiffel Tower for
about ten miles. *Yes . . . there's a black patch to my left.* Lean-

---

* The Trocadero Palace.
† Beacons along airways were red and those at landing fields were green.

ing so far forward the stick touches his shoulder, Lindbergh
peers through the goggles, his eyes tired and strained. It's a big
enough space, and lined with lights, though not the uniform,
neatly spaced patterns of Chicago or St. Louis. *I must remember I'm over Europe, where customs are strange.* Glancing at
his chart, Slim figures this is in the right place, though he had
expected it farther away from the congested areas. The shape
seems to fit, though it occurs to him that he might have marked
the wrong spot on the map.

Twitching the stick slightly, Slim banks up left enough to
see beneath the wing to the ground. There are floodlights, he
sees, clustered down in one corner. Kicking the left rudder,
he brings the stick to his thigh, rolling *Spirit* up farther, and
squints against the glare. There are thousands and thousands
of smaller, weaker lights jammed along the southeast side of
the field. It is a field, too, he sees, rolling up a little more. Those
floodlights are aimed at the bottom corner of it. As he reverses
to the right, Slim makes out building shapes in the shadows. If
it is Le Bourget, why no boundary lights and no beacon?

I'll fly on northeast a few miles more, Slim decides. This
just doesn't seem far enough out of Paris. Maybe, though, he
just doesn't know. Airspeed is 85 miles per hour . . . so that's
1.4 miles every minute. Had he flown seven minutes from the
Eiffel Tower?* He has plenty of gas and the night is clear, so
a bit of caution won't cost anything. *If I see nothing else that
looks like an airport, I'll come back and circle at lower altitude.* Slim has no reason to rush, not after more than thirty-
three hours, and he's well aware of the danger in trying to
land too quickly on unfamiliar ground. After all, even if this

---

* Le Bourget is actually about 6.5 miles from the center of the city, so Lindbergh would have been overhead in less than five minutes. He was temporarily
confused because of the inaccurate information he'd received about the field's
location.

is the wrong airfield, there's no confusion about the Eiffel Tower. This is definitely Paris!

The *Spirit* is wings level again at 4,000 feet heading northeast. Stick and rudder move nearly of their own accord after so many hours, and Lindbergh's muscles are so accustomed to the range of motion that he barely notices. Everything seems better; the seat is less uncomfortable, his eyes can read the gauges in the dim light at a glance, and he's wide awake. Night air, tinged with exhaust, fills the cockpit and Slim leans over to stare from each window. There is a smaller village on the field's northern border, then the lights thin out in the countryside.* It's almost like flying into a dark valley the way the glow abruptly fades, and his eyes take a few moments to adapt. Now there's nothing but the fiery white-orange bursts from the Whirlwind's exhaust ports, and a dribbling trail of faint lights below.

Five minutes later there's still nothing ahead but the scattered yellow dots of farms, and the area off his left wing is especially dark. That *had* to be Le Bourget behind him—it just wasn't as far from Paris as he'd thought. Looking right, Slim dips the wing and boots the rudder, hunching forward again to squint from the window. Through the gray-black light he can see nothing but vast, flat fields below, and he pulls the throttle back.† Clicking the stabilizer trim to neutral, Lindbergh nudges the mixture control up, just a bit less than full RICH, and glances at the altimeter: 3,500 feet.

Halfway through the descending turn and with more airspeed the *Spirit* is suddenly lively. The controls are stiffer; air rushes through the windows and catches in the fuselage behind the seat before dissipating through the fabric. Power vibrates

---

* The village is Gonesse, where Nungesser and Coli detached their landing gear just after takeoff on May 8, 1927.
† This is the future site of Charles de Gaulle Airport. It opened in March 1974, five months before Lindbergh's passing.

back from the engine, up through the floor and rudder pedals to his feet. Lindbergh concentrates on the few lights below and the blaze of lights ahead. The glow bounces from the spinning propellers, creating a weird circular sheen off the blades. Paris floats across the horizon again, a carpet of multicolored lights that makes him blink continuously.

Twenty-five hundred feet and he's still descending toward the darkness under the wheels. But it's actually not so dark. Not like Wyoming or Nebraska at night, and certainly not the heavy blackness of the ocean. It truly is astounding how a pilot's comfort level can go up with experience or training. Why, the possibilities for commercial aviation unlocked by this flight must mean formal training in blind flying, understanding weather better, and maybe one day even landing by instruments alone. Slim can see all that in the future, but at the moment he can't see Le Bourget. Not definitely anyway, though there is nothing else out here that looks even remotely close. As he pulls the stick back, *Spirit*'s nose rises and Slim adds power. The Whirlwind growls and he feels the props bite back into the air.

Two thousand feet. He decides that's low enough for now. Lindbergh has no idea of the terrain and there could be radio towers on top of the hills below. Getting all the way through the perils he's endured just to crack up on a radio tower is too grim to consider. Nudging the stick right, he holds 90 miles per hour and offsets the field to the west. As soon as the floodlights are visible through the left window, Slim dips the left wing and puts *Spirit* into a skidding spiral so he can see better.

The lights are pointing toward him, off in the darkness on the west side of the field. From this angle he can now see an orderly row of buildings and a large slab of concrete. Twitching the stick, he brings the wing up slightly and squints into the lights below. Yes! Excited, he realizes the concrete is a parking apron for aircraft and the buildings . . . one is half-open and despite the glare he can see it is unmistakably a hangar. This is an airport, no doubt about it. It *must* be Le Bourget!

ARCING AROUND THE airfield's southern edge, he stays close to the lights and tries to pick up more details. It's safe to spiral lower now and he drops the wing low again, tugging the throttle back slightly. But the lights . . . they're everywhere, and much worse on the south side. As Paris passes behind him again, the horizon goes with it and Lindbergh feels slightly disoriented. After thirty-three hours of generally flying straight and level, even a gentle spiral at night is tough. Easing the descent, he shallows out in the turns, pulls the throttle back to IDLE, and continues to spiral down, always staying just beyond the lights. There is a whole row of them, little bright lines of lights on the eastern side behind the hangars. Factory windows maybe? Coming around the north side again, Slim flies with the corners of his eyes, using Paris as a guide, staring down and back.

Cars.

They are headlights, he realizes. Thousands and thousands of them clogging the road. But why? *I'll drag the field from low altitude to make sure its surface is clear,* he decides, pushing up the throttle and roaring in a thousand feet over the hangars. The rush of speed is real, the first time he has felt it since his brief acrobatics through the clouds over the Atlantic. Slim's body and inner ear aren't quite caught up yet, so he's careful at this point. No arrival aerobatics like he'd do flying the mail— just a low pass now to let anyone who happens to be down there know that a plane is going to land. He glimpses a wind sock on a big hangar off the right wing. The narrow end is pointed roughly toward him and it's filled up a bit, but not stiff. So the wind is 10 or 15 miles per hour from the northwest, and he now knows from which direction he must land.

Without really needing to think about it, Lindbergh creates a standard rectangle pattern above the airport. Throttle forward, mixture RICH, and he pulls straight up just past the hangars. The lighted area disappears and he flies again into the black wall along the field's western edge. Less than a minute later Slim boots the left rudder, presses the stick to his thigh, and brings the *Spirit* 90 degrees left to the "crosswind" leg. This is the short end of the rectangle, farthest from the landing end, and the idea is to climb high enough, and get enough distance, to turn back for the landing. Holding about 80 miles per hour in the climb, the pilot uses the floodlights as a reference and when they pass a half mile off his wingtip he banks up in another left turn. Playing the stick and rudder to remain just outside the lights, he rolls out 90 degrees later on "downwind," or the long end of the rectangle.

Pulling the throttle back to hold airspeed, Slim gropes for the flashlight with his left hand and shines it over the Luken-heimer manifold. Now is not the time to turn off the wrong tank! He twists the second petcock from the left horizontally, pauses, then switches hands on the stick and turns the right wing tank valve straight up, closing the fuel flow. With the wind behind him, *Spirit* is aiming directly at the east–west road cluttered with the cars. Eyeballing the spotlights, Slim wedges the flashlight under a leg and holds a thousand feet in altitude until the hangars pass under his left wingtip. Kicking the rudder and sliding the stick forward and left, he tugs the throttle back to IDLE and leans into the turn.

Watching the waving white beams below, Lindbergh constantly increases and decreases the bank to adjust the "base" turn. This is the other short side of the rectangle, and if it's done correctly he'll roll out heading into the wind aligned for landing. Crossing the road and all the bright lights, Slim blinks again at the darkness but doesn't look away from the spotlights. They are his best reference and he thinks that at least the area past them is clear enough to land. Wing up . . . wing down, throttle up a bit, then back . . . more rudder . . . and he eases the last part of the turn so the propeller is pointed just short of the spotlights.

The *Spirit* sinks and so does his stomach. As he shoves the throttle halfway up, the prop slices into the air and the plane stops dropping. Slim stares at the ground, eyes wide. Cars, hangars, and floodlights spraying light into the dark sky. Sloppy. He feels sloppy, as though it were his first solo flight. Normally the plane is an extension of his eyes and hands . . . especially for landing. But that isn't working now. It's almost as if he's forgotten how to fly. It could also be that he's never landed the *Spirit of St. Louis* at night before, and now he's trying it after no sleep for three days on an airfield he's never seen. A few more minutes to get the feel of the place . . . that's all he needs.

The row of hangars has a gap a few hundred feet wide, and it's lit well enough to fly through. Maybe that's what they intended since the ground beyond seems flat and clear. This time, lower and better oriented, he can even see a few aircraft parked in the shadows. Over the trees . . . throttle up a bit . . . the car headlights hit the corner of his left eye as *Spirit* thunders past the road into the gap. Hot air from the ground is rising and the plane pitches a bit as he crosses over some buildings, and aims for the lighted grass beyond. Moving . . . there is something moving on the rooftops. Flags? No, too many. Arms? It looks like waving arms.

But he's suddenly over the field and pointed off into the void beyond the lights. As the ground rushes up he sees it's not completely flat. What's out there in the blackness past the lights? Jamming the throttle forward till it stops, Slim holds the nose a few feet off the ground as long as possible, glimpsing blades of grass and sod under the wheels. At full power now the Whirlwind roars and *Spirit* lurches forward, yawing right until he kicks the left rudder. The lighted area vanishes again and night hits his eyes like a thick, black curtain. Stick back, the plane soars up away from the earth and Slim stares from both windows. There are a few tiny lights way out off the nose that might mark the edge of the field. Maybe. *I'll have to take a chance on that,* he thinks. *If I land short, I may stop rolling before I reach it.*

There's no need to circle any longer.

PULLING THE NOSE up in a gentle, climbing turn to crosswind, Lindbergh reaches 1,000 feet and turns downwind. Retrieving the flashlight, he shines the beam around the panel to check the gauges one last time. This is it. Slim runs a hand over his safety belt and makes certain it's fastened. When he looks left, the floodlights seem to be trying to track him, and he darts a glance at the airspeed indicator. Ninety miles per hour. Seems too fast, he thinks. *I'll overshoot if I keep on at this rate.* That would mean missing the gap in the hangars, or landing too far from the lights to see. Back to IDLE again, he clicks the stabilizer trim back a notch and pulls the stick to his chest. Holding it steady, Slim realizes with a start that he can barely hear the motor. Shoving the throttle up for a fast burst, he hears it sputter and slides the knob right back.

Eighty miles per hour.

He's burned up most of his gross weight in fuel, so the *Spirit* is much lighter. It needs less throttle than he's grown accustomed to during these 33 hours and 17 minutes, but his continuing lack of feeling is frightening. *I'll have to pull the nose higher instead of pushing it down.* Fighting a growing fear, Slim summons all he has left; his conviction that this is the correct field, that he has to land, and that he, Charles Lindbergh, has made it to Paris.

One hundred yards to go. The "base" turn is uncoordinated: one wing down, then up, then down again, dropping toward the cars. Left elbow braced against his ribs, he keeps the throttle straight up. The stick feels like a broom, and his feet are blocks of wood in boots. There's a substantial rectangular building close to the road and trees, then a dark spot, maybe a small park, and more buildings right up to the floodlights. Hangars march off into the gloom on both sides, but the ones to the north seem much bigger. Slipping the plane around the final turn so he can see, Lindbergh hunches forward, blinks rapidly and fixates on the gap. Sideslipping is more dangerous than just landing straight in, but he really has no choice. *If I don't sideslip, I'll be too high over the boundary.* He'd float well past the lighted area and land in . . . what? Whatever is out there.

Floodlights.

He peers at the bottoms of the lights and tries to ignore the waving beams. Airspeed . . . 85 miles per hour. More rudder, and he feels the plane's tail whip right. Stick forward . . . the nose drops, and as the *Spirit* skids around the turn Slim straightens out slightly over the road. Cars again. Thousands of cars and people by the road. A sea of arms waving like blades of grass in the wind . . . then they're gone. A bright beam fills the left window and makes him squint, but he can still see the patch of ground beyond the hangars. Flashing over the little park, his eyes register it all; light gray shadows up front, deep black valleys between the hangars, and bodies silhouetted on the rooftops. Ground rush. As he sinks toward the earth it seems to rise up to him.

Thirty feet.

Shoving the throttle forward, Slim kicks left, then right to keep the nose pointed at the tiny area of grass he can see. Hangars flash by both wingtips. Pulling the throttle back the plane drops down through the gap. Twenty feet. The tail is too high and the *Spirit* is too fast. Hold the nose off. Off! He's going to miss the lit area and land past the black curtain.

Careful!

Ten feet.

Lights disappear behind the window and, eyes wide, he searches for something, *anything,* up ahead. It's like jumping from a lit room through a dark window.

Give her the gun and climb. . . .

Lindbergh's hand is moving the throttle forward when the wheels touch at 10:22 P.M., the trombone shocks compress and then come off the ground again. Trying not to squeeze the stick, Slim eases it forward and feels the horizontal stabilizer lift the tail, forcing the nose down. The *Spirit* settles, then lifts again slightly and the wings wobble. Throttling back with his left hand, Lindbergh nudges the stick forward with his right. This time as the tail drops Slim twitches the stick back to catch it, then eases the tail down until he feels the skid make contact. Bumping the throttle several times to make certain it's in IDLE, he cranes his whole body sideways, peering uneasily into . . . nothing.

The field must be clear, he tells himself as the *Spirit* bumps and jolts into the darkness. Boots tapping the rudder pedals, he keeps the nose straight and slows. He's down . . . he's really down! For the first time in more than 33 hours there is something solid beneath him. Leaning out the left window he can see the ground is indeed flat: solid, dry sod covered with grass.

Slowing to walking speed, he taps the left pedal and as the tail begins to swing Lindbergh boots full opposite rudder and clamps the stick against his left thigh to ground-loop, or turn, the aircraft 180 degrees back toward the buildings. Quite literally he is returning to the light. Rolling forward slowly, he peers ahead

past the spinning sliver blades at the hangars and . . . people!
Thousands . . . a surging wall of tens of thousands of tiny black
figures between the plane and the lights. Running, sprinting . . .
at him! The propeller—it will cut them to pieces!

Slim brings the throttle back to IDLE, then reaches for the
magneto switch. Instinctively, he glances through the window
again . . . and yes, he is on the ground. Slowly, deliberately,
his fingers move and click the switch one, two . . . and three
positions right to OFF. For the second time in 33 hours and
30 minutes the magnificent Wright Whirlwind coughs, splut-
ters, and begins to die. The propeller instantly slows, a silver
blade gleaming in the distant light.

Lurching to a stop on Le Bourget field, Lindbergh and the
Spirit of St. Louis are once again part of the human world.* For a
brief moment the plane, and the man inside, are perfectly still. He
can't hear the aircraft creak as it settles on the grass, and the roar
of thousands of voices is just now penetrating the leather helmet
and cotton wadding in his ears. But he can smell hot metal, gasoline, and rich earth; he can see a mass of dark figures silhouetted
against the lights, surging at him like surf on a beach.†

Slim has no thought yet of the startling reality that the
world has altered beyond all belief or expectation, that he has
met the last great challenge of his decade, and revolutionized
human life. Charles Augustus Lindbergh has thrown open a
window that will never close, and for those who witnessed history in Paris on May 21, 1927, and for all of us yet to come, the
future has changed forever.

---

* The *Spirit of St. Louis* touched down, and stayed down, at 10:22 Paris time.
Flight duration was 33 hours, 30 minutes, 29.8 seconds as verified by the
PN-7 barograph and recorded by the Fédération Aéronautique Internationale.
† The crowd, many of whom had been waiting for hours, could not be con-
tained. They broke down and flattened the eight-foot chain link fence protect-
ing the airfield, and overwhelmed the guards.

TEN

A NEW REALITY

PANDEMONIUM.

This is an entirely apt description of the one hundred thousand hysterically exuberant French citizens who poured across Le Bourget's grassy field toward the *Spirit of St. Louis* and its startled young pilot. "I had barely cut the engine switch when the first people reached my cockpit," Lindbergh later wrote about his first moments in Paris. "Within seconds my open windows were blocked with faces."

He was immediately concerned about his beloved aircraft. He felt it "tremble with pressure" from the press of bodies, and then heard wood crack as three fairings gave way beneath the human weight. It was critical to get the *Spirit* covered and under guard, as souvenir hunters were already clawing strips of fabric away from the steel framing. Much has been made of Lindbergh's opening statement on French soil, usually in error, but all he truly managed to yell was "Are there any mechanics here?" He was greeted with excited shouts in French, and screamed back, "Does anyone here speak English?"

The plane was being rolled forward now, but the tail skid dragged in the grass. Slim needed to deal with the problem, so he opened the door for the first time since New York and stuck out a leg. That was as far as he got. The first men around the *Spirit* yanked Lindbergh from his plane and hoisted him horizontally above the throng. Thousands of jumping, stumbling people were cheering and calling his name. Helplessly prostrate "in the center of an ocean of heads that extended as far out into the darkness as I could see," and stiff from hours in the same position, he was unable to break loose from the dozens of hands gripping his body. Inexorably carried off toward the lights, twenty-five years later he reflected on that night and remembered, "After the warnings I had been given in America, I was completely unprepared for the welcome which awaited me on Le Bourget."

HE HAD INDEED been warned.

The French, both proud and nationalistic, had been embarrassed by Nungesser and Coli's failure to reach New York. A rumor, quite incorrect, was circulated that the U.S. Weather Bureau had withheld essential meteorological information from the French aviators in order to give Byrd, Chamberlin, and Lindbergh a better chance at success. Tensions between the United States and France had lingered since the Great War, and Washington was insisting that France's portion of some $10 billion in outstanding loans be paid in full. Many Europeans felt the debt should be forgiven in return for the blood they had spilt, and as the loans were generally used to buy American goods it was unfair for the United States to profit twice. Roughly 1,700,000 French soldiers and civilians had perished fighting the Germans and it was not an uncommon perception that the United States had avoided entry into the war until most

of the fighting was over. Adding to the bitterness was the fact
that Europe's economies were still battered while America was
enjoying the Roaring Twenties.

Conversely, Americans believed that Europe's issues were
Europe's issues, and intervention in a war that did not affect
our national interests had been an act of supreme sacrifice. Britain and France in particular should be properly grateful for
assistance in winning a war not of Washington's making. Large
numbers of tourists, most of whom spoke no French, took advantage of the strong dollar to travel in Europe and this did not
help. It was not unusual for Americans to receive poor service
at restaurants or cafés, and sometimes tourist buses were pelted
with stones. Washington's high tariffs on French imports, combined with American isolationism, angered many Frenchmen
who believed they sacrificed lives to save the world from Imperial Germany, and were owed more aid than they were receiving. As with all such issues there was some truth in both points
of view, but the situation in May 1927 was so bad that Ambassador Herrick cabled Washington advising against any American attempt at the transatlantic prize—Lindbergh's included.

Reports to the contrary aside, the French had planned for
Lindbergh's arrival. A Franco-American welcome committee
was formed to handle the arrangements, and the Élysée Palace
sent Colonel Denain, military aide to the president of France,
with full authority to act as he deemed fit. Commander Richard
Byrd had also dispatched a representative to Paris weeks earlier
to assist as needed. The French priority from the beginning had
been the plane: escorting the *Spirit of St. Louis* to the main
apron near the terminal, shutting it down, and safely securing
it in a hangar. Lindbergh would then be taken to the welcome
reception, then across to the military side of the airfield, where
he would spend the night.

The American priorities were different. Ambassador Herrick, like nearly everyone else, knew nothing about Charles Lindbergh and had no idea how he would behave, or what he would say when faced with the press. Concerned with relations between the two countries, Herrick sought to isolate the young pilot until he could better judge the situation and the man. Above all, he wanted to keep Lindbergh away from the press unless Herrick himself was present.

Enlisting the aid of Commandant Pierre Weiss, commander of the 34th Bombardment Squadron, the ambassador's plan was for the French officer to meet Slim at his plane and immediately whisk him away to the more secure military buildings. Weiss, who was himself a pilot of note, would have a mechanic inspect the plane, as well as have several French aviators nearby who spoke passable English. While this was happening Herrick had arranged for a Lindbergh double dressed in flying clothes, one Jean-Claude d'Ahetze, to make a token appearance and satisfy the crowd.

On the face of it this seemed a logical approach. The French had also augmented the civil police with two companies of soldiers, and the chief of the Paris police sent an extra five hundred men. But no one anticipated the wild response *Spirit*'s landing would generate, so maintaining order over 100,000 ecstatic Parisians and 12,000 vehicles was entirely problematic.

After the *Spirit* landed and turned back toward the lights, the small military group moved out to intercept it. Unfortunately the clustered reporters saw them and believed they were being scooped by other newsmen. Breaking into a run across the field, the reporters apparently set off the stampede that broke down the fences. Lindbergh, of course, knew none of this and only saw the faces at his window. The chances that a senior mechanic and two English-speaking French pilots randomly arrived at his plane are remote and this lends credibility to the story of Herrick's plan.

Two fellow aviators finally rescued Lindbergh from the mob. Michel Détroyat was a French Air Force pilot, and George Delage flew commercial airliners between London and Paris for Air Union. "Come," Delage had shouted. "They will smother him!" He yanked Lindbergh's helmet and goggles off, tossing them to d'Ahetze, the stunt double, to wear, but somehow the gear ended up in the hands of a young, blond American named Harry Wheeler.* As the mob latched on to Wheeler, Delage threw his coat over Lindbergh's shoulders and they managed to get into the Frenchman's little Renault.

Driving away from the madness they made it to the safety of a quiet hangar on the military side of the field called the North Block. Slim's hearing still hadn't fully returned, and since he spoke no French progress was slow. The Frenchmen chuckled at the young pilot's concern over the lack of a visa and his immigration questions, but then Lindbergh asked about Nungesser and Coli and they visibly saddened. No, there had been no news; the men were believed dead. Détroyat scurried off to find a higher-ranking officer who could take charge of the American, and returned with Commandant Weiss.† Weiss, who hadn't known about the double, took one look at Lindbergh and said in French, "C'est impossible . . . Lindbergh has just been carried triumphantly to the official reception committee."

---

* He has been alternately identified as a reporter or a furrier shopping for rabbit pelts. Raymond Fredette, in *The Making of a Hero*, states that Wheeler was a Brown University student traveling in Europe, and this seems most likely.
† Weiss was not the commandant of Le Bourget, which was a civilian field, though the military held sway over half of it. "Commandant" is a French Air Force rank, equivalent to a major.

Once they sorted out that it was, in fact, Charles Lindbergh sitting there before them, all four men piled into the Renault and drove to Commandant Weiss's office. After dropping Lindbergh off with his self-appointed escorts, Weiss decided his superiors should be aware of Lindbergh's location and he left for the welcome reception at the main administration pavilion, near Le Bourget's entrance. Surely there would be someone there who could assume responsibility for the world's newest celebrity. It was bedlam at the pavilion. Poor Wheeler had been carried upstairs and dumped before Ambassador Herrick, who also believed the man was the genuine Lindbergh.

"I'm not Lindbergh!" Wheeler had shouted over and over to the mob, police, and the soldiers. He then said it again to Ambassador Herrick, who came forward to greet him with a bouquet of red roses.

"Of course you are." Who else could he be?

"I tell you, sir, I'm not Lindbergh. . . . My name is Harry Wheeler." He held up the helmet and goggles. "Everyone got confused because of this."

Herrick noticed the young man wasn't wearing a flying suit and was, in fact, missing his coat, belt, tie, and one shoe. Angrily refusing the flowers, Wheeler waved the flying helmet around and said, "I think some French officers took him to the other side of the field while that crazy mob was nearly killing me."

Fortunately Commandant Weiss arrived and managed to quietly inform the ambassador of Lindbergh's true whereabouts. By the time Herrick, his son Parmely, and daughter-in-law Agnes arrived at Weiss's office it was after midnight. Following introductions, Lindbergh was promptly invited to the ambassador's private residence for the night, and he gratefully accepted on one condition: that he could first see with his own eyes that the *Spirit of St. Louis* was safe. No one was enthused to go back to that part of the airfield, and the Frenchmen assured him that the plane was under guard and hangared, but Slim insisted. In the end, all three French pilots took Lindbergh over to the big Air Union hangar so he could see for himself.

He was shocked by the plane's condition. There were gaping holes torn in the fuselage fabric, though at least one of these was caused by the hurried removal of the barograph recorder needed to verify the nonstop flight. Three fairing strips had indeed been cracked, as Slim heard after landing, and a grease reservoir was missing from a rocker arm housing in the engine. Most vexing of all, his logbook was gone; a loss "he would bitterly regret for the rest of his life."

However, the hangar doors were locked and an armed guard posted so there was little else to be done at the moment. The damage was done. The men again piled inside Delage's Renault, and motored off toward downtown Paris.

TAKING BACKSTREETS TO avoid traffic jams and crowds, they cut through St.-Denis and entered the Paris suburbs by way of St.-Ouen. Delage threaded his way through the dark streets near Sacre Coeur, passing between the 17th and 18th arrondissements, then heading south.

Popping out near the Place de l'Opéra, the French pilot turned right and proceeded down the brightly lit Boulevard Haussmann toward the 16th arrondissement, on the Seine's west bank. Reaching the Arc de Triomphe de l'Étoile, which Lindbergh had seen hours earlier from the air, they stopped and motioned for Slim to get out. They wanted to show him the Tomb of the Unknown Soldier, and for a few moments the men gazed quietly at the gleaming brass rectangle surrounding the eternal flame. After squeezing back into the little car, they drove counterclockwise around the big circle. Delage took a spoke to the south onto the wide, tree-lined Avenue d'Iéna, which was sedate and much quieter. Across the river, the yellow outline of the Eiffel Tower was plain to see against the dark sky and they passed the Place des États-Unis. It was a leafy rectangle with a magnificent statue of Lafayette and Washington shaking hands, and the newly dedicated Memorial to American Great War Volunteers.

It had been a long night.

Surviving such a long, dangerous flight was one thing, but then Slim had been mobbed, rescued, and driven through the maze of northern Paris by strangers. Add to it the lack of real communications with the adrenaline of the past thirty-six hours finally subsiding, and Charles Lindbergh was drained. With no clear idea of where he was and no way to ask, he must have felt a profound relief to finally arrive at the curb outside No. 2, Avenue d'Iéna. This was the Residence: Ambassador Herrick's private accommodation in the Chaillot Quarter. Fortunately, when separated from Lindbergh at the Le Bourget, Herrick had telephoned ahead to his house staff so they were prepared and waiting. Both French pilots bid their new friend farewell, leaving him to a hot bath and a late meal of eggs with soup.

Back at the airfield the ambassador had been searching for Lindbergh with Le Bourget's military commandant, Colonel Poli-Marchetti. Eventually arriving at the hangar containing the *Spirit of St. Louis,* even with the French officer he was unable to gain entrance. He later recounted: "A sentinel was inside, apparently with everything tightly bolted. The officer called to him and ordered him to open. He flatly refused. The officer then told him who he was, giving his name and rank and ordering him severely to come out. Still the soldier refused."

Deciding to return to the Residence, the ambassador finally made it through the epic traffic jam and arrived home at 3 A.M. to find the young pilot wearing the ambassador's pajamas. Newspapermen had also found Lindbergh's location and were waiting outside. Herrick, always gracious and seeing an opportunity to further bolster America's image, wished to bring them in. Lindbergh, however, politely declined. Though he had no love for reporters, Slim had given his word to the *New York Times* that they would get the exclusive interview, and he could not go back on his promise. Parmely Herrick eventually found a *Times* reporter, Carlyle MacDonald, who decided that sharing Lindbergh was the most diplomatic option.

MacDonald's own story, attempting to portray the new hero in the best light, was largely sensationalistic and generally erroneous. Lindbergh did not ask for a glass of milk and a bath upon landing, or circle once over the field and land with no doubts that it was Le Bourget. He did not see the "lights of several ships, the night being bright and clear," nor would he have stated, "Anyway, I paid no attention to economy of fuel during the voyage," as MacDonald claimed. The reporter did get the blue and gold color of Slim's guest room correct, though he got the location wrong; the whole episode took place at the ambassador's residence, not the embassy.

It was not the first, nor would it be the last, example of literary license, or simply poor reporting where Lindbergh was concerned. As mentioned, he had a low opinion for most of the press, and for legitimate reasons. In a quest for "the" scoop, reporters invented all sorts of things that unfortunately have been transmitted down through history and are widely accepted as the truth. Hank Wales of the *Chicago Tribune* wrote that Slim "gulped down a swallow of brandy from a flask one of the French pilots offered, and it seemed to revive him." This was nonsense, of course, because Lindbergh was a teetotaler.

Wales went on to invent an entire plane-side interview that never happened because of a bonus he would be paid for the "first" Lindbergh story. Slim also never tied a bicycle to the upper limbs of a tree and sat there dreaming of flight. Nor did he study bird's wings, have a kitten as a mascot in the *Spirit*, or carry a chicken's wishbone for good luck. There was no secret wife or multiple fiancées, and he absolutely never said that "entering my cockpit was like entering a death chamber."

By Lindbergh's own admission after writing *"We"* (1927), and *The Spirit of St. Louis* (1953), he didn't dwell on aspects of his flight that he felt might hurt the image of aviation. Obviously this included the sheer physical difficulties and technical problems of navigation. "Also, believing in aviation's future," he wrote twenty-five years after landing in Paris, "I did not want to lay bare, through my own experience, its existing weaknesses. For reasons such as these, I left out of my story much of greatest interest."

In the end, the interview lasted less than ten minutes; the ambassador intimated that the young pilot had had enough and the reporters left reluctantly. According to Berg, "Lindbergh shook Ambassador Herrick's hand and said there was no need to awaken him in the morning, as he was sure to be up and ready at nine o'clock." What is certain is that at 4:15 A.M. Paris time, sixty-three hours after his head had last touched a pillow, Charles Lindbergh finally got his wish.

He went to sleep.

•   •   •

MOST OF THE Western world did not rest that night, however, and before midnight the president of France sent the following cable from the Elysée Palace:

Paris, May 21, 1927.
His Excellency, Mr. Calvin Coolidge
President of the United States of America, Washington D.C.

On the morrow of the attempt of our aviators, whose misfortune was so keenly felt by the kindly hearts of your countrymen, Charles Lindbergh made true the dream of Nungesser and Coli, and by his audacious flight brought about the aerial union of the United States and France.

All Frenchmen unreservedly admire his courage and rejoice in his success. I congratulate you most heartily in the name of the Government of the Republic and of the whole country.

Across America, fire engines and police cars sounded sirens; boats in harbors everywhere blew their horns, and homemade confetti was tossed from windows. At 5:30 P.M. Eastern Daylight Time, eight minutes after Lindbergh had landed in Paris, the *New York Times* received official confirmation and the excitement was too much for some to bear. In Aberdeen, Washington, sixty-year-old Richard Barrett "dropped dead on the street here this afternoon as he reached for a newspaper extra." Newborn boys were impulsively named "Charles," and the first of 55,000 telegrams began pouring into St. Louis from all over the country.

Newspapers went into overtime; 25,000 tons of newsprint produced 114,000 extra copies of the *New York Evening World*, 16,000 of the *Washington Star,* and at least 40,000 additional papers for the *St. Louis Post-Dispatch*. Nor was the excitement confined to Europe and America. President Coolidge received congratulatory wires from Tokyo and Moscow; Rodolfo Chiari, president of Panama, cabled that "Lindbergh's flight will leave a luminous track in the history of your great country and of the whole world."

This was certainly true in the United States.

And the country was in need of some good news. By 1927 some of the glitz from the Roaring Twenties was wearing thin. Though consumer spending stood at record highs, wages were down in most agricultural and manufacturing sectors, presaging the crash that would soon follow. The vast majority of Americans were fed up with the Anti-Saloon League and being told what to drink or not drink. Street gangs, armed with Thompson submachine guns, roamed the streets of major cities, and with the rise of organized crime the homicide rate leapt 25 percent in seven years.

Suicides were even higher, with more than 16 deaths per 100,000 people, and the number of people committed to mental hospitals had nearly doubled from the turn of the century. Marriage rates were about the same, but the number of divorces had increased. Interestingly though, nearly 70 percent of divorces were granted to women.* Weary from political scandals like Teapot Dome, spectacles such as Billy Mitchell's court-martial or the Sacco-Vanzetti trial, Americans everywhere were ready for a hero.

"For years the American people had been spiritually starved," Frederick Lewis Allen wrote in *Only Yesterday*. "They had seen their early ideals and illusions and hopes one

---

* At odds with modern perceptions of the times, Oregon, Wyoming, and Ohio had the highest divorce rate per 1,000 marriages.

by one worn away by the corrosive influence of the events and ideas."

And who better to restore faith in themselves than a modest, fresh-faced pilot who had just accomplished the greatest death-defying feat of his age? A young man who did not fly across the Atlantic for money or personal glory, but because the challenge was there to meet. In a matter of hours Charles Lindbergh single-handedly restored some measure of chivalry to a jaded nation and romance to a world unbalanced by intellectual cynicism, and the perceived shallowness of a new modern age. Americans were captivated, including a nineteen-year-old boy on his way to study architecture at Princeton. Jimmy Stewart would go on to become one of America's most iconic actors, but he never forgot being inspired by Lindbergh's flight.* "Lindbergh's problem was staying awake," Stewart later recalled. "Mine was staying asleep that Friday night while he was unreported over the Atlantic between Newfoundland and Ireland."

Witnessing the Spirit of St. Louis dropping out of the darkness and landing at Le Bourget, Maurice Rostand promptly sat down and put into words what so many felt. In part, the composition read:

> *That which brought you, predestined one,*
> *Through all these risks where others fell;*
> *It was the rendezvous which they gave you*
> *At their fresh graves†*

Blissfully unaware of the full effect his flight had had on the world, and equally unknowing of the traumatic changes

---

* Stewart would portray Lindbergh in Billy Wilder's 1957 classic film, *The Spirit of St. Louis*.
† Translated and printed on May 24, 1927, in the *New York Times*.

coming to his own life, Lindbergh slept for at least ten hours, awaking in early afternoon to the sight of Walter Blanchard, Ambassador Herrick's valet, standing near the bed holding a robe. After a huge breakfast of bacon, eggs, crisp buttered toast, oatmeal, and grapefruit, Slim dressed in a borrowed blue suit until a tailor arrived to measure him for a new wardrobe. Shoes were a problem as no one had feet as large as Lindbergh's, so his flying boots were carefully shined and he wore them temporarily.

All through the morning a crowd large enough to warrant extra police had slowly gathered outside. Some two hundred reporters, fifty photographers, and two dozen movie cameramen were also waiting for the first glimpse of the world's new idol. This startling attention, combined with personal telegrams from the king of Spain, the French minister of war, and the Prince of Wales, may have given Lindbergh an inkling that everything had changed. Unintentionally, but irrevocably, the young pilot won French hearts by holding up their flag on his balcony and uttering the only phrase he knew: "Vive la France!"

His first request that Sunday morning was to speak to his mother in Detroit. Through an operator in London who was connected by telephone to Paris and to New York by radio, Slim did just that. Upon learning her son had safely landed, Evangeline Lindbergh spoke to the press saying, "He has accomplished the greatest undertaking of his life, and I am proud to be the mother of such a boy."

As she should be. On his own initiative and to the delight of the public, Lindbergh asked to meet Charles Nungesser's mother. With Ambassador Herrick they made their way to the 3rd arrondissement, off the Boulevard du Temple, and climbed to the elderly woman's sixth-floor apartment. She kissed the American pilot's cheeks and through her tears said, "You are a very brave young man. I congratulate you from the bottom of my heart. I, too, have a brave son, who I have never ceased to believe is still fighting his way back to civilization."

Lindbergh attended a formal dinner that night in borrowed evening clothes, and then turned in early. The next day, Monday, May 23, was his first chance to visit the *Spirit of St. Louis* at Le Bourget. There was a line of five big hangars on the north side of the administration complex, and the plane had been secured in the southernmost of the group. The French had wanted to get the *Spirit* under cover as soon as possible, and this had been the logical spot to secure the aircraft in a hurry after control was lost on the airfield.*

Through the gathered French military pilots Lindbergh managed to return George Delage's borrowed Air Union coat, and then spent a few quiet minutes with his plane. Slim discovered he had actually landed with eighty-five gallons of fuel remaining, enough for another thousand miles, and more than fourteen gallons of oil. The magnificent Wright Whirlwind engine was cold now, and the holes hadn't been replaced, but the plane was in far better condition than he recalled from those surreal minutes following his landing. When a pilot and aircraft share something so dangerous an extraordinary bond remains; the man becomes less human, the machine more so. When discussing the flight, Charles Lindbergh quite naturally referred to himself and the *Spirit of St. Louis* as *we*.

As Ambassador Herrick recalled, "While he was talking to the reporters about the flight, he constantly said what 'we' did: 'We were flying over such a place; the fog began to thicken and we decided,' etc., etc. I finally asked him, 'What do you

---

* Remarkably, the hangar is still in use today. It is labeled H5 and belongs to Advanced Air Support, a luxury private charter outfit at Le Bourget. AAS also proudly advertises the fact that the facility housed the *Spirit of St. Louis*.

mean when you say *we*?' He replied, 'Why, my ship, and me.' "
From that day on, many of the few moments of peace Lindbergh managed to hoard were at the controls of his beloved
Spirit, just the pair of them, beyond the reach of everyone and
everything else. Flying doesn't last, though; you must always
return to earth however much a pilot would wish otherwise. As
his situation became clearer one wonders how much Lindbergh
thought of hopping back into the little plane, lifting off, and
disappearing back to a simpler existence. Back to the freedom
of just being himself.

It was not to be, and the new reality of his situation was
disconcerting. Several hours after running his hands over the
Spirit's fabric, smelling the familiar dust and oil of a hangar,
the grass of an airfield and wind on his face, Lindbergh was
walking through the Élysée Palace to meet the French president. For the first time in history the Republic of France conferred its highest award for bravery, the Ordre National de la
Légion d'Honneur, on an American. Gaston Doumergue himself pinned the crimson ribbon with the suspended white Mal-
tese cross of the Chevalier order on the flier's chest.

Later that afternoon Slim spoke at the Aéro-Club de France.
When the members tried to present him with a gift of 150,000
francs, he politely refused, suggesting that it be given to the
families of fallen French aviators. Before another roaring crowd
Lindbergh said, "The name of my ship, the *Spirit of St. Louis*,
is intended to convey a certain meaning to the people of France,
and I sincerely hope it has."

All day the red, white, and blue from thousands of American flags added bright splashes of color against Paris's green
parks and broad avenues. By order of the foreign minister, the
Stars and Stripes would also fly over the Foreign Office. Every
day he was in the city Lindbergh was escorted to monuments

or official functions, and feted at event after event. He was especially honored to take a private lunch with Louis Blériot, who first flew a powered aircraft across the English Channel nearly eighteen years earlier. Deferential toward the older Frenchman, Lindbergh had always thought of him with awe and told him so. Blériot responded, "You are the prophet of a new era."

ON THURSDAY, MAY 26, Lindbergh was paraded down the Champs-Élysées on the Seine's Right Bank before half a million screaming Frenchmen, and given a gold key to the city. In the shadow of Notre Dame at the Hôtel de Ville (City Hall), Slim delivered an impromptu speech.

It began with the usual platitudes expected from an unworldly young man who had accomplished something great, yet then the pilot showed the world that its portrayal of him as a simple country boy was not entirely accurate. "I cannot adequately express my appreciation of the honor which you are doing me and my country to-day," Lindbergh began—but the speech soon veered into more compelling territory. "I think I have already said everything I have to say with respect to my flight," he continued, "but I want to express one remaining desire. I hope my flight is but the precursor of a regular commercial air service uniting your country and mine as they never have been united before. That is my hope to-day as I believe Blériot hoped his flight across the English Channel in 1909 would be the forerunner of the commercial aviation of to-day; and I believe that if those gallant Frenchmen, Nungesser and Coli, had landed in New York instead of me here in Paris, that would also be their desire.

"I have one regret, and that is that New York was not able

to accord to these brave Frenchmen the same reception that Paris has accorded to me."

Such gestures were very real and offer insight into the true man. Though thoroughly human and with faults enough, in 1927 Lindbergh undeniably still possessed that rarest of qualities: honor. He was truly modest and it was no act. Naïve in many respects, he was certainly no bumpkin. It is well to recall that Lindbergh, raised in a prominent family with two highly educated, professional parents, spent his formative years with his father at the very center of power in the United States. As an adult he simply marched to his own drum and, unlike most people, was utterly unconcerned with their opinion of him. Those who mattered to Charles Lindbergh—his family and a few close friends—mattered. Those who did not, did not. As Ambassador Herrick phrased it, "He was afraid of nothing for himself, but only worried about those who were dear to him."

In a satisfying twist of fate, eight years after Raymond Orteig sent his challenge letter to the Aero Club of America, he was personally on hand in Paris to greet the pilot who won his prize. Orteig and his wife, Marie, had been vacationing near Louvie-Juzon in the French Pyrenees when his son Raymond Jr. cabled Lindbergh's departure. Orteig senior immediately departed for Paris, and was able to meet Lindbergh at the U.S. embassy on the Place de la Concorde.

"I am delighted to hear of Captain Lindbergh's triumph," the younger Orteig stated to the *New York Times*. "The fact that he accomplished this feat all alone adds to his glory." Lindbergh's competitors, at least the flyers, were equally gracious. Commander Richard Byrd, who would take off for Europe in late June, had this to say: "It seemed an almost impossible thing for one man to do, but he has done it. I think Captain

Lindbergh's feat is one of the greatest individual feats in all history. It will be of great value for the purposes of aviation. Captain Lindbergh has in a little over a day made for himself a page in American history."

Floyd Bennett, in traction at a Hackensack, New Jersey, hospital, added, "He deserves all the credit in the world. He has done something that most people won't be able to appreciate as much as they should." From Oyster Bay, Long Island, Theodore Roosevelt Jr. enthusiastically stated to the *Times,* "I'm glad to see that a thoroughgoing sportsman and a man who I believe is a representative American has done the trick. My personal admiration is unbounded. He is just a modest, likeable fellow."

LINDBERGH WOULD REMAIN in Paris until the afternoon of May 28, when, just days after its triumphant landing, the *Spirit of St. Louis* lifted off from Le Bourget. It took about five minutes for Lindbergh to fly six miles down to the Eiffel Tower, and how different this trip was from the last! To begin with, nearly everything is friendlier and easier in daylight and this time he knew precisely where he was going, having now seen much of Paris from the ground. Finally, Slim was well rested and better fed than he'd believed possible.

Circling counterclockwise, left wing down, Lindbergh could clearly see the horn-shaped Trocadero across the Seine, and the tree-lined peace of the ambassador's residence along the Avenue d'Iéna. Dropping low, he flew over the Arc de Triomphe, then pulled the *Spirit* into a chandelle that rolled him out heading southeast above the Champs-Élysées. In the daylight it was such a magnificent view. Wide, leafy spokes close to the center gave way to thinner, less pronounced thoroughfares that covered Paris like an enormous spiderweb. Sluggish and green, the Seine flowed south toward the Île de France and into the heart of Paris.

Huge green parks broke up the streets, interjecting a bit of very French orderly disorderliness into the cityscape. The glass barrel vaults of the Grand Palais caught the afternoon light, and its steel framework gleamed in the sun. Across the boulevard to the left lay the thick trees and gardens surrounding the Élysée Palace. Bordering it to the south along the Avenue Gabriel was the embassy of the United States, set well back on its own grounds and just beyond the wide, hard rectangle of the Place de la Concorde. Lindbergh circled overhead long enough to drop a message weighted to a small sandbag, and tied to a French flag. It plopped to the ground near the obelisk in the center of the square. Flanked by two fountains the monument was hard to miss, and Lindbergh did not.

Goodbye! Dear Paris. Ten thousand thanks for your kindness to me.

Charles A. Lindbergh.

With that he looped and barrel-rolled out of town, heading north for Evere, Belgium, outside Brussels. One hundred eighty miles of peace and seclusion, free of reporters, free from adoring girls and fawning men, free to hear his own thoughts and be who he really was. It would not last. Two hours and fifteen minutes later he landed for more of the same. However, the Belgians had heard of the Parisian chaos and were determined to make a better impression. King Albert had the airfield guarded by five thousand soldiers with fixed bayonets who kept the respectful crowd at bay. After changing clothes at the American embassy, Lindbergh was taken to lay a wreath at the Tomb of the Unknown Soldier and was then presented to the Belgian king, who made him a chevalier of the Order of Leopold. Lindbergh showed King Albert and Queen Elisabeth the *Spirit of St. Louis* before attending the Brussels Opera that evening.

The next day, May 29, he flew forty miles west to one of the Great War's bloodiest battlefields. Circling the town of Waregem, he found a perfectly tended square of green grass surrounded by trees. In tribute to his 411 fellow Americans buried there, Lindbergh dropped a wreath near the unmistakable white chapel of Flanders Field American Cemetery, then continued west across the channel to England.

London was not what Lindbergh expected. There was a crowd of more than 150,000 waiting at Croydon, thirteen miles south of downtown, and when the *Spirit of St. Louis* landed they broke through the rope barriers. As people swarmed onto the field, Slim made a snap decision that no doubt saved lives. Firewalling the throttle he accelerated, lifting off just above stall speed and avoiding cutting his fans in half with the propeller. Circling for five minutes he gave the police a chance to clear spectators away, then landed again. Unlike at Le Bourget, this time he would not leave the cockpit until the plane was roped off and guarded.

Events, interviews, and all manner of dinners and receptions filled Lindbergh's days. He met the British prime minister, Stanley Baldwin, at No. 10 Downing Street and was awarded the Air Force Cross by King George V at Buckingham Palace. Slim enjoyed the English, finding them less reserved (on occasion) than he had been told, and no doubt the slightly peculiar British sense of humor appealed to a man whose own mischievousness was well known. During one dinner at the Savoy,

Lindbergh found only five sandwiches and a jar of water at his place. Puzzled, the joke became clear when the toastmaster informed the crowd that "Captain Lindbergh will now partake of his customary meal."

Lindbergh had hoped to fly himself back to the United States—by way of Siberia, the Bering Strait, and Alaska. But while in London he was informed that President Coolidge would not permit this. Ambassador Alanson B. Houghton, obviously quite diplomatic, explained that acquiescence to "the wish of Washington and those who have your best interest at heart" was truly the only option at this point. Willful young man that he was, Lindbergh knew that bucking the president of the United States was not wise.

Though not a regular military officer, Slim retained his commission in the Missouri National Guard and was well aware that he could be ordered to obey, so, with no real choice, Lindbergh flew the *Spirit* to Gosport, on England's south coast, on May 31.* His beloved plane was carefully disassembled, packed up in two crates for the return voyage, and safely loaded on the deck of the USS *Memphis,* a light cruiser serving as the flagship for the commander of U.S. naval forces in Europe.

WITH HIS WINGS gently but very definitely clipped, Lindbergh's flight was truly over. There were other planes, to be sure, and he flew a borrowed British Woodcock back to London, thence departing RAF Kenley for Le Bourget on June 3. The following morning, with no fanfare, he arrived back in Cherbourg. There, in the same port he'd flown over fifteen days

---

* 110th Observation Squadron, 35th Air Division, Missouri National Guard.

earlier, Lindbergh boarded the *Memphis* amid cheers from ten thousand Frenchmen. Ironically, as the warship put to sea, Clarence Chamberlin was finally taking off from Roosevelt Field bound for Berlin.* Having had the singularly useless Charles Levine (who could neither navigate or fly) aboard, Chamberlin deserves more credit than he received for his essentially solo 43 hour, 49 minute, 33 second flight to Germany.

But nothing could eclipse Lindbergh's glory at the moment. He had made it from New York to Paris, and he had done it alone. He did not seek personal fame, or initially commercialize it once this was gained. Other pilots nipping at his heels seemed somehow coarser, and motivated by less pure goals. This is unfair, of course, but in America's eyes Slim, with his modesty and boyish good looks, could do no wrong—at least for the moment. His warmth and unaffected manners on the passage home confirmed this to the crew. He ate with the men, dined with the officers, answered innumerable questions, and never lost his polite demeanor. The warship's radio room handled more than 100,000 words in private dispatches and press releases.

One day Lindbergh climbed the forward yardarm in the face of a 50 mph wind and took a bird's-eye snapshot of the two crates containing the *Spirit*. He joked, allowed pictures of himself to be taken, and stated, "I have enjoyed every minute . . . they are a fine lot of fellows." Slim also worked. As quickly as he could write them, articles were wired ahead and printed for a voracious public. Anything "Lindy" was a hot item, and he did not disappoint, even beginning to write his eagerly anticipated life story. "I have got the book pretty well outlined,"

---

* They actually landed 100 miles short of Berlin, in Lutherstadt-Eisleben, with mechanical issues. Nevertheless, the 3,911-mile flight was a new nonstop distance record.

he explained in a June 9 piece for the *Times*, "with ample material rounded out to make it complete and will do more work on it tonight before going to bed."

Early in the afternoon of June 10, 1927, while the *Memphis* was still a hundred miles east of the American coast, four U.S. destroyers appeared on the horizon, sighted the cruiser's smoke, and intercepted her.* The *Reuben James, Brooks, Sands,* and *Worden* were to escort the *Memphis* to the Virginia Capes. The USS *Humphreys* had rendezvoused much earlier at 4:34 A.M., and passed over Richard Blythe, Slim's long-suffering public relations man, plus a new Army officer's uniform. Charles Lindbergh was now a colonel in the Missouri National Guard, having skipped the ranks of major and lieutenant colonel altogether. The destroyer removed all the photographs and newsreels, then sped for shore at flank speed. She was replaced by the USS *Goff,* another destroyer, crammed full of reporters and photographers. They sighted the famous pilot on the cruiser's bridge and reported, "He appeared to be little different since the morning of his take-off from Roosevelt Field. Apparently his contact with Kings and Princes had not changed him at all."

The *Memphis* had set a new record to get him home fast; holding an average speed of 22.4 knots, she made the 3,337 miles from Cherbourg in only six days. At 5 P.M. on Friday, June 10, 1927, the *Memphis* and her escorts steamed into Chesapeake Bay past the lighthouses on Cape Henry and Cape Charles. Three weeks to the day after the *Spirit* slowly climbed out over the Long Island tree line and turned northeast, Charles Lindbergh got his first look at home.

---

* The *Memphis* passed very close to, if not directly over, the spot where Billy Mitchell's bombers sank the battleship *Ostfriesland* in 1921.

• • •

MOTORBOATS, FISHING VESSELS, and yachts swarmed near the coast; whistles and horns blew, sirens wailed, and thousands of Virginians lined the shore. The Cape Henry Weather Bureau Station blinked out "WELCOME HOME" in Morse code and the *Memphis* ran up a flag in response. Twenty-five aircraft from Langley Field appeared, dropping out of the sky to give the pilot a pilot's welcome. Navy seaplanes spread into a huge V and made simulated torpedo attacks, passing within one hundred feet of the cruiser as Lindbergh, in a gray suit with a red necktie, stood on the bridge and waved. Two airships, an Army TC-3 out of Langley and a Navy J-3 from Naval Air Station Lakehurst, passed over the warship, then took up stations alongside.*

Clearing the capes, the *Memphis* turned north into the Chesapeake, passing Hampton Roads and Cape Charles on her sixty-mile trip to the mouth of the Potomac River. The normal run up to the capital was twelve hours, but as they weren't supposed to arrive until 11 A.M. the following day, the warship traveled slowly. Virginia governor Harry F. Byrd, the older brother of Lindbergh's competitor Commander Richard Byrd, had graciously deferred his celebration plans in favor of President Coolidge's desire to give Lindbergh his first official welcome. By 9 P.M. the *Memphis* dropped anchor off Piney Point, Maryland, fifteen miles into the Potomac and less than sixty from Washington. All through the night preparations continued; 500,000 airmail letters and at least 37,000 telegrams had already been received.

"Blythe tells me everyone in New York wants to see me,"

---

* The giant airship USS *Los Angeles* was expected, but remained at Lakehurst due to high winds.

Lindbergh cabled from the cruiser that night. "Well, I will do my best. I am going to bed early to store up lots of pep for tomorrow's arrival at Washington."

And what an arrival it was.

The *Memphis* weighed anchor early and made her way slowly up the winding river. Marines lined the shores at Quantico and Indian Head, waving and cheering when the gray warship passed. As she approached Mount Vernon a patrol boat spotted the cruiser, and an escort of eight Coast Guard vessels formed up around her. Closer to the capital, where the Potomac narrowed, all types of boats put out from the shore. Dozens of aircraft appeared in the blue morning sky, adding their roaring engines to the shouting and waving.

At 10:30 the *Memphis* steamed past Alexandria with noise rolling over the water from both the Maryland and Virginia shores. Pennants flew from boats and brightly colored flags and buntings festooned the banks. Trains from the Potomac Railroad yard blew till they ran out of steam; fire engine sirens wailed, automobiles honked, and shrill factory whistles split the air. Rooftops, ships, and wharves were packed with cheering, screaming people indifferent to the 92-degree heat. Through it all, Lindbergh stood on the bridge and "viewed it all with an expression of curiosity."

As the Potomac split below Washington the warship turned east into the Anacostia River. At precisely eleven o'clock a cannon on Hains Point began the national salute, a twenty-one-gun honor normally reserved for the president of the United States. Each minute for seven minutes it fired, then Lindbergh crossed to the starboard side of the bridge as seven more roared their tribute from the Anacostia Naval Air Station. When the cruiser glided slowly into the Washington Navy Yard, fifteen guns thundered out to recognize the arrival of Vice Admiral

Guy Burrage and his flagship. She answered, her thirteen-gun salute adding to the deafening noise from shore. At 11:17 the final seven rounds were fired.

Heaving to at 11:45, the USS *Memphis* at last came to a stop. Lindbergh descended to the main deck, hat on, composed and calm in a blue suit as the gangplank lowered to the dock. Admiral Burrage, resplendent in his dress whites, went down first to meet a small woman standing between a pair of White House aides. Wearing a black straw hat with a brown dress, Evangeline Lindbergh was then escorted onto the warship's deck. Minutes later, both mother and son appeared together and the crowd exploded with cheers. Sirens and whistles shrieked, flags waved, and three hundred thousand Americans screamed their heartfelt welcome, wildly proud of their returning son.

Charles Augustus Lindbergh was home.

EPILOGUE

A victory given stands pale beside a victory won.

—CHARLES LINDBERGH

WHEN THE DUST settles, men who have accomplished extraordinary deeds often go on to attempt others, or they retreat to a well-deserved retirement. At age twenty-five, although catapulted into instant wealth and global fame, Lindbergh had no intention of retiring. There was, he fervently believed, a real chance to influence the growth of commercial aviation and give it a rightful place among the land and sea lovers of his day.

"My future is definitely tied up with aviation," he would write. "I think the United States will inevitably lead the world in aviation, but before that goal is reached there is considerable ground to get over, and we must adapt ourselves to our needs at home." He was quite correct.

Europe at that time was far ahead of America in both

military and commercial aviation. Though the Wrights and Henri Farman both took up riders as early as 1908,* arguably the first true commercial passenger was Abram Pheil who, on January 1, 1914, paid four hundred dollars to take the inaugural flight between St. Petersburg and Tampa, Florida. Europe's progression into commercial aviation had been delayed by the Great War, but in October 1919, the Dutch airline Koninklijke Luchtvaart Maatschappij, better known as KLM, began operations. Aeromarine West Indies Airways started flights a year later between Key West, Florida, and Havana, Cuba. Others followed, but as Lindbergh noted in 1927, the United States was lagging far behind. This was also becoming a strategic security concern as the Colombo-German Air Transport Society (SCADTA) had initiated commercial operations in Colombia eight years earlier.

Perhaps the biggest reason for this progressive attitude was the fact that Europeans were convinced of the necessity and economic viability of air travel. To this end, there was already a network of air routes and, most revealing to Lindbergh, well-established airports, which America lacked. Tempelhof (serving Berlin), Le Bourget, and Croydon (London) all functioned with the precision of railway stations, "with planes from as many as twenty different cities and seven or eight countries arriving and departing on schedule."

Lindbergh did not advocate government subsidization, after the European model, nor did he believe airlines should be built for quick conversion to military use in time of war. Lindbergh understood the rationale behind this but felt America, with its lack of hostile borders, was more secure than Europe. And anyway, Lindbergh felt that America might not need govern-

---

* Charles Furnas and Léon Delagrange, respectively.

ment support; with its common language and better weather it was a more favorable environment for commercial flight. Washington agreed and for some time there was talk of creating a cabinet-level secretary of aviation position with Lindbergh as its first appointee.

More realistic, and definitely closer to the young pilot's liking, was a ninety-day tour through all forty-eight states to promote aviation. The Daniel Guggenheim Fund for the Promotion of Aeronautics arranged the jaunt and a $50,000 fee for Lindbergh. He was always more comfortable around aircraft so this was just the sort of activity that suited him, and he accepted with a proposed July start date. There was one task, however, Lindbergh had to complete before he was free for such a trip: the book.

G. P. Putnam arranged for Carlyle MacDonald, who had returned from Paris, to ghostwrite the New York–Paris account based on his interviews with Lindbergh. Within weeks he had done so, and during the last days of June the pilot had a chance to read the manuscript. It was terrible; a largely first-person work of fiction written by a nonpilot who used shreds of the truth and liberally expanded it into self-aggrandizing drivel. MacDonald apparently believed that the power of the pen granted him the privilege of rewriting factual events to suit his story line. "Cheaply done," Lindbergh called it, and utterly unacceptable. But he'd made a contract and wanted to get back in the air as soon as possible, so the only solution was to rewrite the book himself.

And he did.

Slim's new friend Harry Guggenheim gave him use of Falaise, his Sands Point estate, and some much-needed privacy. No doubt enjoying the solitude, Lindbergh wrote every day, in blue ink on plain white paper, and three weeks later delivered his handwritten, forty-thousand-word first draft. There was no time for a second. "I had little experience in writing," he would later admit, "limited facilities for research, and no extra hours to work on shading or balance." It was direct and unassuming, much like the man himself, though because of the loss of his logbook, it lacked some detail. Years later Lindbergh would explain: "Being young, and easily embarrassed, I was hesitant to dwell on my personal errors and sensations." Nevertheless, "*We,*" as it was titled, arrived in bookstores within a few weeks and sold two hundred thousand copies in the first month.*

During this time, bids for his attention, viable and otherwise, rolled in, as did money. It is estimated that within his first month of returning home, Lindbergh received offers in excess of $5 million, with as much again in potential royalties. Many of these enticements were real: $25,000 from the Woodrow Wilson Foundation and another $25,000 for the Orteig Prize. He was also offered $1 million from four prominent businessmen so he would be free to reject other cash offers!

Lindbergh passed on this as he also did on other, more legitimate offers. Media magnate William Randolph Hearst proposed a $500,000 fee, plus 10 percent of the gross, for an aviation motion picture starring the man himself, but Lindbergh politely refused. Other suggestions were just silly: "Lucky Lindy Bread," or a ridiculous lady's hat with wings and a gray felt propeller called the "Lucky Lindy Lid." A production company even offered to make a film during which Lindbergh actually got married.

Slim was not scornful or contemptuous of money, and he was certainly not a "tin saint," as he put it. Contrary to myth,

---

* Lindbergh did not choose the title and always disliked it. The publishing house, and most likely his editor, Fitzhugh Green, picked the name.

he was not raised poor, but neither was his family so comfortably off that they could ignore money. Lindbergh was, in the beginning, as startled by his newfound affluence as he had been by the worldwide publicity the flight had generated. He came to appreciate financial independence for the freedom it provided, and the chance to escape a public life he never desired, and in which he was never truly at ease.

It was with genuine relief then, on July 20, 1927, that he lifted off in the *Spirit of St. Louis* from Mitchel Field in Long Island and headed out for his three-month American tour. Landing in eighty-two cities and visiting all forty-eight states, Lindbergh delivered 147 speeches and covered 1,287 parade miles. In Richmond, Virginia, on October 16, he took Governor Harry F. Byrd and Harry Guggenheim up flying for ten minutes each. Adding 260 flight hours to the *Spirit*'s log, Slim flew 22,350 air miles before returning to Mitchel Field on October 23.

Later that year, Lindbergh was also awarded two U.S. military decorations. The Distinguished Flying Cross (DFC) had been created in 1926, and was given for "heroism or extraordinary achievement while participating in an aerial flight." Certainly the first New York to Paris solo flight qualified as such, though by executive order civilians were now prohibited from receiving the cross. It is commonly stated that Lindbergh received the first DFC, but this is incorrect. He was presented with the first *medal,* but the ten aviators who participated in the U.S. Army Pan American Flight were awarded the original Distinguished Flying Crosses (without actual medals) on May 2, 1927.*

---

* Eight civilians have been awarded the Distinguished Flying Cross, but it is now exclusively a military decoration unless authorized by a Special Act of Congress.

Then Slim received the highest award America can give for valor. On December 14, 1927, Congress authorized the Medal of Honor which Lindbergh, by virtue of his military status, could receive. The citation read: "For displaying heroic courage and skill as a navigator, at the risk of his life, by his nonstop flight in his airplane, the 'Spirit of St. Louis,' from New York City to Paris, France, 20–21 May 1927, by which Capt. Lindbergh not only achieved the greatest individual triumph of any American citizen but demonstrated that travel across the ocean by aircraft was possible."

Additionally, he was presented with an honorary doctorate of laws from Northwestern University and from the University of Wisconsin, where he had failed as a student five years earlier. Princeton awarded him an honorary master's of science, as did Washington University in St. Louis. Both St. Joseph's College and New York University also conferred honorary masters of aeronautics degrees on the young pilot.

But he always wished to escape the public and the bewildering avalanche of accolades, and so had been planning an extended, international flight to promote aviation and American goodwill. "I wanted to make another long distance nonstop flight before retiring the plane from use," he explained. When his friend and mentor Dwight Morrow resigned from J. P. Morgan to become the U.S. ambassador to Mexico, Lindbergh offered to assist in any way he could. Since relations between the two countries had long been strained, Morrow saw a chance to improve the situation and immediately capitalized on the pilot's offer.

TWELVE DAYS BEFORE Christmas the *Spirit of St. Louis* departed from Bolling Field in Washington, D.C. Twenty-seven hours and fifteen minutes later it landed at Mexico City's Valbuena Airport. The reception was magnificent, and the Mexicans were gracious hosts, flattered that the world-famous American would choose their country as a destination.* Two significant events occurred there, both to Lindbergh's liking. First, his mother, Evangeline, flew in from Detroit for the holidays, pleased to be a guest of the ambassador and to see her son. Second, for the first time in his life, Charles showed visible interest in a girl.

Ambassador Morrow's daughter Anne was a self-contained, quiet young woman of twenty-one. Not as cosmopolitan as her lovely older sister, Elisabeth, or as exuberantly vivacious as fourteen-year-old Constance, Anne was nevertheless winsome, thoughtful, and poised. She was, in fact, a perfect match for the shy, introspective pilot—and he knew it. For the next seventeen months they wrote, cabled, and telephoned whenever possible. Despite their differences—few but significant—the couple was married at Next Day Hill, the Morrow estate in Englewood, New Jersey, on May 27, 1929.

In many ways this was a turning point, an event that would, as Lindbergh put it, "bend the trends of life and history." He purchased 425 acres north of Princeton, New Jersey, and built a home, which he named "Highfields." On June 22, 1930, Anne gave birth to Charles Augustus Lindbergh Jr., a healthy baby they called Charlie who grew into a happy, blond-headed toddler. In the meantime Charles Sr. wrote for magazines, continued to promote commercial aviation, and worked as a technical advisor for Transcontinental Air Transport and Pan American

---

* This tour ended at Bolling Field, Washington, D.C., with Lindbergh donating his plane to the Smithsonian Institution. In her short career, the *Spirit of St. Louis* flew 174 flights, totaling 489 hours, 28 minutes in the air.

Airways.* He was no less famous than before, yet some of the hysteria was dissipating after nearly two years and for the first time Lindbergh was able to live as a family man.

Unfortunately tragedy, which so often seems to follow good fortune, was looming just ahead for the young couple. On March 1, 1932, twenty-month-old Charlie was kidnapped from his nursery at Highfields and for the second time in five years Lindbergh was front-page news. Ransom was demanded, theories abounded, and for seventy-two days the boy's fate was unknown.† Then on May 12 his tiny body was discovered in the woods just four miles from Highfields.

Lindbergh had always been at odds with the press, and their behavior following the kidnapping cemented his loathing. He was constantly pursued, and never allowed the privacy needed to grieve for his lost child. A photographer broke into the morgue in Trenton, New Jersey, and snapped a picture of the dead toddler, then sold copies for five dollars each. Slim hired an armed guard to protect his infant son Jon, but photographers still followed the boy to school and took pictures. The Lindbergh estate became an attraction; vendors sold food near Highfields for sightseers, and one carload of tourists ran over Lindbergh's dog. These deplorable incidents, and many others, convinced him that taking his family abroad was the only way to obtain some measure of security and peace. Everything, it seems, was beyond his control except the ability to control himself.

---

* Transcontinental would merge with Maddux Air Lines in 1929 and Western Air in 1930 to become Transcontinental & Western Air (T&WA, later shortened to TWA).

† H. Norman Schwarzkopf was chief of the New Jersey state police, and responsible for the investigation. Al Capone, from prison, offered a $10,000 reward for information leading to the baby's safe return.

On December 22, 1935, after three tumultuous years, Charles, Anne, and three-year-old Jon quietly sailed from Pier 60 in New York, bound for Liverpool on the SS *American Importer.* They took up residence at Long Barn house, in Kent. Among the English, who valued privacy, they succeeded in living quietly.

During this time, Lufthansa, the German state airline, invited Lindbergh to tour airfields and factories, no doubt hoping the most famous aviator in the world would propagate stories of German aviation might. After privately conferring with Major Truman Smith, the U.S. military attaché in Berlin, Lindbergh agreed to accept the invitation and use the trip to gather intelligence for the United States.

He did this, and was even permitted to tour the top-secret test base at Rechlin, as well as fly the Bf-109, the Luftwaffe's most advanced fighter. While there was much negative publicity about his visit and his reputation suffered, Lindbergh revealed nothing of his true mission. The information he obtained was valuable; a unique look inside German factories at last convinced Washington of Germany's rearmament. Smith would write, "I don't believe anybody else in the world could have succeeded in doing what you did."

Always restless, Lindbergh purchased a four-acre island off the coast of Brittany, in northwest France, in 1938. Situated below the English Channel he had crossed nine years earlier, Île Illiec was secluded, difficult to reach, and one of the most beautiful spots in France. After his overwhelming 1927 reception in Paris, Lindbergh had an affinity for the French and always wished to return though, as with so much of his life, the brief calm and happiness would not last. He was aware, as were many others in the late 1930s, that another war in Europe was nearly certain and that this cataclysm would even eclipse the Great War.

Much has been made of Lindbergh's position regarding the war and any involvement of the United States in such a conflict. A great deal of this was true, but much was also exaggerated. Doubtless, contemporary reports of Lindbergh's opinions were colored by his long-standing animosity for the press, and some Americans' distaste for his fame and fortune. Lindbergh certainly didn't help himself with his own political naïveté and, like his father, he tended toward vitriolic, strident, and uncompromising attitudes.

Like Walt Disney, Sinclair Lewis, a young Gerald Ford and many others, Lindbergh joined the America First Committee (AFC) to oppose U.S. involvement in a future war. The U.S. economy had suffered a recession following the Great War, and billions of dollars in debts remained unpaid by the Europeans. With that in mind, many Americans did not desire the sacrifices inherent in "policing" the rest of the world. Lindbergh initially did not regard the situation in Europe as an American concern, and he was certainly not alone in that. Though the majority of Americans were sympathetic to the Allied cause they did not condone active military involvement, nor would they until December 7, 1941.

In the late 1930s barely 20 percent of Americans supported intervention in Europe. If Britain and France had not prepared for such a conflict, and could not protect themselves *again*, how was that the concern of the United States? Less than half of Americans would vote to aid Mexico if it were invaded by Germany, and even in June, 1940, at the height of the battle for France, American attitude was still two-to-one against fighting for Europe. At its peak, the AFC numbered more than 800,000 members, including many prominent and highly decorated soldiers who felt as Lindbergh did in opposing Washington's current foreign policies.

Yet due to Lindbergh's celebrity and passionate views on the subject, he was widely ostracized. Though he had resigned his commission to enter the antiwar movement, Slim was, first and foremost, an American. If his nation decided to fight then he would as well; he fervently desired to be "effective in case our country is ever involved in war."

Vividly remembering the Great War and well aware that the Treaty of Versailles had solved nothing for the long term, Lindbergh would write, "The flame of war has never been difficult to light but while it has burned in the past it is more likely to explode in the future." If America joined the fight, Lindbergh believed his skills and experience would be best utilized in the Army Air Corps.

The problem was the president of the United States, Franklin Delano Roosevelt. A supremely able politician, an extremely savvy operator and a formidable enemy, Roosevelt held long grudges against those he did not like, or those who had wronged him. Unfortunately, Charles Lindbergh fit both categories, and any move to put him back in a uniform was blocked by the commander in chief himself.

And Lindbergh had wronged him.

Several years earlier, in an effort to portray "honesty in government" and bolster Democrats' chances in the 1934 midterm elections, Roosevelt's men had begun digging up dirt, real or fabricated, on former Republican president Herbert Hoover. A report was compiled alleging widespread collusion and fraud between the U.S. Post Office and commercial carriers that were awarded lucrative airmail contracts. As these were granted in the 1920s while Herbert Hoover had been the commerce secretary, it was a perfect opportunity to smear the Republicans, discredit Hoover, and show that the new president would crack down on big-business corruption. So without real proof, an investigation, or a hearing of any sort, Roosevelt unilaterally canceled all existing airmail contracts and issued an executive order directing the Army Air Corps to carry the mail.

Lindbergh, who was a paid technical consultant for several airlines but had no role in running the businesses, was outraged. In early 1934 he sent a telegram to the president that read, in part, "Your action of yesterday affects fundamentally the industry to which I have devoted the last twelve years of my life. Your cancellation of all air mail contracts condemns the largest portion of our commercial aviation without just trial."

All of this was quite true, but Lindbergh committed two tactical errors. He did not request to see the president in person to discuss this issue with him, and he released the telegram to the press *before* Roosevelt had a chance to read it. Enraged, the president told his press secretary, Stephen Early, "Don't worry about Lindbergh. We will get that fair-haired boy."

And he did.

Though the president was proven wrong politically and eventually forced to very publicly reverse himself, his decision cost the lives of twelve Air Corps pilots who were not trained to fly the mail, nor proficient at night or bad weather flying. Roosevelt never forgave Lindbergh and his embarrassment, plus the latter's conspicuous involvement in the America First movement, was enough to keep the pilot out of uniform. After December 7 and the Japanese attack on Pearl Harbor, with war now unavoidable, Slim wrote that "we had no practical alternative but to enter the fighting." Aggressors had provoked the conflict and only through aggression could they be halted. America, he knew, had not chosen to become freedom's guardian but no other nation could do it. Denied any other way to serve, Lindbergh accepted a position as an aviation consultant helping Henry Ford mass-produce B-24 Liberator bombers. "It was," he later recalled, "a significant place where I could help my country at war."

Lindbergh took a similar position with the United Aircraft Corporation and assisted them in improving the F-4U Corsair, currently in wide use with the Navy and Marines. Fighters were more his area of expertise and Slim toured bases all over the country learning about weapons, tactics, and gunnery. During these visits he mastered the basics of dogfighting and ground attack, so his request to the Navy Bureau of Aeronautics for an open-ended assignment to the forward combat areas was not so far-fetched. Unlike other celebrities who were happy to put on a uniform but go nowhere near the fighting, or those who sought deferments and stayed safe at home, Lindbergh believed it was his duty to physically fight.*

Finally, in March 1944, he received authorization through Admiral DeWitt C. Ramsey to depart for the South Pacific as a "technical representative." Ostensibly, he was to evaluate single-engine versus twin-engine fighters, then assist in any engineering evaluations of combat aircraft and their various components. His first fighter sortie in the Pacific, though not a true combat mission, was on the last day of April 1944, in a F-4U Corsair with VMF-113 off Midway Island.†

Lindbergh continued traveling deeper into the forward area, talking to pilots and maintenance troops, flying test flights, and

---

* There were exceptions, of course. Jimmy Stewart, who idolized Lindbergh, refused to "play war" on a movie set and flew twenty-five combat missions in Europe. Fellow actor Lee Marvin, a combat Marine, was badly wounded on Saipan. On the other hand, there were those like John Wayne who, because he was married with children (like millions who fought anyway), sought and obtained a 3-A deferment, thus remaining clear of combat for the entire war. Wayne would be booed by wounded soldiers when he visited a hospital during a photo op.
† VMF is the designation for a U.S. Marine Fighter Squadron.

conducting equipment evaluations. He worked out solutions for landing gear issues, wing tank feed problems, and water injection improvements, among other things. Eventually, on May 22, 1944, from Guadalcanal's Henderson Field, Slim would fly his first combat mission over Rabaul in a Marine Corsair. This was amazing given that he was a civilian and expressly prohibited from flying such missions, but local commanders turned a blind eye due to the technical assistance he was providing, and the inescapable fact that he was Charles Lindbergh.

The personal risk went far beyond that of a fighter pilot in a war zone. As a civilian he was officially a noncombatant and legally should not have engaged in combat. If he were shot down or captured his status would be uncertain at best, and he would have no real protection. Given that the Japanese, who had never ratified the 1929 Geneva Convention, were notoriously brutal to Allied prisoners, Lindbergh faced tremendous danger. One Marine colonel told Lindbergh after a mission, "You're on civilian status. If you'd had to land and the Japs caught you, you would have been shot."

Nevertheless, Slim flew A-20s, F-4Us, P-61s, and P-47s, to name a few, deriving practical solutions for problems with oxygen systems and wing-folding mechanisms and, perhaps most significantly, passing on cruise techniques that allowed pilots to considerably stretch their usable fuel. On July 28, while flying a P-38J with the 475th Fighter Group (Satan's Angels), Lindbergh went head to head with a Mitsubishi Ki-51 over Amahai Airstrip on Ceram Island. Though not a fighter, the "Sonia," as it was called, had two forward-firing machine guns plus a tail gunner. Slim put a long burst of .50-caliber and 20mm cannon shells into it very likely killing the pilot, and the plane dove into the sea.

When word of this got out, it was suggested by General

George C. Kenney, the Allied Air Forces commander, that Lindbergh fly in a much safer bomber. To this Slim replied, "I wasn't any bomber pilot. . . . I didn't like to get shot at unless I could shoot back." Kenney, himself a decorated fighter pilot, laughed and said he liked fighters better as well.

By the time Lindbergh returned to the United States in September 1944, he had flown fifty combat missions and solved dozens of pressing technical problems. In his wartime journal, Slim revealed many personal misgivings about his experiences, and though he believed in the necessity of this war, he had trouble with killing. As with many aspects of the man, this was paradoxical; he had demonstrated during combat that he had no hesitation in attacking enemy positions or even dogfighting, knowing that this usually resulted in a death.

"I felt great freedom of action during those missions," he recalled nearly thirty years later. "There was freedom even in the duel of life and death—his bullets and my bullets, the freedom of life if they passed, the freedom of death if they struck."

Lindbergh seems to have been troubled by the perceived callousness of those doing the killing. What he failed to appreciate was that this is a natural attitude for men who are yanked out of their lives, put down thousands of miles away in hostile territory, and then told to do dangerous things every day. It's hard to be compassionate or, as Lindbergh wrote, to have "respect for the dignity of death," when your friends die and there is no end to the war in sight.

Charles Lindbergh was a natural marksman and completely understood the concept of using aircraft and pilots as weapons. He did not hesitate at critical moments and, like many before and since, relished the utter uniqueness of combat flying. How he would have performed if recommissioned as a regular combat officer, making life-and-death decisions every day, is another question entirely. "But I realize," he would write in May 1944, "that the life of this unknown stranger—probably an enemy—is worth a thousand times more to me than his death."

In the end, for Charles Lindbergh, it was certainly not a matter of ability or courage—he possessed both—but one of temperament, so perhaps it is just as well that his time in combat was limited. The salient point is that he didn't have to be there at all. He could have remained a stateside consultant, rested on his laurels, or retired altogether and remained perfectly safe, but he did not.

FOR CHARLES LINDBERGH, life after the war was as restless and polarized as before. Combat had matured him, as only it can do, and made him realize that though war was to be avoided whenever possible, there were, and always would be, times when one had to fight. "Nations are always faced with the menace of conquest," he believed, and to that end he promptly went to work countering the next global threat: the Soviet Union. Lindbergh's wartime record removed any stigma from the America First days, and with Roosevelt dead in 1945 there were no obstacles to his continued service. Through the Army Ordnance Department he developed better weapons and worked directly for the newly appointed secretary of the Air Force in streamlining the Strategic Air Command.

"What fools men were, I among them," he wrote in *Autobiography of Values,* "when they found security by keeping lethal weapons pointed toward each other! But what was the alternative? A country had to have arms to keep its freedom." Deeply desiring to better understand the world and its people, Lindbergh began consulting again for Pan American Airways, largely because this provided unlimited travel opportunities. He flew all Pan Am's routes: above the Arctic Circle, through Europe, the Philippines, the Middle East, and Africa. Observing the explosive growth of the Cold War decades, Lindbergh became a committed environmentalist. Through the International Union for the Conservation of Nature and the World Wildlife Fund, he used his influence to preserve natural resources and vanishing wildlife. He lectured and wrote, took part in an expedition to the "cave dwelling, stone-age" Tasaday tribe, lived in a Masai *boma* along the Kenyan border, and at last returned to New York where he could continue working with the Rockefeller Institute for Medical Research.

Charles Lindbergh was a restless man, a lonely man and, above all, a complex man. As Scott Berg so eloquently phrased it, "Greatness came at the inevitable price of being misunderstood," and this absolutely applied to Lindbergh. He was a natural fighter, but abhorred war; loved his family, yet was remarkably undemonstrative. Lindbergh has been harshly judged for his antiwar beliefs, yet fought courageously for his country.

It was always the sky—its freedom and vast emptiness, where he was liberated from the distraction of other men—that attracted Slim the most. "I wanted to regain close contact with the land and sea," he would write in *Autobiography of Values*. "We reach a point in observation and analysis where the human intellect stares past frontiers of its evolutionary achievement, toward unreached areas infinitively vast." It was fitting then, following his conquest of the air that Charles Lindbergh lifted his eyes still higher to the next great unknown: space.

He'd spent nearly a decade on various military related ballistic-missile committees, and on the morning of July 16, 1969, Lindbergh stood near Launch Complex 39A at the Kennedy Space Center on Florida's coast. As Wernher von Braun, famed rocket engineer and head of the Apollo Applications Program famously stated, "the moon is our Paris." Atop a Saturn V rocket the Apollo 11 crew of Michael Collins, Edwin Aldrin, and Neil Armstrong lifted off on NASA's twenty-sixth manned spaceflight. Armstrong had personally invited Charles Lindbergh who, by crossing a great frontier proving aviation's potential in 1927, had paved the way for crossing another frontier—walking on the moon.*

Three years later, during a yearly physical exam, Slim was diagnosed with lymphoma and informed it was likely cancerous. After beginning chemotherapy in January 1973 at Columbia-Presbyterian Medical Center in New York, he suffered a severe anemic reaction that cost him thirty pounds of weight. Lindbergh decided to recover in Hawaii, where he had established a home in Maui. And he did—for a time. But by August the following year he was back in New York undergoing blood transfusions, and Slim knew the end was fast approaching.

"I have eight to ten days to live, and I want to come back home to die," he argued from his bed. On August 18, against medical advice, Lindbergh was placed on a commercial flight from Kennedy Airport. Less than a week after returning to Maui, he slipped into a coma and peacefully passed away on the morning of August 26, 1974.

Before his death, Lindbergh had purchased a thirty-foot plot on a sweeping cliff-top vista overlooking Kipahulu Bay. Earth, sea, and sky unite in a beautiful setting that is at once dangerous, unpredictable, and enduring. Difficult to reach, the grave is set well apart from others; like but unlike, near but not

---

* Armstrong also carried two pieces of the original Wright Flyer with him; a sliver of the left propeller and a bit of wing fabric.

too close, and lonely—like the man himself. A massive stone cut from Vermont granite lays flat over the grave facing skyward, and simply reads:

CHARLES A. LINDBERGH
Born Michigan 1902   Died Maui 1974
". . . If I take the wings of the morning,
and dwell in the uttermost parts of the sea . . ."
C.A.L.

Though we all belong to nature, Slim needed to be within it, to commune in a way he never quite managed with his fellow humans. One wonders if this restless quest wasn't irrevocably stoked during his magnificent solo flight across the Atlantic. This was a man who was only comfortable with his place in the world a very few times during his long, eventful life: so perhaps his greatest, and only true peace, came during those fateful, thirty-three hours between New York and Paris in May 1927.

Despite everything that came later, what Charles Lindbergh did, what he *truly* accomplished, was to remind us that we have more similarities than differences, and are capable of great deeds. His immortal flight clearly, unequivocally, and irrevocably demonstrated the tremendous capacity of the universal human spirit, in which we all can take pride.

ACKNOWLEDGMENTS

IN 2015 PETER HUBBARD, my talented, tireless editor at HarperCollins, suggested this book. "No one," he said, has written about Lindbergh's flight from the cockpit. "It would take a pilot to do that," I replied without thinking, and walked directly into his trap.

Peter's enthusiasm was infectious. I realized, as I usually do with my books, how much I was not taught about such an event, or in this case about the man himself. In creating *The Flight,* I have been privileged to have had a great deal of valuable professional assistance. Ric Gillespie, executive director of The International Group for Historic Aircraft Recovery (TIGHAR), made the prologue possible. His exhaustive compilation of reports and personal experiences concerning the disappearance of the White Bird are unparalleled.

Charles Lindbergh was a meticulous note taker, journalist, and record keeper. Over the span of his life, he would routinely take suitcases of his papers to the Yale University Library, where they now reside under the watchful eyes of Judith Schiff and Michael Frost, both of whom generously gave their time in answering my repeated inquiries. So did Dr. Bob Van Der Linden and Elisabeth Borja of the National Air and Space

Museum, who answered my sporadic and continuous questions as only experts can.

Sharon Smith, Dennis Northcott, and Jaime Bourassa gave me several days at the Missouri Historical Society and full access to an amazing collection of Lindbergh's maps, logs, artifacts, decorations, and private letters. My grateful thanks also to Jeff Duford, Teresa Montgomery, and Brett Stole of the National Museum of the Air Force. As always, my friends Greg Anderson and Marilyn Chang of the Wings Over the Rockies Museum were quick to volunteer their time to help. My special gratitude to Julia Blum of the Cradle of Aviation Museum, who helped me reconstruct Roosevelt Field as it existed in May, 1927. Additional thanks to Guy Aceto for his inexhaustible list of contacts, and to Loren Hardenburgh, archivist of Sidwell Friends School.

Ron Twellman of the Experimental Aircraft Association was kind enough to host me for a day with his superb, flyable replica of the *Spirit of St. Louis,* answering the technical questions that made writing this from the cockpit possible. Nova Hall, grandson of the *Spirit*'s designer, Donald Hall, was kind enough to provide details regarding the plane's construction. Both Reeve Lindbergh and Erik Lindbergh, after a lifetime of nagging from a procession of authors, were gracious and extremely tolerant of my questions—thank you. My appreciation goes out to John Petersen of the Lindbergh Foundation for putting me in touch with both of them.

I wish to add a tremendous gesture of thanks to my French researcher, Christophe Blondel: pour sa patience et l'assistance gracieuse qu'il m'a apportée pour relever, dans la presse française de l'époque, des détails concernant l'arrivée de Lindbergh au Bourget et son bref séjour à Paris.

As always, I owe a debt of gratitude to everyone at

HarperCollins who turns these ideas into a book on a shelf. I am especially thankful for the patience and professionalism of my friend Peter Hubbard, executive editor at HarperCollins; his able assistant, Nick Amphlett; and their long-suffering boss, Liate Stehlik, who keeps approving my projects. Kaitlyn Kennedy is truly the most energetic, motivated, and professional publicist with whom it has been my pleasure to work. Last but never least, none of this would ever be possible without the tolerance, forbearance, and assistance of my family.

GLOSSARY

AILERON: A control surface mounted on a wing, near the tips, that alters the camber of an airfoil when deflected. Used to bank, roll, and climb.

AIRFOIL: A cross-sectional view of a wing or propeller blade.

AIRSPEED INDICATOR: An instrument that displays the relative, or indicated, speed of an aircraft.

ANGLE OF ATTACK: The angle between the relative incoming wind and the longitudinal axis of the aircraft.

BANK: To turn an aircraft by tilting its wings laterally.

CAMBER: The measured difference between the top and bottom of an airfoil.

CARBURETOR: A mechanical device that combines fuel and air for combustion.

CEILING: The surface of the lowest layer of cloud measured up from the earth's surface.

CHORD LINE: A line drawn from the leading edge to the trailing edge of a wing.

CIRRUS: Wispy, thin strands of high-level clouds.

COMPASS HEADING: A reading from a compass used to maintain a desired direction of flight.

COMPASS ROSE: A 360-degree graduated circle used for navigation.

COURSE: An aircraft's path across the ground. Either plotted or actual, and not corrected for wind.

COWLING: A removable metal cover for an aircraft engine.

CRAB: To angle into a crosswind to maintain a course.

CUMULUS: Heavier, billowing clouds that often develop into thunderstorms.

DEVIATION: Caused by magnetism from the earth and aircraft. For navigation this is an angular difference between the compass heading and magnetic north.

EARTH INDUCTOR COMPASS: Uses variations in electrical current relative to the earth's magnetic field to display navigation information.

ELEVATOR: A hinged airfoil on the horizontal stabilizer's trailing edge used for climbing and descending.

EMPENNAGE: The parts that make up the tail assembly of an aircraft.

FUSELAGE: The main body of an aircraft.

GREAT CIRCLE: A circle cut through the surface of a sphere.

INCLINOMETER: An instrument that displays changes in an aircraft's nose position: up, down, or level.

LANDFALL: Sighting of land following an extended over-water period.

MAGNETIC COURSE: Direction of flight relative to magnetic north.

MAGNETO: A dynamo that produces continuous electrical current for ignition.

MIXTURE: The combination of fuel and air used in the engine's combustion sequence; regulated by the pilot.

OPERATIONS: A building on an airfield from which flying is managed.

PITCH: The aircraft's nose position relative to the horizon.

PITOT TUBE: An open-ended cylinder pointed into the airstream that measures impact air pressure. This is then displayed in the cockpit as miles per hour.

QUARTERING WIND: Either a headwind or tailwind striking the aircraft at 45 degrees or less.

ROCKER ARM: A mechanism that reverses valve pushrods on an internal combustion engine.

ROLL: A complete rotation around the longitudinal axis.

RUDDER: A hinged airfoil on the vertical tail used to turn an aircraft longitudinally in flight, and for directional control on the ground.

RUDDER BAR: Moved by the pilot's feet to operate the rudder.

SKID: An uncoordinated maneuver away from the direction of turn. Sometimes used in an aircraft with poor forward visibility in order for the pilot to see during a turn.

SPAN: The straight distance between an aircraft's wingtips.

SPIN: A degree of roll and yaw together that stalls the aircraft.

STABILIZER: A vertical or horizontal airfoil, smaller than a wing or a tail, for increased stability.

STALL: Insufficient airflow over the wings for flight; caused by maneuvers or a lack of airspeed or a combination of both.

TACHOMETER: An instrument that displays an engine's revolutions per minute.

TURBULENCE: Unstable, rough air caused by convection currents or wind.

VARIATION: Angular difference between magnetic north and true north.

WIND SOCK: A cone-shaped bag used on an airfield to display the relative windspeed and direction. The large end pivots into the wind.

SELECTED BIBLIOGRAPHY

COLLECTIONS

Archives of the First Maritime Region of Cherbourg.
Bibliothèque Nationale de France [National Library of France]. Gallica. http://gallica.bnf.fr. Accessed April 25–30, 2016.
Cradle of Aviation Museum.
Missouri Historical Society: Lindbergh Collection.
Musée de l'Air, Paris.
National Air and Space Museum, Smithsonian Institution: Lindbergh Collection.
National Museum of the Air Force.
Regional Archives from Paris and the Île-de-France Region.
Wings Over the Rockies Air & Space Museum.
Yale University Library, Manuscripts and Archives: Lindbergh Papers.

AUTHOR INTERVIEWS

Elizabeth Borja, Christophe Blondel, Julia Blum, Jeff Duford, Ric Gillespie, Nova Hall, Loren Hardenburgh, Erik Lindbergh, Reeve Lindbergh, Dr. Bob Van Der Linden, Judith Schiff, Kermit Weeks.

BOOKS, PERIODICALS, AND GOVERNMENT REPORTS

Abbott, Patrick. *Airship: The Story of R.34 and the First East–West Crossing of the Atlantic by Air.* New York: Charles Scribner's Sons, 1973.

Allen, Frederick Lewis. *Only Yesterday: An Informal History of the 1920s.* New York: Harper & Brothers, 1931.

Allen, Peter C. *The 91 Before Lindbergh.* Shrewsbury, England: Airlife, 1985.

Anderson, John D. *A History of Aerodynamics.* Cambridge: Cambridge University Press, 1997.

Bailey, F. W., and Christopher Cony. *The French Air Service War Chronology, 1914–1918.* London: Grub Street, 2001.

Bak, Richard. *The Big Jump: Lindbergh and the Great Atlantic Air Race.* Hoboken, NJ: Wiley, 2011.

Beamish, Richard J. *The Story of Lindbergh, the Lone Eagle.* New York: International Press, 1927.

Berg, A. Scott. *Lindbergh.* New York: G. P. Putnam's Sons, 1998.

Bouché, Henri, ed. "L'Aéronautique Marchand; L'aéroport de Paris: Le Bourget." *L'Aéronautique* 128–39: 493–94.

British Pathé. http://www.britishpathe.com. Accessed March 18–20, 2016.

Brown, Sir John Alcock, and Sir Arthur Whitten. *Our Transatlantic Flight.* London: William Kimber, 1969.

Byrd, Richard E. *Skyward.* New York: G. P. Putnam's Sons, 1928.

Casey, Steven. *Cautious Crusade.* Oxford and New York: Oxford University Press, 2004.

Cassagneres, Ev. *The Spirit of Ryan.* Blue Ridge Summit, PA: Tab Books, 1982.

Chamberlin, Clarence D. *Record Flights.* New York: Dorrance, 1928.

Coombs, L. F. E. *Control in the Sky: The Evolution & History of the Aircraft Cockpit.* Barnsley, England: Pen & Sword Books, 2005.

Coppens, Willy. "La veridique histoire de l'arrive de Charles Lindbergh au Bourget." *Icare* 81 (Summer 1977): 65–75.

Crouch, Tom, ed. *Charles A. Lindbergh: An American Life.* Washington, DC: Smithsonian Institution, 1977.

d'Ahertze, Jean Claude. "One of Lindbergh's Doubles Tells How It All Happened." *New York Times*, July 13, 1930.

Davies, R. E. G. *Charles Lindbergh: An Airman, His Aircraft, and His Great Flights*. McLean, VA: Paladwr Press, 1997.

Davis, Kenneth S. *The Hero: Charles A. Lindbergh and the American Dream*. Garden City, NY: Doubleday, 1959.

DeBruyne, Nese F., and Anne Leyland. *American War and Military Operations Casualties: Lists and Statistics*. Washington, DC: Congressional Research Service, 2015.

de Camp, L. Sprague. *The Great Monkey Trial*. Garden City, NY: Doubleday, 1968.

de la Croix, Robert. *They Flew the Atlantic*. Translated by Edward Fitzgerald. Derby, CT: Monarch Books, 1958.

Duffy, James P. *Lindbergh vs. Roosevelt*. New York: MJF Books, 2010.

Duford, Jeff. *The 1926–1927 Pan American Goodwill Fliers, Lindbergh, and the First Distinguished Flying Cross*. Dayton, OH: National Museum of the Air Force, 2009.

du Gard, Dr. Rene Coulet. *Nungesser et Coli Disparaissent à Bord de l'Oiseau Blanc, Mai 1927*. Paris: Government of France, 1984.

Dutton, Commander Benjamin. *Navigation and Nautical Astronomy*. Annapolis, MD: United States Naval Institute Press, 1951.

Dwiggins, Don. *The Barnstormers*. New York: Grosset & Dunlap, 1968.

"The English Channel." In *The Columbia Encylopedia*. New York: Columbia University Press, 2004.

Federal Bureau of Investigation. https://www.fbi.gov/philadelphia/about-us/history/famous-cases. Accessed May 25, 2016.

Fife, George Buchanan. *Lindbergh: The Lone Eagle*. Cleveland: World Syndicate, 1927.

Fredette, Raymond H. "The Making of a Hero: What Really Happened Seventy-Five Years Ago After Lindbergh Landed at Le Bourget." In Colonel Walter J. Boyne, *Today's Best Military Writing*, 147–74. New York: Tom Doherty Associates, 2004.

Garreau, Charles. *Nungesser et Coli; premier vainquers de l'Atlantique*. Paris: Acropole, 1990.

Gill, Brendan. *Lindbergh Alone*. New York: Harcourt Brace Jovanovich, 1977.

Gillespie, Ric. *Project Midnight Ghost*. The International Group for
Historic Aircraft Recovery (TIGHAR), 1992.

Grierson, John. *I Remember Lindbergh*. New York: Harcourt Brace
Jovanovich, 1977.

Groom, Winston. *The Aviators*. Washington, DC: National Geographic Society, 2013.

Guggenheim, Harry F. *The Seven Skies*. New York: G. P. Putnam's
Sons, 1928.

Gunston, Bill. *Piston Aero Engines*. Sparkford, England: Patrick Stephens, 1993.

———. *The World Encyclopaedia of Aero Engines*. Sparkford, England: Patrick Stephens, 1995.

Haines, Lynn, and Dora B. Haines. "The Lindberghs: The Family's
Own Story." *McCall's*, 1931, pp. 62–63.

Hall, Donald A. *Technical Preparation of the Airplane "Spirit of
St. Louis."* Technical Notes. Washington, DC: National Advisory
Committee for Aeronautics, 1927.

Hall, Nova. *Spirit and Creator*. Sheffield, MA: ATN, 2002.

Hampton, Dan. *Lords of the Sky*. New York: HarperCollins, 2014.

Heinmuller, John P. V. *Man's Fight to Fly*. New York: Funk & Wag-
nalls, 1944.

Hixon, Walter L. *Charles A. Lindbergh: Lone Eagle*. New York:
HarperCollins, 1996.

Hoare, Robert J. *Wings Over the Atlantic*. Boston: Charles T. Bran-
ford, 1957.

Huttig, Jack. *1927: Summer of Eagles*. Chicago: Nelson-Hall, 1980.

Jones, E. T. "The Development of the Wright Whirlwind Type J-5 Aircraft Engine." *SAE Journal* 19, no. 3 (September 1926): 303–8.

Keyhoe, Donald E. *Flying with Lindbergh*. New York: G. P. Putnam's
Sons, 1928.

Kyvig, David E. *Daily Life in the United States, 1920–1940*. Chicago:
Ivan R. Dee, 2004.

Lawrance, Charles L. "Air-Cooled Engine Development." *SAE Journal* 10, no. 2 (February 1922): 135–41, 144.

————. "Modern American Aircraft Engine Development." *Aviation* 22 (March 1926): 411–15.

"Lighted Airways over Atlantic Predicted." *Popular Mechanics*, December 1923, pp. 26–31.

Lindbergh, Charles A. "And Then I Jumped." *Saturday Evening Post*, July 23, 1927, pp. 6–7.

————. "Appeal for Isolation." *Congressional Digest*. Radio address, October 1, 1939.

————. *Autobiography of Values*. New York: Harcourt Brace Jovanovich, 1976.

————. *Boyhood on the Upper Mississippi*. St. Paul: Minnesota Historical Society, 1972.

————. "Feel the Earth." *Reader's Digest*, July 1972, pp. 62–65.

————. "Lindbergh's Own Story of His New York–Paris Flight." *New York Times*, May 23–24, 1927.

————. "Making of an Air Mail Pilot." *World's Work*, September 1927, pp. 472–81.

————. *Of Flight and Life*. New York: Charles Scribner's Sons, 1948.

————. "Our Best Chance to Survive." *Saturday Evening Post*, July 17, 1954.

————. *The Spirit of St. Louis*. New York: Scribner, 1953.

————. "Thoughts of a Combat Pilot." *Saturday Evening Post*, October 2, 1954, pp. 20–21.

————. *The Wartime Journals*. New York: Harcourt Brace Jovanovich, 1979.

————. *"We."* New York: Grosset & Dunlap, 1927.

Lindbergh, Reeve. *Under a Wing: A Memoir*. New York: Delta, 1999.

Little Falls High School. *Lindbergh the Flier of Little Falls*. Little Falls, MN: Little Falls High School, 1928.

McCutcheon, Kimble D. "Aero Engines." http://www.pilotfriend.com. Accessed January 2013.

Mencken, H. L. *Heathen Days, 1890–1936*. New York: Knopf, 1943.

Milton, Joyce. *Loss of Eden: A Biography of Charles and Anne Morrow Lindbergh*. New York: HarperCollins, 1993.

Mindell, David A. *Between Human and Machine: Feedback, Control, and Computing Before Cybernetics*. Baltimore: Johns Hopkins University Press, 2002.

Mosley, Leonard. *Lindbergh: A Biography*. Garden City, NY: Doubleday, 1976.

Mott, Bentley T. *Myron T. Herrick: Friend of France*. Garden City, NY: Doubleday, 1929.

National Center for Education Statistics. *120 Years of American Education: A Statistical Portrait*. Edited by Tom Snyder. Washington, DC: U.S. Department of Education, 1993.

National Oceanic and Atmospheric Administration. http://www.noaa.gov/maps. Accessed March 12–13, 2016.

New York Times Archives. http://query.nytimes.com. Accessed January–May 2016.

Okrent, Daniel. *Last Call: The Rise and Fall of Prohibition*. New York: Scribner, 2010.

Pisano, Dominick A., and F. Robert van der Linden. *Charles Lindbergh and the Spirit of St. Louis*. New York: Harry N. Abrams, 2002.

Rare and Early Newspapers. http://www.rarenewspapers.com. Accessed December 2015–March 2016.

Ross, Walter S. *The Last Hero: Charles A. Lindbergh*. New York: Harper & Row, 1976.

Seeger, Eric H., ed. *A Century of Manned Powered Flight*. Tampa, FL: Faircount, 2003.

Smithsonian National Air and Space Museum. http://airandspace.si.edu. Accessed November 15–20, 2016.

Sullivan, Mark. *Our Times: The Twenties*. New York: Scribner's, 1935.

United States Census Bureau. http://www.census.gov. Accessed November 2015–May 2016.

United States Department of Commerce. *Statistical Abstract of the United States 1919*. Washington, DC: U.S. Government Printing Office, 1920.

———. *Statistical Abstract of the United States 1925*. Washington, DC: U.S. Government Printing Office, 1926.

———. *Statistical Abstract of the United States 1928*. Washington, DC: U.S. Government Printing Office, 1928.

United States Department of State. *The Flight of Captain Charles A. Lindbergh from New York to Paris, May 20–21, 1927.* Washington, DC: U.S. Government Printing Office, 1927.

United States Postal Service. http://about.usps.com/who-we-are/postal -history. Accessed December 5–7, 2015.

Van Every, Dale, and Morris de Haven Tracy. *Lindbergh: His Life.* New York: Appleton, 1927.

Waller, Douglas. *A Question of Loyalty.* New York: HarperCollins, 2004.

Wildenberg, Thomas. *Billy Mitchell's War with the Navy.* Annapolis, MD: Naval Institute Press, 2013.

Works Progress Administration. *Inventory of County Archives of Minnesota.* Minnesota Historical Records Project, 1940.

Wright Aeronautical Corporation. *Wright Aviation Engines: Technical Features of the 1927 Production Model of the Wright Whirlwind 200-225 H.P. Nine Cylinder Air-Cooled Radial Engine.* Paterson, NJ: Wright Aeronautical Corporation, 1927.

NEWSPAPERS

Baltimore Sun, Boston Post, Chicago Evening Post, Chicago Tribune, Dearborn Independent, Humanité, La Presse, Times (London), *Milwaukee Journal, New York American, New York Daily News, New York Herald, New York Sun, New York Times, Philadelphia Evening Bulletin, San Antonio Evening News, Washington Herald, Washington Post, Washington Times.*

NOTES AND SOURCES

ONE: THE FIRST HOURS

13 *Fueling was finished at Roosevelt* Davis, *The Hero,* p. 85.

14 *I must hold the plane straight* Lindbergh, *The Spirit of St. Louis* (SOSL), p. 186, para. 2.

14 *and not take my eyes from its edge for an instant* Ibid., p. 186, para. 3.

14 *It felt more like an overloaded truck than an airplane* Ibid., p. 185, para. 5.

15 "TRANSOCEAN FLIERS DOGGED" *New York Times,* April 27, 1927.

17 *I could probably stay in the air* Lindbergh, *SOSL,* p. 18, para. 17.

18 *I'm above the trees* Ibid., p. 187, para. 1.

19 *French newspapers like La Presse* Quoted from *Project Midnight Ghost Report,* p. 3.

19 *Why smother the flavor* Lindbergh, *SOSL,* p. 176, para. 1.

20 *I've never flown across that much water before* Ibid., p. 190, para. 3.

20 *I'm also a mile or two southeast off course* Ibid., p. 189, para. 3.

21 *But he had left all that behind* Ibid., p. 190, para. 1.

21 *"One boy's a boy"* Lindbergh quoting his father, Ibid., p. 191, para. 4.

24 *Carl Schory of the National Aeronautic Association* Pisano and Van der Linden, p. 67.

24 *"To hell with the money"* Lindbergh, *SOSL*, p. 169, para. 3.

27 *It's a compact place to live* Ibid., p. 191, para. 1.

28 *"Are you only taking five sandwiches?"* New York Times, May 21, 1927.

TWO: HOPE

35 *"he adopted the surname"* Berg, *Lindbergh*, pp. 12–13.

43 *"We are exceedingly poor in cash"* Lindbergh quoted in Ibid., p. 30.

47 *"I used to imagine myself with wings"* Lindbergh, *SOSL*, p. 245, para. 4.

49 *"As I grew older"* Ibid., p. 245, para. 5.

50 *"It was explained at the Department of Health"* New York Times, September 22, 1918.

54 LONDON GIVES READ *New York Times*, June 2, 1919.

54 *The* London Chronicle *added* Quoted from the *New York Times*, June 2, 1919, p. 2.

56 *"I don't want to go to"* Lindbergh quoted in Berg, *Lindbergh*, p. 53.

56 *"[a] pity, to permit so many"* Ibid., p. 55.

59 *"Behind every movement"* Ibid., p. 248, para. 3.

THREE: HOUR FIVE

60 *I'm a little tired* Lindbergh, *SOSL*, p. 201, para. 2.

61 *Why should he tear leaves from a notebook* Ibid., p. 203, para. 1.

62 *I'm half-asleep!* Ibid., p. 203, para. 3.

62 *I've let myself be caught off guard at a critical moment* Ibid., pp. 173–74, paras. 4-5.

65 *How accurately have I held my course?* Ibid., p. 205, para. 2.

65 *When flying low* Ibid., p. 205, para. 2.

67 *What amazing magic* Ibid., p. 209, para. 4.

67 *"On course, plenty of fuel"* Ibid., p. 210, para. 1.

68 *No, I'll leave the windows* Ibid., p. 210, paras. 3 and 4.

68 *Why didn't I put them in before?* Ibid., p. 210, para. 2.

68 *"an enclosed cockpit"* Ibid., p. 88, para. 1.

69 *It's certainly bad country* Ibid., pp. 207, para. 1.

69 *Their supple trunks and thick, green boughs* Ibid., p. 208, para. 2.

69 *"It was a mistake"* Ibid., p. 211, para. 2.

70 *"Yes . . . but we considered all that at the factory"* Ibid., p. 211, para. 3.

72 *If only I had a parachute!* Ibid., p. 212, para. 3.

72 *I can't carry everything* Ibid.

74 *I don't dare check the magnetos now* Ibid., p. 217.

77 *If the fog will hold off a few hours more* Ibid., p. 224, para. 3.

79 *"I don't mind reading it through a mirror"* Ibid., p. 225, para. 5.

79 *"Will this do?"* Ibid., p. 226.

80 *His mother, teaching in Detroit* Ibid., p. 231, paras. 1–3.

80 *The sea is no longer a stranger* Ibid., p. 229, para. 2.

FOUR: **DOORWAY TO THE ATLANTIC**

81 *"You don't plan on making that flight alone"* Lindbergh, *SOSL*, p. 83, para. 4.

81 *"I'd rather have the extra gasoline than an extra man"* Ibid., p. 83, para. 5.

82 *I'm beyond the stage where I need a bed* Ibid., p. 233, para. 3.

82 *Sleep is winning* Ibid., p. 233, para. 4.

82 *And the sun is sinking* Ibid., p. 233, para. 5.

82 *How can I get through the night* Ibid., p. 233, para. 5.

82 *I must think about problems* Ibid., p. 236, para. 5.

85 *a forced landing, over mountains* Ibid., p. 138, para. 2.

87 *I feel that I'm entering the Arctic* Ibid., p. 239, para. 2.

87 *what would I do now if my engine failed?* Ibid., p. 241, para. 3.

87 *Under such conditions* Ibid., p. 97, para. 5.

88 *It was impossible to increase safety* Ibid.

90 *A fishing schooner* Ibid., p. 269, para. 4.

91 *I've never been as conscious of the minuteness* Ibid., p. 269, para. 5.

93 *Still, a search had to be attempted* Ibid., p. 270, para. 2.

93 *a gesture, the payment of a debt felt by living men* Ibid., p. 270, para. 2.

93 *Sometimes, flying feels like man* Ibid., p. 288, para. 3.

96 *"a monoplane, believed to be"* New York Times, May 21, 1927.

96 *"Captain Lindbergh passed over New Tusket"* Cable, printed in the *New York Times*, May 22, 1927.

96 *"Captain Lindbergh passed over Mulgrave"* Ibid.

96 *"Captain Lindbergh got his last sight"* New York Times, May 21, 1927.

96 *"He has my best wishes for his success"* Ibid.

98 *There are no more reassuring islands ahead* Lindbergh, SOSL, p. 297, para. 3.

FIVE: INNOCENCE LOST

101 *"dedicated more than the last"* Fitzgerald, *This Side of Paradise*, New York, Charles Scribner's Sons, 1920, p. 255.

102 *loss of 53,402 combat deaths* DeBruyne and Leland, CRS Report, p. 2.

103 *3,500 American soldiers arrived* Editorial, *New York Times*, December 1, 1918.

104 *Illiteracy would decrease* Snyder, *120 Years of American Education*, 1993.

106 *"the sky is a vast dome"* New York Times, February 1922.

108 *"God's worst enemy and hell's best friend"* Okrent quoting Sunday, in *Last Call*, p. 97.

111 *"The music is sensuous"* Lewis, *Only Yesterday*, p. 78.

111 *"a pathological, nerve-irritating"* Bryson, *One Summer*, p. 69.

111 *"a stupid, sodden, vicious lot"* Okrent, *Last Call*, p. 46.

114 *"terrorist movement"* FBI (Philadelphia Division), "History of the 1919 Bombings."

118 *"I do believe in the ethical teachings"* De Camp, *The Great Monkey Trial*, p. 91.

119 *"The one beauty about"* Mencken, *Heathen Days*, p. 177.

121 *Running into a squall line* Waller, *A Question of Loyalty*, p. 15.

123 *totaling 1,481 planes* Wildenberg, *Billy Mitchell's War with the Navy*, p. 25.

123 *"are a direct result of incompetency"* New York Times, September 6, 1925.

124 *"be suspended from rank"* Waller, p. 324.

125 *"They could not endure"* Allen, *Only Yesterday*, p. 105.

SIX: THE EMPIRE OF THE NIGHT

126 *The last gate is closing behind me* Lindbergh, *SOSL*, p. 297, para. 1.

132 *"If we buy a plane"* Ibid., p. 75, para. 6.

135 *I'm giving up both land and day* Ibid., p. 296, para. 3.

135 *Now, I'm heading eastward* Ibid., p. 296, para. 3.

135 *I won't run out of fuel over the ocean* Ibid., p. 300, para. 2.

135 *The engine sounds smoother* Ibid., p. 301, para. 3.

137 *I wonder if man ever escapes* Ibid., p. 301, para. 4.

137 *You fly by the sky on a black night* Ibid., p. 301, para. 3.

138 *Why try to hold on to those stars?* Ibid., p. 305, para. 3.

138 *But if I start flying blind* Ibid., p. 305, para. 3.

138 *What about God?* Ibid., p. 320, para. 2.

139 *It's hard to be an agnostic* Ibid., p. 321, para. 5.

139 *If one dies, all this goes on existing* Ibid., p. 322, para. 1.

139 *That means I'm gaining on the storm* Ibid., p. 314, para. 2.

140 *too much warmth would make want to sleep.* Ibid., p. 322, para. 2.

140 *How high should I climb tonight?* Ibid., p. 316, para. 3.

142 *There is no doubt now that a storm area lies ahead* Ibid., p. 315, para. 1.

142 *The body's reflexes must be* Ibid., p. 323, para. 5.

142 *The mind must operate as mechanically* Ibid., p. 324, para. 2.

143 *my world and my life are compressed* Ibid., p. 324, para. 3.

143 *When a single one strays off* Ibid., p. 324, para. 4.

143 *there are things to be considered outside the cockpit* Ibid., p. 326, para. 4.

144 *He knows he must get back into clear air* Ibid., p. 327, para. 2.

144 *"Kick rudder hard . . . no time to lose"* Ibid., p. 327, para. 3.

144 *"No, faster; turn the right amount"* Ibid., p. 327, para. 8.

145 *"Turn faster! You see the airspeed's dropping"* Ibid., p. 327, para. 13.

145 *"It's not ice"* Ibid., p. 327, para. 14

145 *I ought to be turned around by now* Ibid., p. 328, para. 3.

146 *if he can keep heading eastward* Ibid., p. 331, para. 1.

146 *What I do depends largely on what I have to do* Ibid., p. 310, para. 4.

SEVEN: PHANTOMS IN THE MIST

147 *Last night I couldn't go to sleep* Lindbergh, *SOSL,* p. 338, para. 4.

147 *I cup my hand into the slipstream* Ibid., p. 343, para. 3.

147 *the earth inductor is hopeless* Ibid., p. 337, para. 5.

148 *Is it possible that I'm entering a magnetic storm?* Ibid., p. 337, para. 4.

148 *I'd almost forgotten the moon* Ibid., p. 340, para. 3.

151 *Night surrendering to morning* Ibid., p. 353, para. 3.

152 *I've waited for morning the whole night through* Ibid., p. 353, para. 4.

152 *I've burned the last bridge behind me* Ibid., p. 351, para. 2.

152 *Now my anchor is in Europe* Ibid., p. 351, para. 2.

153 *Possibly if I eat a sandwich* Ibid., p. 360, para. 1.

153 *Should I have taken along a thermos* Ibid., p. 360, para. 1.

153 *If I could get down through the clouds* Ibid., p. 360, para. 2.

154 *The slightest relaxation of pressure* Ibid., p. 363, para. 3.

155 *I can work it all out then* Ibid., p. 364, para. 2.

156 *this is morning* Ibid., p. 367, para. 2.

156 *Suppose I start down through these clouds* Ibid., p. 367, para. 2.

157 *Two thousand feet now* Ibid., p. 368, para. 6.

157 *The air down here is thicker, humid* Ibid., p. 369, para. 2.

158 *It would have to blow with great* Ibid., p. 369, para. 4.

159 *I have a strong feeling that I'm too far south* Ibid., p. 371, para. 3.

160 *I've done almost as much on this single trip* Ibid., p. 372, para. 2.

160 *I should climb to 1,500 feet* Ibid., p. 378, para. 4.

161 *"It's clear up above"* Ibid., p. 379, para. 3.

164 *These phantoms speak with human voices* Ibid., p. 389, para. 2.

164 *In fact, these emissaries* Ibid., p. 390, para. 4.

165 *Rain may be an indication of better weather* Ibid., p. 388, para. 5.

165 *Am I crossing the bridge* Ibid., p. 390, para. 2.

166 *in fourteen hours, with any luck* Ibid., p. 394, para. 4.

166 *but I'm in mid-Atlantic* Ibid., p. 399, para. 4.

167 *I know there's no land out here* Ibid., p. 400, para. 1.

167 *It's nonsense, pure nonsense, to be lured* Ibid., p. 400, para. 4.

168 *If I keep putting it off for fifteen minutes* Ibid., p. 401, para. 2.

168 *How can I pass through such ordeals* Ibid., p. 423, para. 3.

168 *can I even reach the Irish coast?* Ibid., p. 423, para. 3.

168 *I'm passing out* Ibid., p. 424, para. 1.

168 *God give me strength* Ibid., p. 424, para. 2.

EIGHT: CROSSING THE BRIDGE

171 *I've finally broken the spell of sleep* Lindbergh, *SOSL*, p. 424, para. 4.

174 *Whatever may come later, these sun-filled hours are mine* Ibid., p. 433, para. 2.

175 *the first living thing I've seen since Newfoundland* Ibid., p. 434, para. 2.

175 *I feel that I've safely crossed the bridge to life* Ibid., p. 434, para. 3.

175 *why do I find such joy, such encouragement* Ibid., p. 434, para. 3.

175 *This ocean ... which for me marks the borderland of death* Ibid., p. 434, para. 4.

177 *They make it seem like evening ... make me want to sleep* Ibid., p. 451, para. 2.

179 *No ... I won't clip* Ibid., p. 452, para. 5.

181 *"encourage commercial aviation and to authorize"* H.R. 7064

182 *"The Army schools taught me"* Berg, *Lindbergh*, p. 75, para. 3.

183 *A second sign of life!* Lindbergh, *SOSL*, p. 453, para. 3.

183 *They are really children of ocean and air* Ibid., p. 453, para. 4.

183 *in three hours, if I haven't sighted land* Ibid., p. 455, para. 2.

184 *"Your mail planes fly over"* Lindbergh quoting a letter, *SOSL*, p. 38, para. 5.

184 *The greatest test of my navigation* Ibid., p. 457, para. 3.

185 *The ocean is no longer a dangerous wilderness* Ibid., p. 458, para. 2.

185 *The coast, the European coast, can't be far away!* Ibid., p. 457, para. 6.

186 *"WHICH WAY IS IRELAND?"* Ibid., p. 459, para. 3.

186 *It looks like a severed head* Ibid., p. 459, para. 4.

186 *Why don't they pay attention to my circling and shouting?* Ibid., p. 460, para. 1.

187 *Can it possibly be land?* Ibid., p. 462, para. 2.

189 *Yes, there's a place on the chart* Ibid., p. 463, para. 1.

190 *I've never seen such beauty before* Ibid., p. 463, para. 3.

191 *I know how the dead would feel to live again* Ibid., p. 464, para. 1.

191 *Only six more segments to fly* Ibid., p. 464, para. 2.

192 *Have I lost ability to distinguish fact from fancy?* Ibid., p. 464, para. 3.

NINE: DREAMS

194 *It's as though a curtain has fallen behind me* Lindbergh, SOSL, pp. 465–66, para. 1.

195 *What limitless possibilities aviation holds* Ibid., p. 469, para. 3.

196 *the voices that spoke with such authority* Ibid., p. 467, para. 3.

198 *I feel like the western pioneer* Ibid., p. 469, para. 4.

198 *But of course!* Ibid., p. 470, para. 4.

200 *I have enough fuel to reach Rome* Ibid., p. 472, para. 2.

201 *No, he decides this flight is from New York to Paris* Ibid., p. 473, para. 5.

201 *he can reach France before darkness* Ibid., p. 471, para. 1.

202 *How, he wonders, can a farmer make his living* Ibid., p. 476, para. 1.

202 *"far from being so good looking"* Lindbergh quoting his great-grandmother, ibid., p. 476, para. 3.

204 *I've crossed England so quickly* Ibid., p. 477, para. 4.

205 *How safe the people on those ships have been* Ibid., p. 479, para. 1.

207 *The coast of France!* Ibid., p. 480, para. 1.

207 *Could they have flown off* Ibid., p. 480, para. 1.

207 *They too rode on a magic carpet* Ibid., p. 480, para. 1.

208 *I'm over the country of my destination* Ibid., p. 481, para. 1.

208 *I don't speak a word of French* Ibid., p. 481, para. 5.

209 *I didn't get a visa before I took off* Ibid., p. 481, para. 5.

209 *I'm so far ahead of schedule* Ibid., p. 481, para. 5.

209 *I'll have to buy a new suit of clothes* Ibid., p. 482, para. 1.

210 *I've broken the world's distance record* Ibid., p. 483, para. 3.

211 *Why, it's past suppertime* Ibid., p. 484, para. 3.

211 *No . . . These fields are so clean* Ibid., p. 484, para. 4.

212 *Yes, it's an air beacon!* Ibid., p. 485, para. 3.

212 *nobody told me it had lights* Ibid., p. 485, para. 3.

212 *They have shared this experience together* Ibid., p. 486, para. 1.

213 *It's truly a magic carpet* Ibid., p. 482, para. 3.

213 *I see it* Ibid., p. 487, para. 1.

215 *I shouldn't be hunting for a beacon* Ibid., p. 488, para. 1.

215 *Yes . . . there's a black patch to my left* Ibid., p. 488, para. 2.

216 *I must remember I'm over Europe, where customs are strange* Ibid., p. 488, para. 3.

216 *I'll fly on northeast a few miles more* Ibid., p. 488, para. 4.

216 *If I see nothing else* Ibid., p. 489, para. 1.

219 *It* must *be Le Bourget!* Ibid., p. 489, para. 5.

219 *I'll drag the field from low altitude* Ibid., p. 489, para. 6.

222 *I'll have to take a chance on that* Ibid., p. 490, para. 4.

222 *I'll overshoot if I keep on at this rate* Ibid., p. 491, para. 2.

223 *If I don't sideslip, I'll be too high* Ibid., p. 492, para. 1.

224 *Give her the gun and climb* Ibid., p. 492, para. 1.

224 *The field must be clear* Ibid., p. 492, para. 1.

TEN: A NEW REALITY

226 *"tremble with pressure"* Lindbergh, *SOSL*, p. 495.

226 *"Are there any mechanics here?"* Ibid., p. 495.

227 *"in the center of an ocean of heads"* Ibid., p. 496.

230 *"Come . . . They will smother him!"* Ibid., p. 497.

230 *"C'est impossible . . . Lindbergh has just been carried"* Ibid., p. 498.

231 *"I'm not Lindbergh!"* Davis, *The Hero*, p. 209.

231 *"Of course you are"* Ibid., p. 209.

231 *"I tell you, sir, I'm not Lindbergh"* Fredette, *The Making of a Hero*, p. 154.

231 *"I think some French officers took him"* Ibid., p. 209.

232 *"he would bitterly regret for the rest of his life"* Ibid., pp. 210–11.

234 *"lights of several ships"* MacDonald, *New York Times*, May 22, 1927.

234 *"Anyway, I paid no attention"* Ibid.

235 *Slim also never tied a bicycle* Lindbergh, *SOSL*, p. 547, para. 3.

235 *"Also, believing in aviation's future"* Ibid., p. 547, para. 2.

236 *"On the morrow of the attempt"* Doumergue to Coolidge, *New York Times*, May, 1927.

236 *"dropped dead on the street"* *New York Times*, May 22, 1927.

237 *"Lindbergh's flight will leave"* Davis, *The Hero*, p. 214.

237 *"For years the American people"* Allen, *Only Yesterday*, p. 190.

239 *"He has accomplished the greatest"* Berg, *Lindbergh*, p. 136.

241 *"The name of my ship"* Ibid., p. 142.

242 *"You are the prophet"* Ibid., p. 143.

243 *"I am delighted to hear"* Raymond Orteig Jr., *New York Times*, May 22, 1927.

243 *"It seemed an almost impossible"* Ibid.

247 *"Captain Lindbergh will now partake"* Berg, *Lindbergh*, p. 148.

247 *"the wish of Washington"* Davis, *The Hero*, p. 224.

248 *"I have enjoyed every minute"* *New York Times*, June 10, 1927.

250 *"Blythe tells me everyone"* Ibid., June 11.

INDEX

ABOUT THE AUTHOR

DAN HAMPTON is the *New York Times* bestselling author of *Viper Pilot, Lords of the Sky,* and *The Hunter Killers.* During his twenty years (1986–2006) in the United States Air Force, Hampton received the Distinguished Flying Cross with Valor, a Purple Heart, and numerous other citations. His next book, *Chasing the Demon,* recounts the quest to break the sound barrier.

BOOKS BY DAN HAMPTON

THE FLIGHT
CHARLES LINDBERGH'S DARING AND IMMORTAL 1927 TRANSATLANTIC CROSSING

"Outstanding. ...Riveting. ...Recommended. ...A painstaking account [that] succeeds in placing readers in the cockpit of the Spirit of St. Louis."

—*Library Journal* (starred review)

THE HUNTER KILLERS
THE EXTRAORDINARY STORY OF THE FIRST WILD WEASELS, THE BAND OF MAVERICK AVIATORS WHO FLEW THE MOST DANGEROUS MISSIONS OF THE VIETNAM WAR

"A gripping classic. Exhaustively researched, *The Hunter Killers* puts you directly into a Wild Weasel fighter cockpit during the Vietnam War."

—Colonel Leo Thorsness,
Wild Weasel pilot and Medal of Honor recipient

LORDS OF THE SKY
FIGHTER PILOTS AND AIR COMBAT, FROM THE RED BARON TO THE F-16

National Bestseller

"An excellent, well-researched, literate overview of 20th century warfare and the development of the fighter plane. *Lords of the Sky* will captivate history and aviation buffs alike."

—Stephen Coonts,
New York Times bestselling author of *Flight of the Intruder*

VIPER PILOT
A MEMOIR OF AIR COMBAT

***New York Times* Bestseller**

"Offers a gripping cockpit view of modern air combat. ...Hampton is a vivid writer and an unabashed warrior. ...An outstanding work."

—*Booklist* (starred review)